I.B.TAURIS SHORT HISTORIES

I.B.Tauris Short Histories is an authoritative and elegantly written new series which puts a fresh perspective on the way history is taught and understood in the twenty-first century. Designed to have strong appeal to university students and their teachers, as well as to general readers and history enthusiasts, *I.B.Tauris Short Histories* comprises a novel attempt to bring informed interpretation, as well as factual reportage, to historical debate. Addressing key subjects and topics in the fields of history, the history of ideas, religion, classical studies, politics, philosophy and Middle East studies, the series seeks intentionally to move beyond the bland, neutral 'introduction' that so often serves as the primary undergraduate teaching tool. While always providing students and generalists with the core facts that they need to get to grips with the essentials of any particular subject, *I.B.Tauris Short Histories* goes further. It offers new insights into how a topic has been understood in the past, and what different social and cultural factors might have been at work. It brings original perspectives to bear on the manner of its current interpretation. It raises questions and – in its extensive bibliographies – points to further study, even as it suggests answers. Addressing a variety of subjects in a greater degree of depth than is often found in comparable series, yet at the same time in concise and compact handbook form, *I.B.Tauris Short Histories* aims to be 'introductions with an edge'. In combining questioning and searching analysis with informed history writing, it brings history up to date for an increasingly complex and globalized digital age.

www.short-histories.com

'Helen Parish's exciting new book is a timely, assured, well-written and thoroughly engaging account of this key episode of early modern European history. Drawing on the most recent scholarship, and making extensive use of primary sources, it provides readers with an excellent introduction to the subject while at the same time offering something quite distinctive. Not only does this volume cover essential topics such as Reformation theology and the role of printing, but it also does a great job of drawing our attention to less conventional themes, such as the visual arts, women and marriage and the supernatural. It is a key contribution from one of our leading Reformation historians.'

– Kenneth Austin, Senior Lecturer in Early Modern History, University of Bristol

'This book is an excellent and up-to-date treatment of the Reformation. Helen Parish has produced a splendid summary, based on the latest research, of those major themes that characterized the Reformation in both its coherence and its diversity. Though underpinned by solid scholarship, it deserves a wide readership.'

– Scott H. Hendrix, Emeritus Professor of Reformation History and Theology, Princeton Theological Seminary, author of **Martin Luther: A Very Short Introduction**

'This is much more than just another history of the Reformation. Helen Parish not only gives us Luther's story, she expertly traces its impact deep into ordinary life. We learn how a theologians' quarrel ended up reinventing the arts, family life and even ghosts. And while she digests the best of recent scholarship for us, the book is also filled with vivid vignettes, from the inferno of a Dutch church torched by iconoclasts to an Anabaptist radical's letter to her infant son written as she went to her death.'

– Alec Ryrie, Professor of the History of Christianity, Durham University, author of **Protestants: The Radicals Who Made the Modern World**

A Short History of . . .

the Normans	Leonie V Hicks (Canterbury Christ Church University)
the Ottoman Empire	Baki Tezcan (University of California, Davis)
the Phoenicians	Mark Woolmer (Durham University)
the Reformation	Helen L Parish (University of Reading)
the Renaissance in Northern Europe	Malcolm Vale (University of Oxford)
Revolutionary Cuba	Antoni Kapcia (University of Nottingham)
the Risorgimento	Nick Carter (Australian Catholic University, Sydney)
the Russian Revolution	Geoffrey Swain (University of Glasgow)
the Spanish Civil War	Julián Casanova (University of Zaragoza)
the Spanish Empire	Felipe Fernández-Armesto (University of Notre Dame) and José Juan López-Portillo (University of Oxford)
Transatlantic Slavery	Kenneth Morgan (Brunel University London)
Venice and the Venetian Empire	Maria Fusaro (University of Exeter)
the Vikings	Clare Downham (University of Liverpool)
the Wars of the Roses	David Grummitt (University of Kent)
the Weimar Republic	Colin Storer (University of Nottingham)

A SHORT HISTORY OF THE REFORMATION

Helen L. Parish

I.B. TAURIS
LONDON · NEW YORK

Published in 2018 by
I.B.Tauris & Co. Ltd
London • New York
www.ibtauris.com

HB ISBN: 978 1 78076 609 6
PB ISBN: 978 1 78076 610 2
eISBN: 978 1 78672 470 0
ePDF: 978 1 78673 470 9

A full CIP record for this book is available from the British Library
A full CIP record is available from the Library of Congress

Library of Congress Catalog Card Number: available

Typeset by Free Range Book Design & Production Limited
Printed and bound in Great Britain by TJ International, Padstow, Cornwall

Contents

List of Maps
and Illustrations

MAPS

FIGURES

Helen L. Parish

All figures are public domain.

Acknowledgements

I am, as ever, grateful to my colleagues and students at the University of Reading who have done so much to see this book through to completion. Particular thanks are due to staff in the Department of History and the Early Modern Research Centre for their insights, comments and companionship, and to my undergraduate and postgraduate students whose critical questioning has shaped the content of what follows. As a work of synthesis, this book perches like a dwarf on the shoulders of giants; the commemorations of Reformation 500 have spawned a new enthusiasm for discussion of Martin Luther and his legacy and a range of publications that have made researching and writing the 'short history' an altogether pleasurable and thought-provoking task.

I owe a substantial debt to Alex Wright, both for his invitation to write for this series and for his unfailing conviction that the manuscript would be worth the wait. Working with the production team in the final stages before publication has been a pleasure. Any errors in the text that remain are my own.

A final expression of gratitude is offered to my family, and particularly my children, whose sense of what makes a good book does not yet extend into the realms of Reformation studies. I dedicate this book to them, in thanks for their blunt questioning of the endeavour, and in the hope that I have provided an adequate answer to the most fundamental question, 'But why?'

Timeline

1506 Julius II lays the foundation stone of the new St Peter's Basilica in Rome. Martin Luther makes his final vows as a member of the Augustinian Order.

1507 Martin Luther ordained as a priest.

1510 Martin Luther visits Rome.

1512 Fifth Lateran Council, first session.

1516 (March) publication of Erasmus' Greek New Testament, *Novum Instrumentum*. Luther begins first lecture series on Galatians.

1517 Pope Leo X declares indulgence for rebuilding of St Peter's. Luther writes his 95 Theses.

1518 Heidelberg Disputation.

1519 Leipzig Debate: Luther debates with Johann Eck (1486–1543) and argues that *sola scriptura* (Scripture alone) is the basis for Christian faith and doctrine. Ulrich Zwingli begins preaching on the New Testament in Zurich.

1520 Leo X issues the papal bull *Exsurge Domine*. Three key works set out Luther's theology: *To the Christian Nobility of the German Nation*, *On the Babylonian Captivity of the Church* and *On the Freedom of a Christian*. Luther burns the papal bull and books of Canon Law.

1521 Henry VIII of England takes up the pen against Luther in the *Assertio septem sacramentorium* (*Defence of the Seven Sacraments*). Pope Leo X rewards Henry by granting him the title *Fidei Defensor*, or 'Defender of the Faith'. Luther excommunicated by papal bull *Decet Romanum Pontificem*. The Diet of Worms is held and Luther's refusal to recant leads to his excommunication by Pope Leo X and condemnation at the Imperial Diet. Charles V issues *Edict of Worms*, declaring Luther a public outlaw. Elector Frederick the Wise provides Luther with protection and refuge in the Wartburg castle.

1522   Luther preaches the *Invocavit Sermons* against radicalism of the Zwickau prophets. Printing of Luther's German *New Testament*. City of Zurich embarks on Reformation.

1523   Nuns fleeing convent in Nimbschen, including Katherine von Bora, arrive in Wittenberg. Heinrich Voes and John Esch, first Lutheran martyrs, burned at stake in Antwerp.

1524   Outbreak of German Peasants' War. Printing of *Achtliederbuch (A Book of Eight Hymns)*, first Lutheran hymnal.

1525   Rebaptism of George Blaurock by Conrad Grebel seen as the origin of Anabaptism. Luther marries Katherine von Bora. William Tyndale's English New Testament is printed in Worms.

1526   Diet of Speyer permits German princes to determine the religion of their territory.

1527   Luther writes 'A Mighty Fortress'. Imperial troops of Charles V sack Rome.

1528   Execution of Patrick Hamilton, Protestant martyr, in St Andrews.

1529   (April) Second Diet of Speyer, including the issue of the *Protestio*, giving rise to the label 'Protestant'. Colloquy of Marburg: Luther and Ulrich Zwingli debate the issue of the presence of Christ in the Eucharist, but are unable to reach an agreement.

1530   *Augsburg Confession* presented to Charles V at Diet of Augsburg.

1531   Formation of Smalkaldic League. Ulrich Zwingli dies in battle at Kappel am Albis.

1533   The marriage of Henry VIII and Catherine of Aragon is declared invalid, against the will of the Pope.

1534   Act of Supremacy: Henry VIII becomes supreme head of the Church in England. Ignatius of Loyola founds the Jesuit order. Hans Lufft publishes first edition of Luther's complete German Bible.

1535 Thomas More, former Lord Chancellor, is found guilty of treason for refusing to take the Oath of Supremacy and is executed on the orders of Henry VIII.

1536 John Calvin publishes first edition of *Institutes of the Christian Religion*. Execution of William Tyndale in Antwerp. Smaller monasteries suppressed in England.

1540 Martyrdom of Robert Barnes, Lutheran, in England. Society of Jesus (Jesuits) confirmed by Pope.

1541 Colloquy of Regensburg attempts to reach an agreement between Rome and Lutherans on justification.

1545 Council of Trent's first sessions.

1546 Luther dies at Eisleben, and is buried at the Castle Church in Wittenberg.

1547 Smalkaldic League defeated by Charles V at the Battle of Mühlberg.

1548 *Augsburg Interim* published.

1552 Death of Katherine von Bora in Torgau.

1555 Peace of Augsburg grants toleration to Lutherans within the Holy Roman Empire using the principle of *cuius regio, eius religio*, or 'Whoever the prince, his the religion'.

1563 Closing session of the Council of Trent.

1566 Iconoclastic Fury (*Beeldenstorm*) in the Low Countries.

1572 St Bartholomew's Day Massacre of Protestant Huguenots in France.

1598 *Edict of Nantes* grants religious freedom to French Huguenots.

Maps

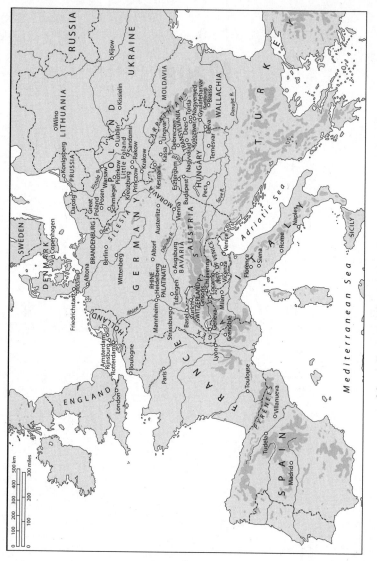

Map 1: Europe at the end of the sixteenth century

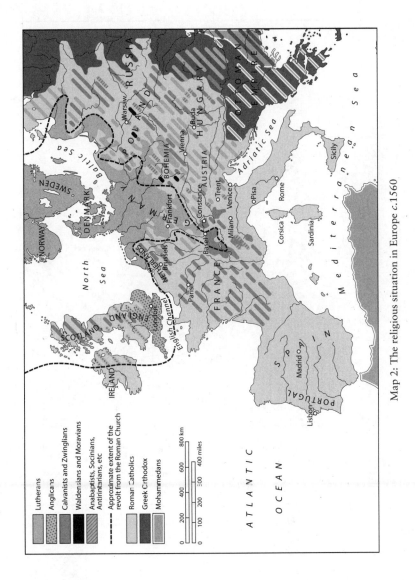

Map 2: The religious situation in Europe *c*.1560

Map 3: The religious situation in Central Europe c.1560

Introduction

500 YEARS

'The eternal, all powerful God has looked upon us graciously and delivered us from the horrible darkness of the papacy and led [us] into the bright light of the Gospel.'

Abraham Scultetus, New Year Sermon delivered in Heidelberg on the centenary of the Reformation, 1617[1]

'Ad Lutherum igitur nostrum revertimur, &, ipsius potius effigiem in incendiis singulari Dei providentia conservatam fuisse, probamus ...' ['Then we go back to Luther, and his portrait in the fire, preserved by the providence of God ...']

Justus Schoepffer, *Lutherus non combustus*, 1717[2]

'The reformation brought instead of the word of man the word of God, instead of constrained interpretation, free enquiry into Holy Scripture, instead of dark, blind faith, the rational clarity of free conviction, instead of the coercion of conscience under priestly power, the freedom of the spirit and heart under God's power.'

August Ludwig Hanstein *Das Jubeljar der evangelischen Kirche: Vie vorbereitende Predigten*, 1817)[3]

'Martin Luther als Vorkämpfer deutschen Geistes.' ['Luther, champion of the German spirit.']

Erich Brandenburg, *Martin Luther als Vorkämpfer deutschen Geistes: eine Rede zur 400jährigen Jubelfeier der Reformation*, 1917

'On 31 October 1517, Martin Luther nailed his 95 theses against the abuse of the sale of indulgences on the door of the Castle Church in Wittenberg, thereby not only changing the ecclesiastical world but setting in motion a reformation in politics, business, science, art, and culture.'

Lutherstadt Wittenberg, Tourist Information,
https://lutherstadt-wittenberg.de/en/luther-2017/

1517

The 500th anniversary of the Reformation was marked on 31 October 2017. Few anniversaries have attracted such global and diverse interest, much of it focused upon the beliefs of one man, Martin Luther, and the sense that the events of October 1517 have exerted a transformative influence upon Europe and the wider world. The Protestant Reformation has been denounced as a source of division and strife, religious war and cultural destruction, and lauded as a force for progress, in which are anchored the roots of capitalism, democracy and secularism. Its history began to be written in Luther's own lifetime, and has continued to be written in the five centuries that have elapsed since then. Over the course of half a millennium, the act of writing that history has shaped history itself, and the memorialization of events, times, people and places has reshaped memory and recreated the past. The Reformation is a palimpsest upon which each generation has imposed a meaning, a meaning which is in turn effaced under pressure from new contexts and methodologies. But the consistency with which 1517 appears in word, image and memory is indicative of a broad appreciation of the significance of the events that occurred in Wittenberg, and the ripples that they sent across European and global history.

Martin Luther occupies a central position in that historical memory and in the discussions that follow here. The publication of this volume coincides with the quincentenary of what has been seen as Luther's Reformation; although most current scholarship would contend that the picture is rather more complex than this implies, the story of the 'renegade friar' is intricately tied up with the history of the Reformation. There is an inherent attractiveness in this narrative, from which Luther emerges as a man of conscience,

Fig. 1: Lucas
Cranach the Elder,
Martin Luther,
1529

a man who could 'do no other' when armed with the word of God
and confronted by the institutional Church. Luther was the figure
of David who stood up to the might and tyranny of Goliath, who
challenged authoritarianism and presented a cogent defence of the
authority of the faith of the believer, and the relationship between
the individual and God over the traditions and superstitions of the
medieval Church. It was Luther who put the Bible, the word of
God, back in the hands of the faithful, wresting control of the
Gospel from those who asserted the primacy of the papacy and
the laws of the Church, proclaiming the freedom of the Gospel
to those who were prepared to accept it. It was Luther who swept
away the constellation of devotional practices that set physical and
doctrinal barriers between priest and people, positioning mankind
in a direct relationship with God, freed from the obligations and
disciplines of an oppressive and interventionist institution. And
it was Luther, whose name became synonymous with reform and

regeneration, whose destructively simple theology cut a swathe through the complexities and corruptions of a Church that had fallen under the influence of the devil, and set Christendom on an iconoclastic path towards true religion, salvation and intellectual and economic progress.

But start to dissect the language and assumptions in this narrative and it becomes clear why the Reformation has been contested, debated and reconstructed for the last 500 years. In the eyes of his opponents, Luther's Reformation was not anchored in Scripture, but in an arrogant and stubborn approach to the Church that had been founded upon the rock of Peter. Luther was not the hero of the hour, but the 'wild boar' who trampled in the vineyard of the Lord. The wide circulation of his vernacular polemic spread poison among the faithful, and encouraged disobedience and rebellion, spiritual and physical. The decrees and councils of the Church, guided by the Holy Spirit, affirmed the truth of Scripture and provided the normative exegesis, and yet Luther's pride and obstinacy led him to assert that his opinions held greater authority. As other self-appointed reformers had done before him, Luther encouraged the faithful to indulge in wild fantasies that tarnished the sacred mysteries of the faith. Standing against 1,500 years during which the Church had exercised custodianship of the Gospel, 'one single monk is hallucinating and is deceived by a certain opinion of his own, which is contrary to all Christendom'.[4]

Within that rather polarized set of narratives lie a range of more nuanced and engaging possibilities. As the scale and range of Reformation scholarship has proliferated, so general narratives have been modified, a more thoughtful vocabulary has been deployed to understand and explain ideas and events, and the cultural, political, social, economic and pastoral undercurrents that shaped early modern religion have been explored and understood in more detail. The history of the Reformation has been shaped by the discipline of history, and by the intellectual pressures exerted upon it by changing contexts and ideologies. The result is perhaps more, rather than less, uncertainty, and a more detailed but also more confusing narrative that challenges the very foundations of the Reformation that it seeks to depict. The relationship between Luther and Lutheranism, between the man and the ideas enacted in his name, is far from binding. The

Fig. 2: Workshop
of Lucas Cranach,
*Posthumous
Portrait of Martin
Luther as an
Augustine Friar*,
after 1546

Reformation, that neatly labelled file of theological certainty, has become a collection of reformations, each shaped by their own ideas, concerns and realities. The age of reformation is no longer confined to the sixteenth century, but reaches back into the High Middle Ages, and stretches over the horizon of the late seventeenth century. Historians of the Reformation(s) have been efficient colonists, seeing the roots and the ramifications of their topic across an ever expanding chronology, and in the context of debates not only over theology, but over the relationship between Church and state, the interaction of print and oral culture, economic and social imperatives, material culture, gender, magic, superstition and the sacred topography of early modern Europe. To tie this intellectual dynamic to the personal crisis of one Augustinian friar may seem ill advised, but the history of early modern Christianity has remained inseparable from the name of Martin Luther since the Reformation was first historicized and memorialized.

The creation of a history for the Reformation was intricately bound up with its own search for a useable past. The construction of a new narrative of sacred history which connected the past with the present in a symbiotic relationship that has, in many respects, endured to the present day. History was read through the prism of Scripture, which imbued events and narratives with an eschatological colour, and the leaders of reform with the status of prophets, possessing both Scripture and the past. A respect for history encouraged a process of memorialization that was most evident in the accounts of the martyrs who suffered for their faith in the sixteenth century as they had in the early Christian centuries, but that process of memorialization also had the potential to create its own imperatives and history.[5] As Howard Louthan has suggested, the Reformation 'fuelled the need to reconstruct a convincing narrative of the Christian past that could robustly withstand the most rigorous of Renaissance humanist critiques'.[6]

The commemoration of the centenary of the Reformation provides us with a clear illustration of this process. The anniversary of Luther's death, or the date on which the Reformation was established, had been marked in some imperial cities as early as the 1540s, but the celebrations of 1617 ushered in a more wide-ranging and specific form and focus for commemoration. The desire to mark the 100th anniversary was anchored less in Lutheran piety than in the political and cultural context of the early seventeenth century in which decades of confessionalization and confessional strife within Protestantism were played out against a resurgent Catholicism. In the Rhineland Palatinate, the Elector Frederick took the lead in a series of events intended to build an identity and unity within Lutheranism. In Wittenberg, celebrations of the Luther 'jubilee' were shaped by a more energetic anti-Catholic rhetoric, with sermons preached over three days based on biblical texts that constructed an image of the papal Antichrist, the whore of Babylon, and the persecuted little flock of true believers who had held fast to their Lutheran faith in the face of suffering and persecution. The commemoration of Luther exploited a range of weapons in the polemical armoury. Sermons featured prominently, but woodcuts, pamphlets, theatre, coins and medals all presented and celebrated Luther as the founding father of a reformed faith. Luther the monk had been chosen by God to break apart the superstition and idolatry of monasticism, one man empowered by God to stand up against the power and authority of the medieval Church. The memory of Luther was carefully constructed. Sermons were preached to an agreed template, and secular and ecclesiastical authorities provided a visual and verbal vocabulary that would enable the faithful to think in the right way about the Reformation as a set of ideas and as a historical event. In this commemoration, the key moment was not Luther's death, but the events of October 1517 when Luther, so the story ran, had nailed his 95 Theses to the door of the castle church in Wittenberg.[7] The very language of jubilee resonated with the theology of purgatory and the devotional practices that it had spawned, but the positioning of the jubilee in the calendar created an iconic moment for an iconoclastic Reformation. Perhaps the most famous illustration of this is to be seen in the 1617 broadside *The Dream of Friedrich the Elector.*[8] Frederick of Saxony confided in his brother, John, the content of his dream. After praying for the souls in purgatory, Frederick fell asleep,

[...] then dreamed that Almighty God sent me a monk, who was a true son of the Apostle Paul. All the saints accompanied him by order of God, in order to bear testimony before me, and to declare that he did not come to contrive any plot, but that all that he did was according to the will of God. They asked me to have the goodness graciously to permit him to write something on the door of the church of the Castle of Wittenberg. This I granted through my chancellor. Thereupon the monk went to the church, and began to write [...] The pen which he used was so large that its end reached as far as Rome, where it pierced the ears of a lion that was crouching there, and caused the triple crown upon the head of the Pope to shake. All the cardinals and princes, running hastily up, tried to prevent it from falling [...]

The lion, still annoyed by the pen, began to roar with all his might, so much so that the whole city of Rome, and all the States of the Holy

Empire, ran to see what the matter was. The Pope requested them to oppose this monk, and applied particularly to me, on account of his being in my country [...]

Then I dreamed that all the princes of the Empire, and we among them, hastened to Rome, and strove, one after another, to break the pen; but the more we tried the stiffer it became, sounding as if it had been made of iron. We at length desisted. I then asked the monk (for I was sometimes at Rome, and sometimes at Wittenberg) where he got this pen, and why it was so strong. 'The pen,' replied he, 'belonged to an old goose of Bohemia, a hundred years old. I got it from one of my old schoolmasters. As to its strength, it is owing to the impossibility of depriving it of its pith or marrow; and I am quite astonished at it myself.' Suddenly I heard a loud noise — a large number of other pens had sprung out of the long pen of the monk. I awoke a third time: it was daylight.[9]

Fig. 3: Reformation Centenary broadsheet, *The Dream of Frederick the Wise*, 1617

A century after Luther composed his attack on purgatory and indulgences, the events of 31 October 1517 were cast as the starting-point of a religious reformation, inspired by God and enacted in accordance with the providential design. In the sermon delivered by Abraham Scultetus with which we started, preached within the framework of the 1617 commemorations, that sense of Luther as divinely chosen is apparent. 'The eternal, all powerful God has looked upon us graciously and delivered us from the horrible darkness of the papacy,' Scultetus proclaimed, 'and led [us] into the bright light of the Gospel.' The 1617 centenary celebrations did much to create the image of Luther as prophet and messenger, but also shaped a new narrative of events from which the 95 Theses emerged as the 'moment' at which the Reformation began.

This depiction of Luther as the chosen messenger of God, marked out by the Almighty and preserved and protected in order to fulfil this calling, was still evident in the commemorations of the bicentenary of the Reformation in 1717. Luther was once more the focal point, but the implicit supernatural validation of his actions in Frederick's dream was articulated more explicitly in the multiple reports of the 'incombustible Luther', images and objects associated with Luther that were immune to fire and flame. The most substantial presentation of such events was the work of Justus Schoepffer, *Lutherus non combustus*, published in 1717 in Latin and in German. Schoepffer provided an account of a growing number of 'wonders' associated with Luther, including the widely reported case of the pastor and dean of Artern who in 1634 had retrieved from the ashes of his study an image of Martin Luther, unharmed by the flames. The pastor dispatched the engraving to the Consistory in Mansfeld, where it was displayed with the inscription 'the image of Luther, miraculously preserved in a fire in Artern'. This image is generally regarded as the first such 'incombustible Luther', but other examples soon followed.[10]

Whether or not fabricated and accepted consciously or subconsciously by the Lutheran Church, the apparent indestructability of Luther's image resonated with the language of incorruptibility of the relics of the saints, and opened up a new theme in the commemorations and memories of the Reformation. The miraculous preservation of an image of Luther seems paradoxical given the rhetoric that Luther himself deployed in an assault upon the idolatry and superstition of Catholic image worship. As we will see, the destruction of images was a priority of the early Reformation in Wittenberg, but the relationship between the Reformation and the image was more complicated than the rhetoric of iconoclasm suggests. Lucas Cranach produced popular visual propaganda for the Reformation, but also a series of altar pieces, each decorated in a way that endorsed and enacted Lutheran theology. These altarpieces depicted not only biblical scenes, but scenes from church services and liturgies, which allowed the celebration of the Lord's Supper to take place against the backdrop of a Cranach image of the same.[11] In much the same way, the account of the incombustible Luther involved the reader in a dialogue in which the narrative of the Reformation shaped memory, and memorialization constructed the narrative.

The message of the 1717 celebrations, shaped by the rhetoric of 1617 and expressed in popular song, was that God's word and Luther's teaching shall never perish (Gottes Wort und Luthers Lehr wird vergehen nimmermehr).[12] There was an implicit anti-Catholicism in some of this rhetoric, which echoed the language of 1617 in presenting Luther as the godly reformer engaged in battle with the church of Antichrist. By 1817, however, the focus had become more politicized, with Luther presented as a German national hero, and with confessional conflict downplayed in celebration of human progress since the Reformation. Commemorative medals depicted not just Luther, but Luther and Calvin, and the king of Prussia participated in a sharing of communion with Lutheran and Calvinist clergy. In keeping with the emerging teleology of reform, Hegel declared the Reformation to be the 'transfiguring sun, the morning dawn that signifies the end of the Middle Ages'.[13] Such language inspired Leopold von Ranke to pen the 'Luther fragment', a biography of the reformer that situated Luther firmly among the founding fathers of German nationhood. Ranke asserted the value of history rather than hagiography in the representation of Luther, although, as on other celebratory occasions, there was plenty of hagiographical writing to be had in 1817. A more substantial articulation of Ranke's interpretation was set out in the six-volume *Deutsche Geschichte im Zeitalter der Reformation* (1839–47), which exerted a profound influence upon the narrative and history of the German Reformation until the end of the century. Here, the centrality of faith to the Reformation was argued, motivated by the *ewig freie Geist,* the eternally free spirit, that guided events.[14] Luther's message, it seemed, was ingrained in the heart and soul of German nationhood, as a political history took shape that drew a line stretching from Luther to Bismarck, and provided what amounted to a creation myth for the land over which Bismarck presided. The achievement of the Reformation, and its triumph, was to create the political and cultural environment that allowed such ambitions to come to fruition. 'Luther and the German Nation' was both an inspiration and an outcome. In Heinrich von Treitschke's exuberant presentation of Luther's influence, the reformer was 'the pioneer of the whole German nation' whose 'German defiance' and willingness to defy unjust authority shaped and reflected the German character. Luther inspired German modernity, in politics, religion and culture.[15] Ranke's terminology of *freie Geist* continued to shape German Reformation historiography well into the twentieth century. An editorial in the influential academic journal *Archiv Fur Reformationsgeschichte* for 1938 asserted the Reformation to be 'a major achievement of the German spirit [*Geist*], and its historical understanding must be preserved by the whole of the German people'. However, the journal was not intended to cement the link between Luther and the German nation, but rather to adopt a more universal approach. Reformation studies would not be constrained by ideas about 'church history' or 'secular history' or 'political history', or the history of the Protestant churches, but rather focus on the global history of the impact of the Reformation that stretched from the sixteenth century to the Enlightenment: 'truly modern Reformation research that unites theological, political, legal, and socioeconomic and philosophical methods'.[16]

This approach, laid out eight decades ago, has continued to exert a profound influence over the study and writing of Reformation history, which has come to encompass theology, politics, social and economic context, material culture, print and oral culture, and debates over gender and religion. Such an approach is fuelled by a desire to contextualize events, to debate the reception of ideas, to reflect upon the processes by which hearts and minds were persuaded (and the success of such endeavours) and to position the lived environment within discussions of the relationship between Protestantism, history and memory. Encouraged by alternative approaches and methodologies, notably the social, cultural, linguistic and material 'turns' of modern scholarship, histories of the Reformation have become histories not only of 'the Church', or even 'religion', but, increasingly, of 'belief'. The chronology of the Reformation has shifted, but so has the mental landscape against which Reformation as process, less than event, played out. The indebtedness of Reformation theology to the intellectual framework of the late medieval Church is recognized, and the argument that the roots of Protestantism lay in the 'harvest of medieval theology' rather than the mind of Luther alone articulated with more vigour. The poetic language of Carter Lindberg conjures images of 'evangelical sprouts [that] not only hardened into many of the contemporary branches of Protestantism, but also intertwined with the growth of early modern Catholicism. The taxonomy of the Reformation focuses on the reformers with the supposition that without them there would have been no Reformation. At the same time, to carry our garden image a bit further, it is clear that any analysis of growth must take into account the soil and environment.'[17] That same connection between Catholicism and Protestantism was asserted in John Bossy's authoritative and still influential discussion of *Christianity in the West, 1400–1700*, from which the Reformation emerges as a chapter in a much more complex process by which the religious homogeneity of Latin Christianity was shattered.

Bossy's conclusion was that the outcome of this pluralism was a Protestant piety that was focused upon the individual rather than the community, and which undermined any possibility of social cohesion and sense of Christian commonwealth. The extent to which Protestantism constructed or imposed a confessional identity was debated with energy in the scholarship of the 1980s, fuelled substantially by the work of Heinz Schilling and Wolfgang Reinhard, and the language of 'confessionalization' in which politics and religion shaped the development of the modern state. Here, the creation of a confessional allegiance went hand in hand with social discipline.[18] The underlying hypotheses have since been explored and debated in a variety of geographical and chronological contexts, exploring the extent to which political structures interacted with religious identities through a process by which social discipline imposed a pattern of acceptable belief and behaviour. The emerging analyses expose both the plausibility and the dangers inherent in the vocabulary of confessionalization, which has the potential to downplay the extent to which post-Reformation communities were able to exercise control over their beliefs and to exaggerate a hostile polemic that obscures a willingness to entertain toleration or irenicism. Such debates have encouraged a more thoughtful reflection upon the implications of religious diversity for individuals and communities, and the extent to which the Reformation required a conscious individual negotiation of the relationship between faith and practice, believer and Church, and a pluralism in belief that had profound implications for social relationships.[19] Within the context of these interactions, recent work has also highlighted the value of an understanding of the dynamics of the community and household, and the impact of the Reformation upon marriage, family and women, and the very personal responses to the Reformation that shaped, and were shaped by, a reordering of the traditional structures and models.[20]

Such a recognition of the diversity of responses to Reformation is often a far cry from the certainties and stark polarities of polemical debate. The effort to win over hearts and minds, beyond simple coercion, relied upon the communication of a message that was persuasive and self-evident, and anchored in the eschatological language of two-church ideology in which the faithful exhibited an allegiance to the true congregation of the Gospel (at least in evangelical rhetoric) or the false idolatrous church of Antichrist. In the heat of polemical exchange, one's opponents were not simply misguided, but the very agents of the Antichrist. References to the medieval Church as the 'synagogue of Satan' and the 'whore of Babylon' punctuated polemical and theological treatises and provided a recognizable iconography in cheap broadside prints.[21] The value of such language and imagery in the history of sixteenth-century religion was exposed in the seminal works of Bob Scribner in the 1980s, which fuelled an ongoing debate over exploitation of the printing press as a weapon of confessional conflict in the sixteenth century, and the effectiveness of printed propaganda, word and image.[22] The allure of the printed book as a means of shaping minds is obvious: it is recognizable and tangible, and for most scholars reassuringly familiar as a repository of ideas and analysis. However, the broader 'culture of persuasion' discussed in the work of Andrew Pettegree and others has widened the scope of the debate over the nature and impact of propaganda during the Reformation. Given the relatively small size of the reading public in early modern Europe, and the constraints imposed by the price of books, the availability of education, and, on occasion, the efficient use of censorship, just how important was the printing press to the dissemination of the Reformation? And if print no longer reigns supreme as the channel through which new assumptions were disseminated, through what medium did that dissemination occur, and how easily controlled was its content? A growing sensitivity to the interactions and intersections of oral and literate culture has led to a greater recognition of the role that oral and material culture played in the communication of the Reformation and the construction of belief, history and memory. Sermon, song and the senses provide new routes into debates about communication and conversion, the reception of the Reformation and the experience of Protestantism as a theological and cultural force.[23] A willingness to engage with the material remains of the past has encouraged reflection upon the often complex relationship between Protestantism and the image, the book as object, and the sacred topography by which evangelism and belief were shaped.[24] As a result, the interactions between belief and action, and between the physical and spiritual, have been reimagined, recognizing the importance of the object, as much as the idea, in the construction of community, memory and faith.

A further and far-reaching consequence of this analysis of the wider culture of Protestantism has been the emergence of a more detailed and sympathetic understanding of the relationship between the Reformation and the supernatural. Recent work has undermined the assumption that a clear path existed from popish superstition to the Protestant rejection of numinous beings and objects to the rational world of the Enlightenment. These studies explore the presence of the sacred within the Reformation, and debate the construction of a Protestant sacralized universe that was not mere survival, but a more conscious attempt to mould the relationship between the supernatural and the physical. The discursive exchange that characterized this relationship exposes the extent to which attempts to redefine the interaction between mankind and its environment were orchestrated as much by negotiation as by coercion and conversion. Post-Reformation religious culture was heterogeneous and multiform, an often capacious set of ideas and principles formed at the point of collision between the old and the new, delineating the past and mapping the present.[25]

This interchange between the present and the past has been evident in the commemorations of the Luther anniversary over the last five centuries, and is no less relevant now. As the Reformation is 'remembered' in the present, it acquires an increasingly amorphous shape. After 500 years, the Reformation defies classification as a simple religious, political, social or cultural 'event', it lacks an agreed start or end, and the dogmatic certainties that shaped its relationship with the past, and its own history and identity, have proved to be far more malleable than its language suggested. But for this very reason, as attention shifts once more to the events that took place in Wittenberg in October 1517, it is hard to escape from the sense that the history of the Reformation will continue to be written for another 500 years.

1

IN THE POWER OF GOD ALONE?

MARTIN LUTHER AND THE THEOLOGY OF THE REFORMATION

For a variety of reasons, some more compelling than others, the theological debates and controversies that defined and shaped the Reformation have receded from our view in recent years. There are, of course, some honourable exceptions to this assertion, but the same emphasis upon the culture of reform, the reception of religious change and the long-term impact of the Reformation upon belief that has made recent scholarship so exciting has also run the risk that the theologies of reform become increasingly marginalized. The subtle but important shift from the history of the Church to the history of religion in the final quarter of the twentieth century has diverted attention away from the doctrines and apologetics of the intellectual and theological elite, towards what we might loosely term 'popular religion', or the faith of 'simple folk'.[1] These were not the passive recipients of new ideas, accepting unquestioningly the sermons and polemic that defined and explained justification by faith, *sola scriptura*, or any of the other guiding principles of early evangelicalism. Rather, through the prism presented by histories of early modern culture and society, the laity and local clergy emerged as active agents, participating in, and remodelling, a new religious understanding. Where older, traditional narratives depicted the crystallization of Reformation

17

theology in the minds and works of the 'great men' of the nascent Protestant churches, the origins of these ideas seemed to matter less than their impact.

It is quite right that the history of the Reformation should be more than the history of academic theology, but the process of understanding the means by which theological and pastoral change was adopted and adapted in the parishes, in lay religion and in the hearts and minds of the faithful still needs to start with a sense of where these 'new' beliefs came from. Of course the narrative of the evolution of belief is never simple. The discussion of Reformation theology (or perhaps more accurately, theologies) over the last few decades has become increasingly anchored in the faith and practice of the later medieval Church: the history of the Reformation begins not in 1517, but some 200 years before.[2] A growing interest in the ideas that underpinned the collapse of Christian unity in the first half of the sixteenth century has been a natural concomitant of the burgeoning interest in the origins and impact of reform. Study of the reformation in the parishes, or of the operation of religious belief in the social and cultural sphere, has in many respects served to refocus our attention on the competing theologies that drive this change. The narrative of the Reformation as a history of doctrine or a history of society need not be mutually exclusive, and an intermingling of these strands has greatly enhanced our appreciation of both. Cultural and social histories of religious change have drawn upon analyses of theological debate, while scholars of intellectual dialogue and disputation have rejected any assumption that these ideas were of no concern to a popular culture that was grounded in superstition rather than faith. As the editors of one of the best recent studies of Reformation thought have reminded us, theology may once more be centre-stage in scholarship, but its position is *contextual* and no longer tethered to the intellectual pillar of historical theologians. Rather, debates over Reformation theology are to be found in works of history and literary studies, cultural and social analyses of the age of reform. Theological principles did not arise in a vacuum, but grew out of the broader environments into which they were planted. The discussion of theology therefore requires a similar willingness on the part of the scholar to reflect upon that context and to seek out the practical impulses that acted as a catalyst or a brake on doctrinal change. Salvation was a practical, rather than abstract, theoretical concern, and the question of how to secure the fate of one's eternal soul mattered across the broadest demography. The theologians of the Reformation were themselves its pastors and preachers, and our ability to access their ideas and ambitions derives from a reading of the means by which they were communicated: sermons, polemical treatises, letters of support and exhortation.[3]

THE START OF THE REFORMATION?: 31 OCTOBER 1517

In February 2015, the toy manufacturer Playmobil announced that its figurine of Martin Luther was the fastest-selling model in its range. Within 72 hours of its release, some 34,000 figures of Luther, complete with hat, quill and German Bible, had been sold.[4] A spokesman for the company conceded that the popularity of the Luther figurine had come as something of a surprise, attributing the rapid sales, primarily in Germany, to a growing interest in history and the desire of parents to ensure that their children grow up with an understanding of how 'a totally normal person [who] shared the belief of the majority of the people of the time' could still speak to a twenty-first-century audience. The mass production and consumption of the Playmobil Luther pays homage to the traditional legend and imagery of the origins of the Reformation. Luther, in this story, articulated his grievances against the Roman Catholic Church by hammering his 95 Theses to the door of the castle church in Wittenberg. This open expression of difference, even defiance, sent ripples across Christendom, presented a new analysis of the relationship between man and God, and rocked the foundations of the institutional Church. The image of Luther, with hammer in hand, emerged as an icon in its own right, leaving an indelible mark upon the representation of the Reformation in art and print and on screen.

Erwin Iserloh's assertion in the 1960s that 'the theses were not posted' was an act of iconoclasm as bold and as controversial as those of the sixteenth century.[5] The legend, Iserloh contended, was the creation of Luther's companion Philip Melanchthon, although the fictional narrative of the Reformation that the legend invited and incited was cemented by the determination of Luther and

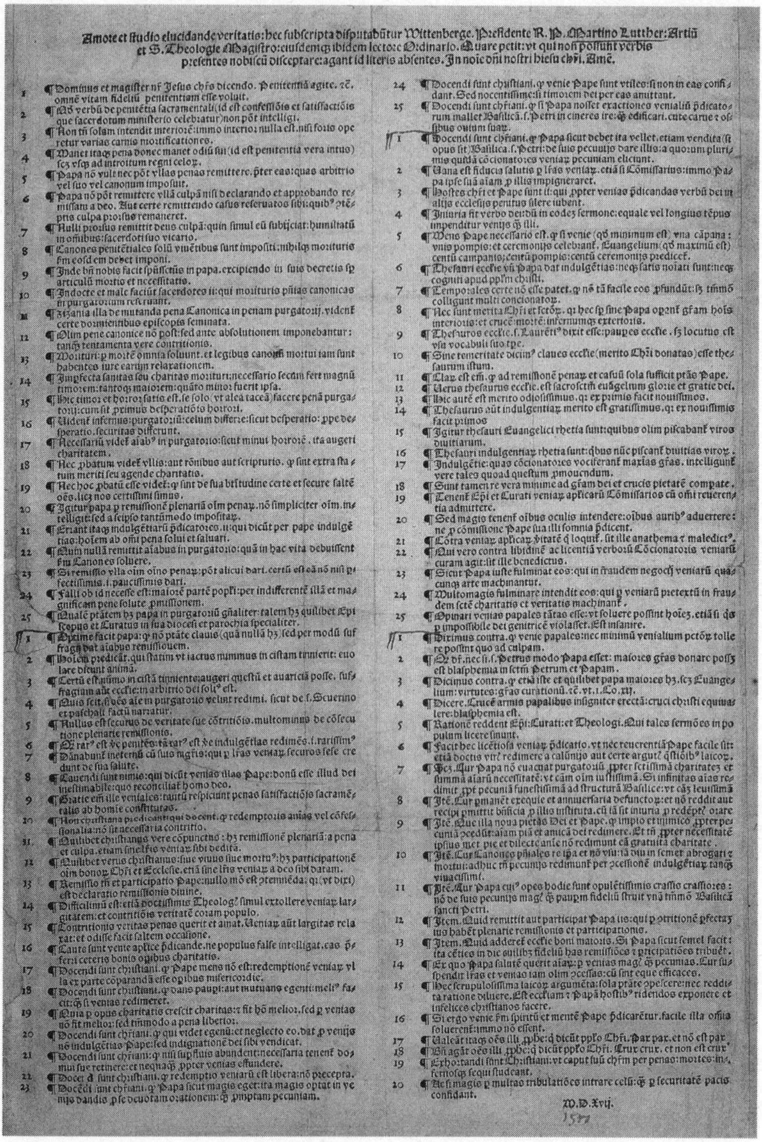
Amore et studio elucidande veritatis: hec subscripta disputabuntur Wittenberge. Presidente R. P. Martino Luther: Artiu et S. Theologie Magistro: eiusdemque ibidem lectore Ordinario. Quare petit: ut qui non possunt verbis presentes nobiscum disceptare: agant id literis absentes. In noie dni nostri hiesu chri. Ame.

M.D.Xvij.

Fig. 4: Martin Luther, 95 Theses, 1517

his followers to establish a date on which the 'foundation' of the Reformation had been laid. The fact that the legend could not withstand scholarly scrutiny, he argued, presented compelling evidence that Luther had not intended to rush headlong into conflict with the Roman Catholic Church, and that the process that we know as 'the Reformation' had been initiated 'quite unintentionally'.[6] The origins of Luther's thought, Iserloh suggested, might be better understood within the context of late medieval nominalism, rather than in the events of October 1517. Iserloh's assertion that Luther's reformation was unintentional perhaps echoes the lexicon of Melanchthon's account of the posting of the 95 Theses on the church door.[7] For Melanchthon, this was the 'beginnings of this controversy, in which Luther, as yet suspecting or dreaming nothing about the future change of rites, was certainly not completely getting rid of indulgences themselves, but only urging moderation'. Yet that failure to appreciate the significance of the event need not be negatively construed. As Michael Mullett has suggested, Luther's lack of knowledge imputed to the events of 31 October an almost providential purpose. Luther, as the human instrument of God's purpose, did not yet perceive the divine plan in its entirety. If Luther was the agent rather than the means in this context, then the work of reformation was also enacted through the will of God, not man.[8]

The reality and symbolism of the nailing of the Theses continues to be energetically debated, but the modelling of 31 October as 'Reformation Day' has ensured the continued presence of the story of the 95 Theses in almost every narrative of early German Protestantism. Frederick Wilhelm IV (1795–1861) sought to make good the damage that had been sustained by the *Schlosskirche* during the Seven Years War and the Napoleonic Wars, arguing that, if nothing else, the door of the church must be restored 'this door is a monument to Reformation History. Let us renew them in kind, poured in ore, and just as Luther attached his 95 Theses, engrave the Theses on the door in gold.' In 1858, the bronze *Thesenportal* were installed at the entrance to the church on Reformation Day.[9] In many respects, the veracity of the story matters less than the content and reception of the Theses themselves. Written in Latin, posted on what amounted to a general bulletin board for debates and news, the physical text that Luther published on the church

Fig. 5: A. Savin, Luther's 95 Theses engraved
above the door of All Saints' Church, Wittenberg

door was undoubtedly less significant than the fact that his ideas spread widely, and immediately, within and beyond the academic community. Martin Luther remains, understandably, the starting-point for the history of the Reformation, although the extent to which either the 'key man' or the 'key moments' of his life set in train a process that transformed the European understanding of God remains contested. This is not to deny that which was significant, or radical, in Luther's evolving theology. But rather than assume that the true import of his thought and actions was perceptible from the outset, it is vital to situate Luther's ideas within the context provided by his life, the social and intellectual context in which he worked, and the response to the first stirrings of reform that did so much to shape the way that the story unfurled.

A copy of the Theses was dispatched to Albert, the Archbishop of Mainz, who drew them to the attention of the Pope Leo X, but at this point, there was no formal response. Leo reportedly dismissed the Theses as an 'argument among monks', an academic disputation and debate rather than a determined attempt to subvert the foundations of the Church. A formal response came in the bull *Exsurge Domine* (1520), but by this point the dissemination of Luther's ideas was more widespread. In 1518, Christoph von Scheurl and a group of Luther's students from Wittenburg translated the document into German and published it, thus spreading Luther's ideas among a broader audience. In order to stand as the nominal or figurative start of the Reformation, the Latin manuscript of propositions needed to find its way into the vernacular culture of the time. And if the Theses were not the intentional start of a reformation, neither were they a fully formed description of Luther's views; criticism of indulgences in the early sixteenth century was neither new, nor unique to Luther, and the key principles that are commonly associated with later Lutheran theology are not yet in the foreground. They contained no outright rejection of papal authority (although there were some strident criticisms of papal conduct), no open statement of schism and no attempt to extrapolate from the specific question of indulgences to the other theological and devotional pillars of the late medieval Church. So what, for Luther, was at stake here, and how did context and concept intertwine in his actions and their outworking?

MARTIN LUTHER

The details of Martin Luther's life are well mapped in a multitude of biographical studies, historical theologies and discussions of the manifold ways in which Luther has been imagined and reimagined across different chronological, geographical and confessional boundaries.[10] Martin Luther was born in Eisleben in 1483, the son of a mine owner, who was encouraged in his youth to pursue a career in law that would be both respectable and financially secure. To this end, in 1501 he enrolled at the University of Erfurt, and seemed set to fulfil his family's ambition. Decades after the event, Luther described a momentous incident in the summer of 1505, which was to change the course of his life. Caught in a thunderstorm on the road near Erfurt in the principality of Saxony, and fearing for his own survival, Luther invoked the intercession of St Anne, and vowed to become a monk if he was spared. In July, he entered the Augustinian house at Erfurt, in fulfilment of his promise. This was no easy way of life, but Luther dedicated himself fully to its demands, spending time in fasting, prayer, the examination of conscience and confession. As he later commented, 'If anyone could have earned heaven by the life of a monk, it was I.' But the pious fulfilment of these obligations did not bring for Luther the comfort and assurance that he sought. Rather, the opposite was true; Luther was to refer to these years as a period of deep spiritual despair in which he 'lost touch with Christ the Saviour and Comforter, and made of him the jailer and hangman of my poor soul'.

The physical and spiritual sufferings that followed from Luther's overriding sense of his own weakness and failings took their toll bodily and mentally, but these months of despair also helped to shape Luther's own understanding of his relationship with God. His confessor, Johannes Staupitz, encouraged Luther to engage with the writings of St Augustine, with which Luther later conceded he had little sympathy at the time.[11] But employed at the University of Wittenberg to lecture on the *Sentences* of Peter Lombard, Luther read and reflected upon *On the Spirit and the Letter*, *On the Trinity* and *The City of God*, and his lectures on the Psalms cited Augustine extensively. It is possible to chart a shift in emphasis and interpretation away from a sense, informed by Biel and Occam, that while man was imperfect, he was certainly not impotent in his own salvation, and capable of loving God. By 1513, in the *Lectures on Psalms*, Luther was borrowing more extensively from Augustine and the vocabulary of *justitia Dei*, the justice of God; by 1515 in his lectures on Romans, Augustine had led Luther to a rather different sense of the righteousness of God (Romans 1.17). A month before the posting of the 95 Theses, in his *Disputation Against Scholastic Theology*, Luther was still more strident in his rejection of any notion that a meritorious human righteousness might be acquired. If it was possible to do, without grace, that which is in oneself (*facere quod in se est*), to argue that humanity was incapable of fulfilling the law without grace was to transform divine grace into an unbearable burden. And, significantly for what was to follow, two months later in October 1517, Luther reworked the relationship between works, faith and grace to argue that righteous deeds did not make one righteous, but rather having been made righteous by God's grace, man was capable of, and motivated to do, righteous deeds. Luther, the devout, perhaps over-conscientious, monk, stood on the brink of breaking apart the very principles that guided monastic life.

To see the seeds of the Reformation in the spiritual crisis of one individual is to downplay the importance of the intellectual and cultural climate in which Luther found himself. Luther was certainly not alone in contemplating the essence and purpose of the Christian life. The decades that preceded Luther's personal discovery of what it meant to be righteous had witnessed calls for reform from inside and outside the institutional Church, some of which had found embodiment in alternative expressions of the religious life, and in more overt rejections of the theology and practice of the late medieval Church. It is no longer acceptable to attribute the 'success' of the Reformation simply to the 'corruption' of the medieval Church, but the reflection of the Reformation as the 'harvest of medieval theology' still provides a useful perspective on the intellectual origins of Luther's crisis, and its apparent solution. Far from being moribund, the late medieval Church was intellectually vibrant, powerful, self-confident and deeply rooted, despite (or perhaps because of) demands for reform.[12] Critics, even heretics, and attempts to suppress them, were not simply a reactionary response, but manifestations of an ever-present reforming spirit within the late medieval Church, and testimony to its institutional vibrancy. Wycliffe, Hus, Erasmus and Luther were all products of this intellectual milieu, as much as the Brethren of Common Life, the Beguines and the Heresy of the Free Spirit were the embodiment of its practical consequences. But if pluralism could mirror vitality, so license ran the risk of exposing vulnerabilities. For Alister McGrath,

[...] an astonishingly broad spectrum of theologies of justification existed in the later medieval period, encompassing practically every option that had not been specifically condemned as heretical by the Council of Carthage. In the absence of any definitive magisterial pronouncement concerning which of these options (or even what range of options) could be considered authentically Catholic, it was left to each theologian to reach his own decision in this matter. A self-perpetuating doctrinal pluralism was thus an inevitability.[13]

The apparent absence of any magisterial guidance gave rise to a situation in which theological opinions became confused with 'authorized' dogma, which eroded the teaching authority of the Church while at the same time permitting a credal pluralism to coexist without repression. A crisis of authority went hand in hand with doctrinal diversity, and provided a stimulating and potentially unsettling context into which Luther's doubts could plunge, spreading ripples across an already far from placid surface.[14] What is clear from this is that Luther's articulation of his criticisms of the Church in the 95 Theses was not simply the beginning of something new. To adopt something of a cliché, the Theses were as much the end of the beginning as they were the beginning of the end, rooted in the theologies of the fifteenth century, fed by the religious, social and cultural concerns of the sixteenth century, and informed by the internal conflict of one man, that was both highly personal, but generally relevant.

THE 95 THESES

The starting point for Luther's 95 Theses was the sale of indulgences, and the soteriology that underpinned them. Luther was, in 1517, a university teacher but also a pastor. His denunciation of indulgences therefore grew out of his own academic training, but also a more immediate alarm that his congregation might be deluded into believing, wrongly, that forgiveness for sins might be obtained via a financial transaction. The ramifications of his criticisms were substantial. Indulgences were part of a much broader theology of sin, forgiveness and penance; to criticize the sale of indulgences in 1517 was, at the very least, to raise questions about the underlying principles that warranted their existence.

The lexicon of the Theses was that of the medieval penitential system, making clear that the sale of indulgences was not to be treated in isolation. The penitential system rested upon three component parts: contrition, confession and satisfaction. In order that sins might be forgiven, the Christian was required to feel sorrow, to confess to a priest and to perform penance appropriate to the offence. The act of confessing to a priest, and absolution, ensured forgiveness, but this forgiveness brought with it a debt to be paid. Penance, or satisfaction, the debt of forgiven sin, could be paid through the performance of good works in this life or through suffering in the next. It enabled the sinner to pay at least some of this debt on earth, but the remainder would be paid in purgatory, where all but the saints expected to spend time preparing and purifying their souls before entry into heaven. The suffering of the souls in purgatory could be alleviated by the prayers of the living, but also reduced by procuring an indulgence, which remitted the temporal penalty due to sin. The remitting of some of the punishment due in purgatory in exchange for charity and good works was, perhaps, consoling, but the practice of commutation, through which any such obligations were fulfilled by a corresponding monetary payment presented ample opportunities for abuse. Successive popes asserted that the indulgence system allowed the faithful to draw upon the treasury of merits, the 'surplus' good works of the saints, in order the alleviate the burden of their own suffering. The living and the dead, the Church Militant on earth, the Church Suffering in purgatory, and the Church Triumphant in heaven, were already united through prayer and good works, and the indulgence system both cemented these bonds and raised questions about the legitimacy of permitting the living to obtain indulgences for the souls in purgatory. Papal confirmation of this practice came in 1476, but at a price. Indulgences that had been tied to the penance due after confession and absolution sat readily alongside the established penitential structures, but indulgences issued to alleviate pain in purgatory seemed to circumvent this process, given that the dead were in no position to confess their sins. Given that indulgences were, increasingly, issued on the basis of a financial transaction rather than charitable deeds, there was a very real danger that the indulgence preacher might be seen to be selling salvation in a way that circumvented the sacrament. The papal indulgence of 1515 did little to assuage these fears. Proclaimed in the bull *Sacrosanctis*, Leo X's indulgence was ambitious in its scope, with revenues supporting both the substantial building project of St Peter's Basilica in Rome and the episcopal and territorial ambitions of Albrecht of Brandenburg, the newly consecrated Hohenzollern Archbishop of Mainz. The campaign was delegated by Albrecht to the Dominican Johann Tetzel, who energetically promoted the sale of the indulgence with the promise that the purchaser could secure a 'divine and immortal soul' in the kingdom of heaven.[15] Tetzel's efforts did not win universal acclaim. Frederick, Elector of Saxony, refused to allow the indulgence to be preached in his territory, and those who heard Tetzel preach were not always convinced by the message. Frederick Mecum heard Tetzel preach at the silver mines at St Annaberg, and noted with horror the amount of money that had been collected by 'this stupid and brazen monk' peddling incredible promises, and assuring

Fig. 6: Jörg Breu the Elder of Augsburg,
A Question to a Mintmaker, woodcut, *c.* 1530

those present that 'as soon as a coin rang in the chest, the soul for whom it was paid would spring up to heaven'.[16] In his criticisms of the indulgence, Luther was no lone voice in the wilderness, but neither did he (at this point) present a manifesto for revolution. Ignorance was, in some respects, a proper defence; rather than argue that the actions of the Pope rendered null the authority of the Church, Luther suggested that 'if the pope knew the exactions of the preachers of indulgences, he would rather have the basilica of St Peter reduced to ashes than built with the skin, flesh and bones of his sheep'.[17] The 11th thesis, 'that the changing of the canonical penalty to the penalty of purgatory is quite evidently one of the tares that were sown while the bishops slept', stopped short of an outright denial of the purgatory's existence, but certainly struck a more critical note. The Theses did not propose a full-scale rejection of penance and good works; neither did Luther argue against the existence of purgatory. Cosmetically, at least, Luther was starting a debate, and inviting the Pope to condemn corrupt practice.

The agenda of penance and forgiveness was established in the first four Theses. 'Our Lord and Master Jesus Christ, when He said *Poenitentiam agite*, willed that the whole life of believers should be repentance,' Luther argued. Penance, he proposed, 'cannot be understood to mean sacramental penance, i.e., confession and satisfaction, which is administered by the priests' , but it also could not be understood to mean mere inward repentance, for 'there is no inward repentance which does not outwardly work divers mortifications of the flesh'. The debt of sin (Thesis 4) lasted as long as self-hatred, the true inner repentance that would continue until the soul entered heaven. The exclusion of sacramental penance in the definition of *poenitentia* offered in the second thesis was less radical than it might seem with the benefit of hindsight; this was not a strident unworking of one of the seven sacraments of the Catholic Church, but rather a reflection of the orthodox line that confession (and satisfaction) presume penitence rather than grant repentance. A prior condition of sacramental confession was a penitent aspect in the heart of the believer. Later propositions were rather more controversial. The suggestion that the penitential canons are imposed only upon the living was not contentious; indulgences for the souls in purgatory were, in reality, petitions to God for the remittance of suffering and punishment, although whether Tetzel's preaching of the 1515 indulgence imparted the subtle detail of that message is perhaps less clear.

Theses 27 and 28 were a direct engagement with the reports circulating of Tetzel's preaching: 'they preach man who say that so soon as the penny jingles into the money-box, the soul flies out', and 'it is certain that when the penny jingles into the money-box, gain and avarice can be increased, but the result of the intercession of the Church is in the power of God alone'. Luther's assertion that it was necessary to separate the financial transaction from the power of God to release the soul from purgatory amounted to a pointed criticism of contemporary practice, but not one that would be out of place with canon law. Similarly, the 32nd thesis, 'they will be condemned eternally, together with their teachers, who believe themselves sure of their salvation because they have letters of pardon', while it might appear a rejection of pardons and indulgences, in many respects reaffirmed the teaching of the Church on the necessity of repentance that precedes the pardon. To assume or assert one's own salvation (on this or any ground) was itself a form of sin, presumption. Theses 40–4 argued for the importance of suffering in the Christian life, and the need for a balance to be struck between providing reassurance to the faithful while at the same time ensuring a true contrition and works of love, rather than a lack of sorrow accompanying a freedom from any sense of penalty due as a result of sin. In a more stridently critical vein, Luther took issue with the notion of the 'treasures of the church' that were an essential part of the mechanics of the indulgence system. Here, the vocabulary is more challenging and barbed. There is an implicit criticism of the Pope in the assertion (Theses 73 and 74) that while the Pope 'justly thunders' against those who obstruct pardons, 'much more does he intend to thunder against those who use the pretext of pardons to contrive the injury of holy love and truth'. This falls short of an overt rejection of papal authority, but perhaps invites an assertion that popes have not treated equally those who obstruct pardons and those who exploit and abuse them. The call for change is apparent, but at this point, the authority of the Pope is not explicitly called into question.

The final section of the Theses raise the questions that might reasonably be posed by the faithful, although the tone of voice is likely Luther's: 'Why does not the pope empty purgatory, for the sake of holy love and of the dire need of the souls that are there'; 'what is this new piety of God and the pope, that for money they allow a man who is impious and their enemy to buy out of purgatory the pious soul of a friend of God'; 'What greater blessing could come to the Church than if the pope [...] were to bestow on every believer these remissions and participations?' But at the root of the abuses, Luther placed the financial transaction and the very real threat that those who preached indulgences were, in essence, selling salvation. The preaching of indulgences to raise revenue for the Church brought with it a temptation to exaggerate their efficacy, and downplay the requirement to contrition that was so central to the penitential system of the medieval Church. Doing so certainly created a demand for indulgences, but it left the Church exposed to more general criticism. To trivialize salvation by turning it into a commodity brought the worldly into the realm of the divine, downplayed the gravity of sin, and ultimately for a pious and soul-searching Augustinian, incited further reflection on judgement, righteousness and the role of man and God in redemption.

But where from here? If the 95 Theses did not, as it seems, present a manifesto for religious reform, we perhaps need to look elsewhere for the emergence of a theological understanding that was recognizably 'different' in the years that followed. What were the distinctive features of theology of the early Reformation? Certainly, the discussion of sin and penance in the 95 Theses has resonances in the formulation of a model of salvation in which the sinner is accepted, unconditionally, by God. Where medieval Christianity had posited a partnership, albeit an unequal one, between man and God in salvation, Luther's overriding sense was that the dreadfulness of sin was so great that man lived in a state of personal rebellion against God. Penances and good works were no remedy for this, hence the despair that Luther felt despite repeated, prolonged unburdenings in confession. The sin of the individual could not be cancelled out by works that seemed to merit grace. Rather the true Christian was simultaneously sinful and righteous, but, by divine grace, justified and cloaked by God's righteousness. Justification by faith reoriented the topography of salvation, positioning good works not as a means by which to earn God's favour, but as acts of love and charity.[18] The kernels of this belief were visible in the 95 Theses, but it was only in the aftermath of their composition and circulation that Luther started to address more actively the relationship between the sacrament of penance and his understanding of the righteousness of God. To deny the importance of works in the scheme of salvation was to run the risk that the faithful might believe that actions had no importance. For Catholic controversialists writing against Luther, this was a slippery slope towards antinomianism, but Luther also perceived the danger and error in this stance. Works, he argued, were neither meritorious, nor capable of earning salvation, but this did not mean that they were not a necessary part of Christian life. Works were rather the fruit of faith, and should derive from faith; works that arose from a misguided belief, without faith and without the clear command of God, were neither essential nor positive, tending towards superstition and error. The message was simple, in some ways alarmingly so. 'This is the true meaning of Christianity,' Luther wrote, 'that we are justified by faith in Christ, not by the works of the Law.'[19] Justification by faith was 'the highest article of our faith', without which the whole of Christian belief was nothing.[20]

In 1520, Luther published *A treatise on good works,* which grew out of a sermon preached in Wittenberg, and which was intended to make clear the meaning and purpose of good works, and address the critics of the principle of 'sola fide' who feared that such an emphasis on faith over works might lead to disorder. There were, Luther argued, no good works except those which God has commanded, and 'truly good works are not self-elected works of monastic or any other holiness'. Those acts of piety and charity ordained by the medieval Church, but without a divine mandate, had no role to play in the salvation of the believer, and simultaneously imposed a narrow definition on acts of love. Even the most mundane of actions, done in faith, might still be good.

> If you ask further, whether they count it also a good work when they work at their trade, walk, stand, eat, drink, sleep, and do all kinds of works for the nourishment of the body or for the common welfare, and whether they believe that God takes pleasure in them because of such works, you will find that they say, 'No'; and they define good works so narrowly that they are made to consist only of praying in church,

fasting, and almsgiving. Other works they consider to be in vain, and think that God cares nothing for them. So through their damnable unbelief they curtail and lessen the service of God, Who is served by all things whatsoever that are done, spoken or thought in faith.

A more strident articulation of Luther's stance came in his *Lectures on Galatians* (1535), in which the discussion of Paul's teaching was set in the context of the dangers of legalism in faith, institutions, false doctrine, scriptural exegesis and religious instruction and understanding. Here, the implications of his stance were set out with clarity and conviction, and the potential consequences laid bare. Justification and the forgiveness of sins came, for Luther, through Christ alone, not through attempts to win God's favour by extreme acts of piety, including the monastic observance that he had once embraced with vigour. It was not the works of men, but the suffering of Christ, that established the righteousness of man before God.[21] Justification by faith offered comfort in the face of the frailty of man, and spoke less of the wrath of God visited upon those who failed in their obligations to the Law.[22]

The consequences of such an assertion were far reaching, and broke apart the medieval penitential system from within. Once cloaked with righteousness, justified by faith, the believer was both sinful and righteous at the same time; he did not set out on a path righteous, fall into sin, and seek restoration through confession, absolution, penance and the sacraments of the Church. There were no sacraments that might cleanse the soul from sin, and no works of supererogation capable of restoring man's relationship with God. A soul that was less than spotless was still accepted by God, and grace became God's act of forgiveness rather than something to be attained by human effort. Those cloaked in God's righteousness were still sinners, and the treasury of merits upon which the theology of indulgences was constructed simply did not exist. The ascetic demands of the monastic life did not 'win' salvation for those who made vows of poverty, chastity and obedience. Indeed to trust in such vows and acts of mortification and suffering for salvation was to erect an idol in one's heart. Pilgrimage brought no spiritual reward. The fasting and abstinence demanded by the Church was inefficacious in salvation, and the open breaking of the Friday fast emerged as one of the most visible signs of doctrinal allegiance. Obedience to the laws of the institutional Church mattered less than obedience to the law of the Gospel.[23]

Such an assertion had radical consequences. If indulgences and the theology that supported them were flawed, on whose authority had they become part of the life of the Church? If the cult of the saints in its multitude of manifestations had become embedded in Christian life, on what basis might it be proven false? If the penitential cycle established by the Church to guide the Christian through the hazard-laden path of life was meaningless, on what might the faithful now trust? If the institutional Church was in error, by what means might that error be identified, and where might the solution be found.[24] Luther's proposed answer was expressed in a striking piece of ecclesiological theatre: when the bull of excommunication, *Exsurge Domine*, reached Luther, he burned it, together with books of canon law and scholastic theology in Wittenberg on 10 December 1520. Luther denounced the Pope as Antichrist and declared that the papal condemnation 'shall neither console nor frighten me'.

After the burning of the papal bull, Luther elaborated on the significance and meaning of the event in a printed defence of his actions, *Why the Books of the Pope and his Disciples were Burned by Dr Martin Luther*. The preceding months had seen Luther engage with Jan Hus's writing on the Church, *De Ecclesia*, in which Hus defined and debated the nature of the Church, the authority of the Pope and the college of cardinals, the papal power to bind and loose and the relative authority of Church and Scripture. The Bible, as the word of God, he concluded, was a sufficient standard of faith and conduct, and held primacy over the laws and tradition of the Church, which were, instead, the works of men. 'We ought,' Hus concluded, 'to obey God rather than men,' and the Bible provided the only necessary rule of life and faith. The laws of the Church were not binding unless grounded in Scripture (*præter expressam scripturam*), and human authority, even that of the Pope, was nothing compared to the Spirit. The Church, catholic and universal, was not the visible edifice but those who gathered together in Christ's name. By this definition, the 'Church' did not mean those over whom the Roman see claimed jurisdiction, and neither was it without error. The head of the Church was Christ, not the bishop of Rome; the rock on which the Church was built,

Fig. 7: Pope Leo X's Bull, *Exsurge Domine*, 1521

as described in Matthew's Gospel, was Christ, not Peter. Perhaps as a result of reading *De Ecclesia*, Luther reported to his confessor and friend Spalatin, 'we are all Hussites'.[25]

At the same time, Luther had been reading Lorenzo Valla's exposition of the Donation of Constantine as a fraud, and had started to set out his own views on the authority of Church and Scripture, popes and princes, in a series of pamphlets addressed to different constituencies of the faithful: *The Address to the Christian Nobility of the German Nation, On the Babylonian Captivity of the Church* and *The Freedom of a Christian*. In these three texts, Luther established the foundation of a new form of Christian life. It was, he argued, the duty of the princes to ensure that the Church was reformed. If man was to be saved, it was to be through faith and the righteousness of God, and not the works of a sinner on earth. Those sacraments that could not be established from Scripture were denounced, and, by ignoring or perverting Scripture, the Pope had led the Church with blindness into superstition. The spiritual and material separation of clergy and laity was rejected; the Church of Christ was, he argued, a priesthood of all believers. The sacrament of ordination had no basis in Scripture, therefore the position of the clergy must derive from faith, not the rites of the Church.

In this model, moral or theological error in the Church had no simple panacaea; more radical action was required. As Brad Gregory has argued, 'institutional abuses and immorality were seen as symptomatic signs of a flawed foundation, namely false and dangerous doctrines'. A new epistemological foundation was found, and explained, in the principle of *sola scriptura*, Scripture alone as the source of authority in the Church.[26] While the ramifications of this were substantial in the decade after 1520, the debate over authority was not in itself new; once again, we can see Luther's theology growing out of internal debates within late medieval Christianity.[27] Luther's early reflection and teaching on Scripture was a necessary step along the way to *sola scriptura*, but he was also influenced by Ockham and his followers, especially Gabriel Biel, and patristic texts, in which he read widely.[28] The potential clash between Church and Bible was evident, if not extensively explained, in the 95 Theses. But under pressure from Johannes Eck at the Leipzig debate in 1518, Luther appreciated more fully the consequences of asserting that it was possible to stay faithful to both the Pope and Scripture, where the decrees of the popes seemed to innovate, or contradict, the word of God. 'I will not permit men to posit new articles of faith and scold, defame, and judge all other Christians as heretics, renegades, infidels only because they do not submit to the Pope,' Luther declaimed, and 'everything that the Pope claims, makes, and does will I receive in this wise that I will first examine it according to the Holy Scripture. It must remain under Christ and be judged by Scripture.'[29] If tested by Scripture, and found wanting, the 'opinions of the doctors' remained only that – opinions, rather than matters of faith.[30] The culmination came at the Diet of Worms in 1521, when Luther declared before the Emperor (in another 'did it really happen moment' in the narrative of the Reformation), 'Here I stand. I can do no other. My conscience is captive to the word of God.'[31] Confronted by the word of the God and the palpable failings of the Church, there could be no compromise.

The iconoclastic force of *sola fide* and *sola scriptura* was to be felt across the full panorama of Christian life. Applied to the structures of the institutional Church, to its sacraments and devotional observances, to the model of salvation that it preached, to the nature and function of the priesthood, the relationship between image and the written and spoken word, to liturgy, private and communal religion, it demanded and delineated a new imagining of man's relationship with God. But these issues raised as many questions as answers. If the Bible was indeed the touchstone of faith, how was it to be accessed? If the word of God was indeed to be placed in the hands of every ploughboy, it needed to be presented in the vernacular. Was the word of God in Scripture both sufficient and autopistic, or did the eyes and minds of the faithful need a guide through the sacred text? How best was the message of the Gospel to be communicated, and understanding rather than blind compliance engendered? If both the conduct and construction of the sacerdotal priesthood was found wanting, and the Church comprised a priesthood of all believers, what then was the role of the priest, pastor or preacher? As Luther's theology found its way into the public domain, its full implications became almost immediately apparent.

2

THE REFORMATION AND DISSEMINATION OF IDEAS

THE BURNING OF LUTHER'S BOOKS IN LONDON, MAY 1521

On 11 May 1521, Antonio Surian wrote to the Signory of Venice with the news that 'Friar Martin [Luther] is to be proclaimed a heretic, and his works burnt. He has already been sentenced, and on Sunday Cardinal Wolsey will publish his condemnation [...] as a heretic; and that all of his books be burnt under penalty of excommunication, according to the brief received from the Pope.'[1] The following day, Surian, alongside the papal ambassador, and representatives of the emperor, gathered to witness Luther's books being consigned to the flames. The spectacle was impressive; Wolsey arrived 'with a great train of nobility', bishops and other dignitaries, although the king was unwell and not present. When Wolsey dismounted from his horse, he was escorted under a 'canopy of gold [...] to the high altar, where he made his oblation'. The Archbishop of Canterbury addressed the assembly, and, after a blessing, the participants moved to the churchyard. Here, a special platform had been erected, upon which Wolsey sat on a gold throne, accompanied by the papal nuncio, the Archbishop, the Bishop of Durham and the ambassadors. The other bishops, clergy, nobility and other spectators, perhaps numbering as many as 30,000, stood in front of the cardinal, while John Fisher, Bishop of Rochester, preached.

During Fisher's two-hour-long sermon, directed against Luther and his works, 'there were many burned in the said churchyard of the said Luther's books'. The assembly dispersed in the early afternoon, and the cardinal invited the ambassadors and higher clergy to a banquet marking the 'Luther festival'. Fisher's sermon against Luther positioned the Wittenberg reformer in a long line of condemned heretics that could be traced back to the early Church. Luther, he argued, had stirred up a 'mighty storm', promulgating heresies that ran contrary to the decrees of the popes and councils, and against the traditions and canons of the Church. A Latin translation of the sermon was prepared by the Dean of St Paul's, and Fisher's text was disseminated in English via the printing press of Wynkyn de Worde before the end of the year.[2]

Luther's name was virtually unknown in England in 1517, but by the following year his writings were beginning to attract attention. Erasmus sent Thomas More a copy of Luther's *Conclusiones* in spring 1518, and a few months later a Basle printer reported that he had exported some more of Luther's works to England. Trade in such items was not yet illegal, but the number of individuals involved, either as sellers or as readers, was likely to be small; the ledger of one Oxford bookseller describes the sale of a handful of Luther's books in spring 1520, each probably costing the equivalent of a day's wages for a worker.[3] However, as the quantity and range of Luther's printed works increased, so did the degree of suspicion in which his views were held. Luther's theatrical show of contempt for the authority of the Church, manifested in the burning of the books of canon law in Wittenberg in 1520, and his condemnation at the Diet of Worms in 1521, perhaps encouraged a revised assessment of the danger that his works, even if not exactly bestsellers, might pose in England. Wolsey attempted to prohibit the importing of Luther's books, but despite this prohibition there were suggestions that the University of Oxford was becoming 'infected' with Lutheranism, and that attempts to prohibit the dissemination of the German heresy were largely ineffective.[4]

What might we learn from this series of events? It is clear that in the few months after Luther penned the 95 Theses, a relationship had been established been print and reform, one that was potentially beneficial to both sides. By 1520, the association between print and heresy was clearly well enough established that the English Church and state believed that some action against the free circulation of texts was necessary to prevent further spiritual contamination. The mechanics of dissemination are also worth considering: how were works of evangelical theology, polemic and propaganda printed, circulated and read? And finally, given the evident role of theatre and spectacle, both for Wolsey and for Luther, above, to what extent was the printed word simply one means – albeit a potentially important one – of getting the message across.

PRINT AND PROTESTANTISM

The close relationship between print and Protestantism has long been recognized, even assumed, in discussions of the spread and impact of the Reformation. In part, this assumption derives from the way in which Luther and other evangelical writers engaged energetically with the medium, but it also stems from the way in which they represented the press as an instrument of divine providence, bestowed for the purpose of ensuring that their message was heard. Luther described printing as 'God's highest and extremest act of grace, whereby the business of the Gospel is driven forward; it is the last flame before the extinction of the world'. The English Protestant martyrologist John Foxe concluded his account of the death of the Bohemian heretic Jan Hus on a note of optimism: the Church might have been able to silence one of its critics, but the message would not be so easily suppressed, for 'God has opened the press to preach, whose voice the Pope is never able to stop with all the puissance of his triple crown'.[5]

This rhetoric has left its mark on the historiography of the Reformation, and on writing about the importance of the printing press in the communication of ideas in early modern society. For Eisenstein, the relationship was two-way: print acted as a precondition for the Protestant Reformation, but it also acted as a precipitant. The printing press was not a neutral format for the dissemination of ideas, but also had the capacity to shape these ideas and the form in which they were expressed. It is not enough simply to note that critics of the Church used printed books as a weapon of evangelization; we also need to examine the extent to which the availability of print affected the way in

Fig. 8: Jost Amman, early wooden printing press, depicted in 1568. In Philip B.
Meggs, *A History of Graphic Design*

which evangelism by the written word took place. There is also a danger that the providential rhetoric that surrounds Protestant engagement with print becomes a self-fulfilling prophecy. To argue that the printing press was given by God for the furtherance of reform of the Church is to prioritize the written word over other media, to position Catholic and Protestant on either side of a line that demarcates 'true religion', and to turn the printing press into something that must be seen to have had some effect. Some of these assumptions may contain a grain of truth, but in order to assess the relationship between print and Protestantism we need to do more than simply point out the rough coincidence of chronology and mere fact of the existence of evangelical literature, particularly in the German context. We also need to consider the extent to which the so-called 'printing revolution' was indeed revolutionary, not only in technological terms but also in terms of its intellectual, cultural and material impact. Again, such an assumption may not be entirely invalid, but it does need to be interrogated in light of what we know not only about book production, but also book consumption.

PRODUCING BOOKS AND PRODUCING PROTESTANTISM

The figures for the sales of Luther's books in England before 1521 need to be set within a broader context. A. G. Dickens' analysis of the book trade on the continent concluded that between 1517 and 1520 sales of Luther's 30 publications had run to over 300,000 copies. On this basis alone, he suggested, 'in the relation to the spread of religious ideas its seems difficult to exaggerate the significance of the press, without which a revolution of this magnitude could scarcely have been consummated'.[6] Lutheranism, he argued, was the 'first child' of the printed book, and, unlike Wycliffe or Hus before him, the German reformer was able to make 'exact, standardised and ineradicable impressions on the mind of Europe'.[7] The ability to exploit a vernacular mass market for revolutionary ideas and propaganda was, for Dickens, a defining feature of the Reformation, and one that made a substantial contribution both to the accessibility of Luther's ideas, and their consistency and durability.[8]

43

Eisenstein's assessment was perhaps more cautious, but still asserted the significance of the relationship between Protestantism and the printed word: even if it did not create the Reformation, she concluded, 'the advent of printing did, at the very least, rule out the possibility of perpetuating the status quo'.[9] In a similar vein, Mark U. Edwards argued that the Reformation saw the first 'major, self-conscious attempt' to exploit the printing press to reach a large audience quickly, and with a transformative message. Thousands of pamphlets penned by evangelical reformers – Luther pre-eminent among them – disseminated criticisms of the old Church and the building blocks of the new.[10]

On a purely numerical basis, the evidence for a connection between print and Protestantism is compelling. Hans-Joachim Köhler estimated that approximately 10,000 pamphlet editions emerged from the German-speaking lands between 1500 and 1530; the years 1517–18 alone witnessed a 530 per cent increase in pamphlet production.[11] But by far the most substantial proportion of these editions, accounting for around three-quarters of the total, were printed in the five years after 1520. The majority were works of religious controversy and debate, and around 20 per cent were penned by Martin Luther. Köhler sampled some 3,000 of these pamphlets, and from these selected 356 that formed a representative sample of the whole. Luther's theology of justification featured in the majority of these, and almost two-thirds engaged with the principle of *sola scriptura* (a higher proportion between 1520 and 1526). Thomas Hohenberger came to similar conclusions based on his analysis of the religious pamphlets published in Germany in 1521–2, which he argued presented the essential topography of justification by faith, albeit in a format that might be communicated through the new mass media of popular print.[12]

The other distinctive feature of this propaganda campaign was its dominance by the vernacular. This, of course, did not prevent the consumption of printed works by the educated, clerical audience that formed the rather narrower market for Latin works, but it did open the possibility of reaching a more general readership. The dominance of the Latin language in print gave way to a predominately German vernacular medium, with Latin titles accounting for barely one-quarter of the print output in the 1520s. In the case of Luther's writing, the dominance of the vernacular was more striking still. The majority of evangelical writers in the 1520s were clergy, Luther included, and their dominance may well have helped to ensure the apparent levels of consistency and uniformity in the message that the printing press promoted in this critical period. As Mark Edwards has noted, this was also the period in which the geographical spread of editions of Luther's writings was at its greatest; as the Reformation fragmented, and other individuals promoted variant theological understandings or responded to more local territorial concerns and circumstances, Luther became, increasingly, an author with a regional audience.[13] As Luther's numerical dominance of vernacular printing diminished, the diversity of works in circulation increased.

Part of Luther's legacy to the Reformation was his recognition of the potential power inherent in the printed word in a popular format, and the close links between print and the spread of Protestantism was as recognizable to those who feared its impact as to those who sought to capitalize upon it. This model has been well demonstrated for the German-speaking lands. However, outside the immediate hinterland of the Reformation, the numbers can potentially add up rather differently. Arguments for the book as the central agent of change and evangelist for the Reformation, and for the centrality of Luther's works to this endeavour, often become less convincing if we move the focus of our analysis to a different context.[14] The successful and productive arrangement between Luther and his printers, the appeal of Luther's message to the audience for which he wrote, and the practical, financial and technological support that enabled the rapid production of cheap and popular pamphlets were in many respects a unique feature of the German, and urban, Reformation. Protestantism did not create the book industry.[15] Instead, the print shops in Wittenberg in particular, but also in other German cities, which had established their position before 1520 were able to capitalize upon this by acting as the printers and promoters of Lutheran polemic, investing resources in early works and generating an income that supported future publications. It was not just printing, but a particular dynamic of printing, that made a significant contribution to the dissemination of the message of the Reformation. In Germany, there were multiple centres of book production, a literate, educated, urban audience, the skilled printers and craftsmen to turn Luther's script into popular *flugschriften*, and an almost entirely absent structure of control and repression. Elsewhere in Europe, where this conjuncture did not pertain, the relationship between print and Protestantism, although still perceptible, is somewhat less compelling.

By 1500, there were more than 1,000 print shops across Europe, and although both the number of print shops and the number of print outputs increased throughout the early modern period, the pattern of this expansion was contingent upon local and regional factors. English printers produced fewer than 500 editions in the first decade of the sixteenth century. Tight restrictions on printing in the 1540s were relaxed during the protectorship of the Duke of Somerset in the early years of the reign of Edward VI, and the number of vernacular, evangelical works in circulation increased; there was, for example, a sudden spike in the printing of anti-Mass tracts in this period. With the breakdown of control and censorship during the Civil Wars in the 1640s, the number of titles printed in this decade rose to 20,000, more than three times the press output of the previous decade. But the centralization of the print industry in London meant that one apparent pre-condition for the successful partnership between print and Protestantism was not met: the dispersal of German printers around the imperial cities enabled them to target what was essentially a local market in a way in which the English print shops could not. In other parts of Europe, the influence of the secular powers, and the institutional Church, was felt rather differently. In England, control or censorship of the printing presses was more readily achieved given their location in London, and the relatively small scale of the market. Royal patronage was sought after, which made the publication of overtly evangelical literature a less attractive and more dangerous pursuit. As had been the case with the works of Luther that were burned by Wolsey in 1521, those contentious books that did circulate in England tended to be imported, rather than locally produced. Likewise, the limited distribution and tight control over the French print industry limited its potential role as an agent for the dissemination of the Reformation. The Swedish print industry secured a stable footing only after the decision was taken to adopt the Reformation, suggesting a close correlation between state-sponsored Protestantism and the emergence of print communication, but a rather different direction of travel.

The invention of printing with moveable type had the capacity to bring a new and challenging range of religious ideas more broadly into the public domain. But the extent to which that actually happened depended not only upon the presence of individuals who were motivated to write such works, but also upon the availability of a printer capable of producing such texts, and willing to do so. Economic factors were an important driver. The ability to produce, cheaply, multiple copies of the same text had become more reliably established in the half-century after Gutenberg's invention. As the costs of production were diminished, so were the financial costs of ownership. But the dynamics of the print industry were often precarious, and fortunes hard to predict. The preparation of a substantial scholarly edition could occupy the entire print shop for months, and the costs of ventures such as the *Polyglot Bible* or Foxe's *Acts and Monuments* needed to be weighed against the potential profit and prestige that they might bring. Patronage mattered, as did protection from interventions. If the name of an author drove up sales, then a breakdown in the relationship between printer and writer could kill the career of either. The print shop of Melchior Lotter, for example, responsible for the preparation of many early editions of Luther's works in Wittenberg, was forced out of existence when Luther withdrew his support. Regional demand might also change the dynamic. Using Mark Edward's example, if there was interest in Strasbourg for a work first published in Wittenberg, it was likely that a printer in Strasbourg would reprint the work. A first edition emanating from Wittenberg was not a guarantee that subsequent editions would come from the same press.[16]

PRINT, READING AND CONVERSION

Whether they printed evangelical works as a result of confessional sympathy or not, printers still needed to generate enough income from their work to make a profit substantial enough to keep them in business. It is unlikely that altruism provided a good economic model; on this basis, the printer probably assumed that there would be a market for the book or pamphlet. However, it would be hazardous to assume that the printer was always correct in his assessment. If public interest fell short of the levels expected, there was a loss to bear, but perhaps one that could be balanced by good fortune or strong sales elsewhere. The printing of a single edition of a work does not give us enough evidence to conclude that it had a readership (although we might reasonably conclude that the printer believed, however optimistically, that it would). The reprinting of a work serves as a rather better measure of public interest. Even this does not guarantee, of course, that the audience had grown in parallel with the print run, but it does indicate that enough of the first printing had been sold to suggest that further copies would be purchased.

However, we still need to be cautious before making any assumptions about the extent to which the printing of books should be read as an indication of their popularity and influence. In some cases, such an assumption may be perfectly valid, but, in the sixteenth century as now, book ownership might not be evidence that the owner shared the beliefs of the author. The argument that print was an effective disseminator of the Protestant message relies upon basic assumptions about the way that books were bought and read, and the extent to which reading impacted upon the views of the reader. For some readers, this might well be the case; an individual might choose to purchase a piece of Lutheran theological writing because, having heard or read about some of Luther's ideas, he wanted to know more. It is not impossible that printed texts might for some readers act as an important mechanism in the process of conversion, and that by reading either anti-Catholic polemical writing, or works of Protestant spirituality, they might be persuaded to embrace the Reformation. The fact that print was censored, and efforts made to suppress the circulation of evangelical literature suggest that this was a danger that was very much recognized by secular and ecclesiastical authorities. And, at one level, those who wrote works of Reformation polemic and propaganda, and those who were prepared to print them, clearly assumed some purpose and efficacy in their endeavour.

However, as Andrew Pettegree has argued, reasons for book ownership were unlikely to be that simple, and the trajectory from print to Protestantism in the heart and mind of the reader less direct and clear. To own a book is not the same as to read it (or to read it more than once; one book might be read multiple times, and another barely touched). To own a book, and to read a book, is not the same as to inwardly digest every word on the page or to agree with the arguments and ideas that it contains. Book ownership might be a sign of shared belief or of cultural and religious identity, or an attempt to create such a thing. Alternatively, book ownership may well reflect a sense of what one ought to read (or what friends and colleagues think one ought to read) rather than a conscious and informed personal decision. Of course the relative cost of book ownership in the sixteenth century was rather higher than today; something that cost the equivalent of a day's wages or more was unlikely to be a frivolous purchase, but it is still worth reflecting upon the unpredictable relationship between the reader and the text.[17]

The sheer scale of cheap book production implies that there was a reading audience available, and one that was prepared to purchase multiple texts. In some respects, the relatively quick and cheap to produce *flugschriften* were attractive to readers because of their price and consumability, and the quick and simple access that they provided to more complex and opaque debates and controversies. Their function might be to persuade and convert, but perhaps also to consolidate opinion among those who knew exactly what the content would be, and agreed with it before reading the first page. The sheer volume of material printed in defence of the Reformation in the 1520s might provide some consolation to the reader that he was not alone in his opinion, but rather part of a wider movement and a growing congregation.

But with writing and publishing on such a scale, maintaining the unity of the message preached by the press would be difficult. If the pamphlets put the Reformation, materially, into the hands of all who wanted to read about it, they also opened up the possibility that divergent, even contradictory ideas might circulate under the banner of reform. Add in the complex process by which these ideas were read, received and understood by their audience, and the problem of control becomes even more apparent. If Luther's message was spread quickly and effectively by those who were prepared to produce an accessible version for mass consumption, it is easy to see how the theological principles might be either simplified or diluted, and the name of Luther attached to ideas that were not, perhaps, his own. The basic tenets of Luther's theology, as we have seen, certainly found their way into the printed pamphlets of the early 1520s, but whether they did so in a form of which Luther approved is a rather different question.

Mark Edwards has reminded us that if we are to regard the printed word as propaganda for the Reformation, we need to be aware that the attempt to persuade was not always successful, and that even where it seemed to be, the measure of success may not be the same as that which was intended or expected by the authors of these texts.[18] Both the power of the printing press, and its dangers, were certainly recognized by Luther, who made a concerted effort to control the spread of his own ideas and to impose some kind of authority upon what was published in his name. However, it was much more difficult to control how the message was read and understood by its audience, and even harder, perhaps impossible, to impose constraints upon what that audience said, wrote or did on the basis of what they had read. In March 1518, Luther wrote to the Nuremberg printer Conrad Scheurl, expressing his anxiety about the rapid dissemination of the 95 Theses in print. Luther claimed that he had not intended that the Theses be published, but had rather expected to discuss them with his colleagues, and then perhaps to destroy them or to edit them in light of these conversations. Once in print, however, the text of the Theses had circulated well beyond the level that he might have expected, and Luther confessed to Scheurl that he now 'felt anxious about what they may bring forth: not that I am unfavourable to spreading known truth abroad – rather this is what I seek – but because this method is not the best adapted to instruct the public'.[19] Whether Luther was concerned about the use of print in the dissemination of his propositions, or the extent to which the Theses, in their original form, were not the best way of getting the message across, is unclear. Nonetheless, the cautionary note struck is still the same: the printing of the Theses had wrested the text from Luther's control in terms of content, form or both.

A similar set of concerns is evident in Luther's response to the German peasant risings of 1525. The articles presented by the rebels in justification of their actions were firmly influenced by the lexicon of Luther's theology, particularly the language of Gospel freedom and the equality of all believers before God. Whether for personal or political reasons, Luther moved swiftly to distance himself from the disorder, and attempted to make clear that his writing and preaching presented no justification for rebellion. The tract *Against the Murdering, Thieving Hordes of Peasants* was a reflection of the dangers posed by the swift and popular dissemination of ideas in the early 1520s. If Luther found it hard to control what was printed in his name, it was harder still to control what was said by those who read, dissected and repackaged Luther on their own terms. Particularly where there was a practical application, as we will see when we examine Reformation iconoclasm in the next chapter, it was all too easy for the intentions of the author to be lost or reinterpreted in the readings and actions of the audience. What Luther 'meant' to the individual reader was, to some extent, imparted by the words on the page, but the meaning of these words was constructed in the mind of the individual, and to reflect not only Luther, but also the personal circumstance of the reader, the nature of his environment and the extent to which he was prepared to turn words into action. Two (or more) people buying and reading the same text could arrive at polarized conclusions as a result.

THE PRIMACY OF THE WORD?

The existence of a vibrant print culture in the Protestant Reformation does not mean that the Reformation was encountered only through the printed word. The rejection of religious images, decoration, ritual and liturgical spectacle certainly did much to position the word at the centre of religious life, but that word might be the written word of Scripture, the spoken word of the sermon or the conversational word of the community. In the imperial cities, levels of literacy were rarely above 30 per cent; in the rural context, much lower. Without denying the potential for pamphlet literature and printed books to be influential in shaping opinion, we need to consider the extent to which exposure to the ideas that they contained might be second-hand, through the spoken word and actions of others. For those who could not read, contact with the Reformation was likely to come indirectly, and refracted through the mindset or requirements of a range of intermediaries. The importance of communication through sermons, rituals, spectacle and informal conversation should not be underestimated. Such forms of communication exposed those who could not read to the message of the printed tracts and treatises, but also imbued that message with a range of personal experience, magisterial objectives and individual interpretations. Miriam U. Chrisman's analysis of the communication of the Reformation in Strasbourg gives a compelling illustration of the ways in which the theological and social message of reform was mediated through the eyes of the learned and turned into something with a popular appeal and broader audience.[20] Clergy who read Luther's message might preach it to their congregations; others might preach outside the walls of the Church, and without its sanction. It was also possible for the spoken word to find its way into print, such as was the case with many of the sermons delivered at the famous Paul's Cross pulpit in London. The potential for an inexact correlation between the written and spoken word in both contexts should not be forgotten, but it is important to remember the extent to which speech and reading might exist alongside one another.

And, of course, the same questions about reception and understanding need to be asked of the spoken word as well as the written. For all the emphasis placed upon the sermon as the focal point of the reformed liturgy, there is plenty of evidence that the enthusiasm of the preacher, such as it existed, was not always shared by the hearer. Susan Karant-Nunn has argued that the sermon was not always the most effective way of rousing a congregation to action or even awareness. The Lutheran liturgy might have kept the congregation awake by retaining physical gestures such as kneeling and standing, but this often had the effect of merely postponing sleep until the sermon: the dead in the graveyard might be thought of as holy sleepers, but those snoring in the pews definitely could not. The printed texts of the Paul's Cross sermons do not make it entirely clear how these would serve as energizing vehicles for the communication of the message to a broad audience. In a similar vein, Alec Ryrie's analysis of what it meant to 'be Protestant' in early modern England presents a broad spectrum of responses to sermons, ranging from those who energetically engaged with the spoken word, to those who complained of the physical and perhaps mind-numbing discomfort that accompanied a lengthy sermon.[21]

Protestant printing and preaching both made demands upon their audience, and, perhaps as a result, often deployed the same tactics. The message, to be understood, needed to be simple and effective, and present the reader or hearer with a clear picture of truth and falsehood. There was polemical capital to be had in holding up a caricature of the enemy, and in its effective mockery. And, perhaps most importantly, the greatest impact for the message was perhaps to be found where it was communicated through multiple media, whether printed, spoken or otherwise. Crick and Walsham argue that 'the intermixture and hybridity of print and script should be seen as a keynote of the culture of communication in this period'.[22] Early modern print culture did not mark, or enact, an immediate or total break with the scribal culture of the past. The same can be said of the relationship between print and oral or visual communication. The primacy of the printed word was not complete, and sermons, as we have seen, but also song, theatre and imagery, remained potent tools in the communication of the message.

WORD AND MUSIC

Music had the potential to act as a powerful tool for evangelism. Lutheran hymns were composed in the language and music of the people, using vernacular words, often set to folk songs and other familiar tunes. They also present compelling evidence of the interaction of print and oral culture. Advances in the technical skills required to print music allowed Lutheran hymnody to reach a large audience, and given that not all members of a congregation could read, the new hymns and psalters provided an important vehicle for religious education. The 1524 *Geystliche gesangk Buchleyn* presented a range of congregational hymns for use in church, of which perhaps the most famous example is Luther's own *Ein' feste berg*, written with a strongly Christo-centric message and set to a German folk melody. This ability to impose a Lutheran message upon familiar, or accessible, melodies helped to create a new and distinctive piety and confessional identity among the German laity. The vernacular

"Ein' feste Burg."

Fig. 9: An early printing of Luther's hymn 'Ein feste Burg ist unser Gott'

Bible, preaching and catechisms were a vital part of this process, but in recent years our understanding of the dissemination of the Reformation has been greatly enhanced by a fuller recognition of the important role played by the learning and singing of vernacular hymns in churches, schools and, especially, in homes.

Most of Luther's hymns were written in a chorale form, and intended to be sung by the whole congregation during services. But hymns were not confined to church; the *Geistliche Lieder auffs Neu gebessert* (1529) was intended for use in the domestic context. The quantity of hymn prints between 1500 and 1600, ranging from broadsheets to full scale hymnals, was in excess of 2,000 (approximately 2 million copies), of which three-quarters were recognizably Lutheran.[23] News of Luther's ideas arrived in Magdeburg as a result of some of his early printed hymns finding their way into the city via a merchant, and in the preface to his hymnal, Luther paid tribute to the role that hymns might play in the promotion and popularization of the Gospel message. The purpose of Lutheran hymns might be to proclaim the Gospel and bring comfort (*Trost*), but music also had the capacity to imbue the remnants of Catholicism with a new cultural meaning. Parallels can be drawn here between the presentation of the cult of the Virgin in Nuremberg after the Reformation, discussed in the next chapter, and the relationship between objects and music in the St Catherine altarpiece, in the Joachimstal *Spitalkirche*. Here, the representation of Catherine's marriage to Christ, symbolized by the Christ-child placing a ring on her finger, was given a new meaning by the song *A dialogue between two Christian Maidens*, set to the tune of a folk dance, in which the ring was represented as a symbol of baptism.[24]

Psalm singing was to emerge as a defining landmark on the reformed cultural landscape. Given by God, and contained in Scripture, the Psalms existed for the purpose of praising God, and the collective singing of Psalms, helped by the production of the Genevan Psalter, was both a powerful pedagogic tool and a mark of confessional identity. Luther had translated the Psalms into verse and stanzas in German; Martin Bucer did the same for the city of Strasbourg, and John Calvin deployed the services of poets including Clément Marot and Théodore de Bèze to create the impressive and enduring Genevan Psalter. The purpose of church music was not to entertain or to distract, but to profit the Church, but the focus upon the word encouraged a shift away from more elaborate polyphony and toward singing without the accompaniment of the organ. Congregational singing was in some respects a form of empowerment: the participants were given a voice in church, and one which acted as a vehicle for the dissemination of the fundamentals of the faith. Psalm singing often accompanied Calvinist preaching in public spaces in France in the 1560s, and music could, quite literally, become a confessional battleground as Catholic and Protestant congregations sought to drown out the sound of their opponents' worship.[25]

THE PRINTED IMAGE

The communication of the Reformation through song, sermon and printed treatise relied variously upon the written and spoken word, and exploited to the full their intersection in the appropriation of popular cultural forms. But it is worth noting that it was not only words that were printed and disseminated by the early presses; the role of the printed image in Reformation propaganda has long been recognized. Positioning the printing press in relation to both oral and visual culture provides us with a more convincing and more compelling sense of its importance. The relationship between the Reformation and the image is complex: at one level, as we shall see in the next chapter, it was destructive and iconoclastic, where images appeared to embody false religion and idolatry; but in other aspects, the Reformation was more willing to embrace and exploit the image. The traditional model of the clash between the visual culture of Catholicism and the focus upon the word in Protestantism is far from watertight, and the printed propaganda for the German Reformation gives us a clear indication of the extent to which word and image could work together to communicate a message.

If the printing press enabled the mass production of identical texts, so it also, in the form of woodcuts, allowed the rapid dissemination of multiple copies of the same image. Seeing was an important part of religious devotion, and the visual had a prominent role to play in the culture and communication of late medieval Christianity. Woodcuts existed prior to the Reformation – and indeed pre-dated the invention of the printing press – but the function of the medium as a means of reaching the illiterate or semi-literate was rapidly recognized and exploited in the 1520s and beyond. The visual propaganda for the German Reformation was appealing and energetic in its form, but, gradually, enhanced by the addition of printed text to aid interpretation. It was at least as easy, if not more so, to misread an image as to mishear a sermon or wrongly interpret a text. Woodcuts accompanied by explanatory text emerged as an important vehicle for the dissemination of both anti-Catholic sentiments and reforming theologies, and had the potential to reach both reading and non-literate cultures at the same time.[26]

In some instances, the message was abundantly clear. The schism that was opening up in Western Christendom was represented – and encouraged – by the visual representation of the clash between true and false religion. The church of the godly, reformed, and the church of the ungodly, the popish, stood back to back, the page riven in two by a pillar or some other seemingly impenetrable divide that sent out the stark message that there could be no compromise between the divine and the demonic. Such was the case on the title page of John Foxe's *Acts and Monuments* in England, and in the famous series *Passionale Christi under Antichrist* (1521). The *Passionale*, with woodcuts commissioned from Lucas Cranach, was a conscious attempt to combine text and image in order to maximize the appeal and impact of the pamphlet across a wide spectrum of literacy. The pamphlet was simultaneously polemical and prayerful, kindling in the reader a sense of fear and hopeful expectation as the end of time approached, while also providing a visual and visible manifestation of the anti-papal rhetoric of Luther's theological and polemical writings, particularly the *Appeal to the Christian Nobility of the German Nation*. By the mid-sixteenth century, the Antichristian nature of Catholicism had become almost a theological principle in its own right, reflected and reinforced in complex images such as *The Difference between the true religion of Christ and the false idolatrous religion of Antichrist* (attributed to Lucas Cranach, c. 1550). The right half of the page set out an image of false piety based upon error, greed and superstition. A rotund monk preached, inspired not by Scripture but by the devil perched on his shoulder, blowing into his ear with bellows. The audience for the sermon included a gambling monk, whose cards and dice could be seen falling from his habit. The Pope is depicted filling his coffers with the revenue from indulgences, a priest saying a private Mass, a bishop using holy water to bless a bell, and God, in the upper right, hurling fire and brimstone in judgement upon such false religion, despite the intercessions of St Francis on behalf of the 'faithful'. In the contrasting left frame, divided from the Catholic Church, stood Luther, preaching the word of God and depicted next to the celebration of communion in both kinds.[27]

By this point, the image of Luther himself would have been instantly recognizable. Visual representations of Luther had been circulating since the early 1520s, beginning with images that drew heavily upon the traditional iconography of a monastic, or doctor of the Church, inspired by the Holy Spirit, and becoming more elaborate and complex in their meaning as the years passed. Luther, wearing a doctor's cap, merged with Luther the prophet, Luther the Bible scholar and Luther the saint.[28] Some such images acquired almost miraculous qualities – the so-called incombustible Luther, whose portrait could survive the flames.[29] The woodcuts sought to establish a personal relationship between Luther and the reader, creating a figure whose face was instantly recognizable, but also connecting Luther with his theological and pastoral principles, liberating the people from captivity by Scripture and faith.

The Reformation, was a written, oral and visual event, shaped by preaching, disseminated by print and communicated in song. The marked intersections between print and oral culture are evident in their shared vocabulary and immediacy, and in their strident assertions and vigorous criticisms of the enemy. Woodcuts in which women and peasants appeared to outwit and overturn the Catholic priesthood and Church occupied the same theological ground as the formal articulation of the principles of *sola fide* and *sola scriptura*. Luther's promise to free the German people from the Babylonish captivity of the Church was expressed in engravings and images in which the robed doctor led his followers out of the deep pit of popish darkness. The supremacy of the Bible as the written word of God was preserved and promoted by the living voice of the Gospel and the sermon, and celebrated in a hymnody that wove together new theologies and traditional tunes.

The marriage of print and Protestantism in the German cities could not be replicated across the continent, but the printing press was not the only agent of change. The burning of Luther's books in London in 1521 recognized the potency of print – why else the fear that Luther's work might be circulating in England? – but also saw the potential for the spoken word and visual symbolism to communicate a powerful message. How that message might be understood was another matter. As we have seen, there was no guarantee that the printed pamphlets of the 1520s would be read in the way that their author intended, or embed an identical religious and cultural understanding in the mind of each believer. Neither was there any way of knowing how those men and women seated in the pews of early modern churches would react to the sermons that they heard. Those who read or heard Luther's message internalized them in a multitude of ways, and disseminated diverse interpretations in writing, sermons and conversations of their own. 'The audience,' Hans Speier suggests, 'seeks the meaning that it needs.' The very mechanisms that the early reformers harnessed in the service of evangelism might also be the means by which doctrinal difference was proliferated and perpetuated.[30] In the encounter between word and action, the outcome was not always possible to predict.

3

THE REFORMATION AND THE IMAGE

ANTWERP, 1566

On Wednesday 21 August 1566, the Welsh Protestant merchant Richard Clough wrote from Antwerp to his colleague Thomas Gresham, describing recent events in the town. Clough described 'a marvellous stir, all the churches, chapels and houses of religion utterly defaced, and no kind of thing left whole within them, but broken and utterly destroyed, being done after such order and with so few folk that it is to be marvelled at'. The disorder had begun at about five o'clock, when the priests singing the divine office were disturbed by a group singing Psalms; within the hour, this company had swelled, breaking up the choir and destroying books. After that, Clough wrote,

[...] they began with the image of Our Lady, which had been carried about the town on Sunday last, and utterly defaced her and her chapel, and, after, the whole church, which was the costliest church in Europe, and have so spoiled it that they have not left a place to sit in the church. And from thence, part went to the parish church, and part to the houses of religion, and made such despatch as, I think, the like was never done in one night, and not so much to be wondered at of the doing, but that so few people durst or could do so much for that, when they entered into some of the houses of religion, I could not perceive in some churches not above ten or twelve that spoiled, all being boys and rascals: but there were many in the church lookers on, as some thought, setters on [...] After I saw that all should be quiet, I, with above ten thousand more, went into the churches to see what stir was there, and coming into Our Lady church, it looked like a hell, where were above 10000 torches burning, and such a noise as if heaven and earth had got together, with falling of images and beating down of costly works, such sort that the spoil was so great that a man could not well pass through the church. So that, in fine, I cannot write you in ten sheets of paper the strange sight I saw there, organs and all destroyed; and from thence I went, as the rest of the people did, to all the houses of religion, where was like stir, breaking and spoiling all that there was. Yet, they that this did, never looked towards any spoil, but broke all in pieces and let it lie under foot. So that, to be short, they have spoiled and destroyed all the churches, so well [St] Mary's as [the] others; but, as I do understand, they neither say, nor did anything to the nuns; but, when all was broken, left it there and so departed. So that, by estimation, they that spoiled, meddled with nothing, but let it lie; and, before it was three o'clock in the morning, they had done their work, and all home again, as if there had been nothing done, so that they spoiled this last night between 25 and 30 churches. And it is thought this day many more shall be spoiled abroad, for that, in divers places in Flanders, they have and do the like; for they that do spoil in Flanders, go by 4 and 500 in a company, and, when they come to a town or village, they call for the governor of the town, and so go into the churches, where, so much silver or gold as they do find, either chalices or crosses, they break and deface, and then delivered it to the head-officer by weight, and, for the rest, utterly destroy.[1]

Two days later, Clough reported that the destructive iconoclasm had spread throughout Zeeland and beyond, including Flushing, Middelburg, Ghent, Mechelen, Lier, Bergen-op-Zoom and Breda. This 'Iconoclastic Fury', was the product of growing religious and political tensions in the region. Anti-Spanish sentiment, blended with the reformed theology of the *hagepreken* (hedge-preachers) who commanded growing audiences by the mid-1560s, created a potent mix. Dutch Protestant clergy were joined by reformed preachers from France, Germany, Switzerland and England, and

Fig. 10: Frans Hogenberg, *Destruction in the Church of Our Lady in Antwerp*, 20 August 1566

increasingly incendiary language encouraged those who heard the sermons to exact vengeance upon the material monuments of Catholicism. On 10 August 1566, after a sermon preached by Sebastien Matte in Steenvoorde, the audience forced entry into the convent and smashed images in its church. Similar events took place in Bailleul and Poperinghe, where outbreaks of iconoclastic destruction were fuelled by evangelical preaching against the Catholic Church, the Pope, false religion and idolatry. Some iconoclasm was spontaneous, but the most violent and destructive incidents need to be seen alongside a more general and systematic process by which Dutch churches were purged of images in order to allow, it was argued, a more pure form of religious worship to be used in these buildings, focused upon the preaching and hearing of the word of God.[2]

Helen L. Parish

ICONOPHOBIA AND ICONOCLASM

The removal of images from churches, either by violent destruction or more ordered purging, provides us with a clear link between the theology of the Reformation and its practical impact. Iconoclasm was both a reflection of the internalization of opposition to traditional religion and a means by which this process of winning over hearts and minds might be achieved. In the words of the Royal Injunctions that accompanied the reformation of the English Church in the reign of Edward VI and Elizabeth I, Church officials were to

> [...] take away, utterly extinct, and destroy all shrines, coverings of shrines, all tables, candlesticks, trindals, and rolls of wax, pictures, paintings, and all other monuments of feigned miracles, pilgrimages, idolatry, and superstition, so that there remain no memory of the same in walls, glass windows, or elsewhere within their churches and houses; preserving nevertheless, or repairing both the walls and glass windows; and they shall exhort all their parishioners to do the like within their several houses. And that the churchwardens, at the common charge of the parishioners, in every church shall provide a comely and honest pulpit, to be set in a convenient place within the same, and to be there seemly kept for the preaching of God's word.[3]

The process was twofold; the monuments of idolatry were to be destroyed, thus (at least this was the intention) removing both the object and any memory of it, and paving the way for the introduction of a reformed worship and liturgy in which the sermons and thus the pulpit were dominant, visually hammering home the message. John Foxe's *Acts and Monuments* in its 1563 edition presented the same message in text and in image at the start of his account of the reign of Edward VI. Papists were depicted 'packing away their paltry' at the top of the page, while the king presented the Bible to his clergy and nobility. A bonfire in the background reduced to ashes the last remnants of popish superstition, while the pulpit in the foreground provided the vehicle by which the word of God would be preached.[4]

If the destination, and the mechanism, for the physical and spiritual transformation of church buildings was clear, what was

Fig. 11: Woodcut depicting the destruction of Catholic images.
In John Foxe, *Acts and Monuments*, 1563

the motivation that underpinned the destructive impulse? The piety of seeing, or looking, *Schaufrommigkeit,* was a central pillar of late medieval religion.[5] The visual, as much as the spoken or written word, guided the believer's encounter with God. There was an immediacy in the visual encounter that enabled the material object to act as a 'book' for the laity, and a means of instruction in a non-literate culture. This was the defence of the place of images in churches that was presented by Pope Gregory the Great and which was to become a commonplace in later medieval writing; William Durandus explained in 1286 that 'when the forms of external objects are drawn into the heart, they are, as it were, painted there, because the thoughts of them are their images'. The Lenten practice of concealing images was, he argued, an allegory of the hidden nature of the divinity of Christ during the Passion.[6] Liturgy and churchgoing were a highly visual experience, and church buildings themselves had a key role to play in the dissemination of the Christian message. If the visible world was indeed a sign of the invisible world, then it was through the signifying quality of the natural or material that the faithful might come to a better knowledge of the divine.[7]

This is not to say that religious images were never debated or contested. The relationship between Christian imagery and the apparent prohibition contained in the second commandment was debated in patristic texts, in discussions between East and West in the eighth century, and in later reflections upon the material culture of the Church both from within (St Bernard, St Francis) and from its critics (Lollards, Hussites) in the century or so before the Reformation. John Wycliffe, writing in the mid-1370s, considered that 'images might be made both well and ill: well in order to rouse, assist and kindle the minds of the faithful to love God more devoutly; and ill, when by reason of images there is a deviation from the true faith, as when the image is worshipped [...] or unduly delighted in for its beauty, costliness, or attachment to irrelevant circumstances'. The nature and function of such objects was not entirely neutral, but rather needed to be considered carefully.[8] Scripture was the essential guide, but there was, he argued, a difference in the discussion of images in the Old Testament and the New. The prohibition of images in the Decalogue was intended to prevent idolatry. God had no physical likeness before the Incarnation, and should not be provided with a corporeal form at the hands of man. After the birth and death of Christ, and once secure roots had been established for the Christian faith, images were permitted both as books for the laity and as a commemoration of the saints and a guide to their proper veneration.[9] It was appropriate to use an image to direct worship towards that which it signified, but not to adore the created object in its own right.

However, Wycliffe's thoughtful and in many respects moderate approach was not reflected in the actions of those who sought to spread his message, or act upon it. Physical opposition to images,

Fig. 12: Hans Holbein, *Desiderius Erasmus of Rotterdam with Renaissance Pilaster*, 1523

iconoclasm, rather than intellectual wariness, was to emerge as a distinguishing feature of the late medieval English Lollard heresy. 'And in England they are called Lollards,' wrote Stephen Gardiner, 'who, denying images thought therewithal the crafts of painting and graving to be generally superfluous and naught, and against God's law.'[10] The rejection of image worship permeated the articles directed against Lollards brought to trial. Images were condemned as idolatry, false religion, as a form of social and economic injustice in which the Church provided its own physical splendour to the prejudice of support for the poor. The Leicester Lollard William Smith gave physical expression to his doubts about the validity of images, burning a statue of St Catherine to test whether the saint's image might bleed, while at the same time finding wood for his cooking fire. He was not alone; many Lollards argued that images, as idols, should be destroyed, and put their ideas into practice.[11]

But there was still some common ground between the theologians and the iconoclasts. As the Lollards had argued, for Erasmus there was also something inherently unsettling about the presence of the poor, lying against the walls of the church, while inside the building was richly decked with images, candlesticks and organs. Such worldly objects had been bought and paid for with money; the souls of the poor had been bought with the blood of Christ. Images might well be the books of the laity, Erasmus argued, but they were all too readily converted to externalism and false belief. Images were the embodiment of human materialism: at best a distraction, at worst a perversion of proper worship. The separation of the sacred and profane was not always clear, and where the saints were depicted in an unworthy manner, their images had the potential to lead the faithful to lasciviousness and physicality. But there was also a note of moderation and caution; despite their inherent dangers, the removal of images might actually cause more harm than the toleration of their presence.[12] The cult of images might be 'a horrible crime', but at the start of the sixteenth century, Western Christendom remained saturated with material objects of devotion, liturgy and worship that engaged the senses, and a piety in which, in many respects, seeing was believing.

OPPOSITION TO IMAGES: DOCTRINE AND DESTRUCTION

The iconoclastic impulse in Reformation Europe has been extensively studied, both from a theoretical point of view and from the point of view of those who engaged in acts of destruction.[13] The rejection of religious imagery was an early, but not immediate, consequence of shifting theological understanding in the decades after 1517. For Luther, the focus of his criticisms of popular piety was the abuses associated with images; far too much money was spent on richly decorated ecclesiastical buildings, which might better be spent upon care for the poor. It was possible, he argued, that images, properly understood, might have a place in Christian practice, but where the presence of images invited the faithful to misunderstand the relationship between man and God, then as such they were an incitement to idolatry. Images of the saints were nothing but wood and stone; they had no inherent power, but might yet have a function. The unsanctioned and uncontrolled destruction of religious art, though, was not justified. By 1524–5, in his most extensive treatment of images and iconoclasm, Luther was prepared to argue for the positive contribution that images might make to the better understanding of Scripture, a line of argument that was not altogether removed from the traditional understanding of images as the books of the laity.[14] Where iconoclasm was warranted, it was to be orderly and with the consent of the appropriate authorities.[15]

The tone of Luther's writing on images in the mid-1520s reflected the escalation of the image controversy, and outbreaks of destructive and unlicensed iconoclasm that had become associated with his message. There had been a small disturbance at the Franciscan house in Wittenberg late in 1521, during which an altar had been smashed, and a further incident on Christmas Eve. In January 1522, the Augustinians in the city had destroyed their own altars and images; hardly an act of mob violence, but perhaps a sign of things to come. In 1522, Andreas Karlstadt published a treatise *On the removal of images*, the first significant incitement to destruction. Karlstadt's ideas had developed in a series of sermons and pamphlets in the period between June 1521 and early 1522.[16] The 1522 treatise was written in German, for a popular audience, and presented both a defence of these iconoclastic instances in Wittenberg, and a rousing call to further action. The text opened with a clear statement of intent:

i.   That we have images in churches and houses of God is wrong and contrary to the first commandment. Thou shalt not have other gods.

ii. That to have carved and painted idols set up on the altars is even more injurious and diabolical.

iii. Therefore it is good, necessary, praiseworthy, and pious that we remove them and give Scripture its due and in so doing accept its judgement.[17]

False and deceitful images, he argued, brought spiritual death to those who revered them. To erect a statue of a saint in a church was a sign of love for the object rather than for God, and the rich decoration of these images was further testimony to the extent to which man had rejected God. If these images were mere signs, he suggested, then such care and attention would not be lavished upon them. Images were idols erected in the house of God, and it was not only desirable but necessary that they be consigned to hell, or to the fiery furnace. The idolatry that permeated the cult of the saints manifested in their images was enacted in the lights that burned before statues, and the offerings that were left in thanksgiving or in hope of intercession. Such honour was due to God alone, and to do otherwise was to violate the first commandment. Both the Old and New Testament warned of the dangers associated with images and their veneration, and there could be no defence of their presence. For Karlstadt, images were both dangerous and useless; they could neither see nor understand, and were certainly not capable of functioning as books for the laity. To believe that an image could lead the mind closer to God was idolatry, both in the veneration of the image and in the erection of a false idol in the heart.

Given the severity of the danger posed by images, it was the will of God that 'you shall overturn and overthrow their altars. You shall smash their images. Their groves you shall hack down and their graven images you shall burn.'[18] An impenetrable divide existed between the flesh and the spirit, and material objects of devotion stood in the way of true worship of a God of spirit. The text was littered with references to Scripture, and Karlstadt used the Old Testament judgements upon images to argue that their presence both witnessed to, and supported, spiritual infidelity. Given the severity of the offence, he argued, it was vital that the authorities act to purge the churches of false religion. It was incumbent upon the 'highest worldly authority' to remove and destroy the works of the devil, or face the punishment of God. Iconoclasm was necessary, but still needed to be controlled. However, if the authorities failed to act, or acted slowly, it would be hard to contain the imperative to purge the churches. In Wittenberg, the Elector Frederick attempted to re-establish control over religion in his territory, and the city magistrates set a date for the orderly removal of images from churches. However, by early February there were instances of spontaneous iconoclasm, and Luther felt compelled to return to the city in an attempt to assert his authority over the pace and nature of doctrinal and material change.

Karlstadt was not alone in his call to action. A year after the publication of *On the removal of images*, a similar set of arguments were presented to the people of Zurich in the form of a pamphlet on *The Judgement of God*, penned by Ludwig Hatzer. The text circulated in the city shortly before a series of three disputations on images, and appeared to reflect the iconoclastic preaching of the preceding months, while at the same time shaping the frame of reference for the disputations.

For all the immediacy and relevance of Hatzer's work, the most significant contribution to the written debate came in the form of Ulrich Zwingli's *Answer to Valentin Compar*, in which he argued stridently that to worship or venerate images was to violate the law of God. The proliferation of images in the city's churches did not bring the faithful into a deeper understanding of God, or a closer relationship with Him. Far from it – the cult of images was the road to idolatry; as material, tangible, external objects, images were the very false gods which Scripture condemned. True religious experience was to be found not in rich decoration and ornamentation, but in the purity and simplicity of the whitewashed walls of reformed churches. The rhetoric was strident and energizing, but despite the temperature of the debate, there were relatively few outbreaks of 'popular' iconoclasm in Zurich, perhaps because of the continued presence of Zwingli in the city, and perhaps reflecting the close relationship between the reform leaders and the city council. In September 1523, three men entered the Fraumünster church in the city, damaging lamps and profaning holy water. However, for the most part, the removal of images from the city's churches remained under the control of the council, and the task was completed by summer 1524 after the death of the mayor, Marcus Roist, whose more conservative leanings on the image question delayed the formal decision to proceed.[19] Heinrich Bullinger summarized the outcome of the process, which took barely two weeks: 'all the churches of the city were cleared; costly works of painting and sculpture, especially a beautiful table in the Waterchurch, were destroyed. The superstitious lamented; but the true believers rejoiced in it as a great and joyous worship of God.'

This same dialogue between those who condemned the presence of images and those who carried out their removal or destruction, evident in the exchanges between Luther and Karlstadt, between reformers and council in Zurich, and the modification of Wycliffe's theology by later Lollards, can also be seen in mid-century Calvinism. Coming back to where we started, the iconoclastic destruction in the Netherlands in 1566, there was a clear correlation between incendiary preaching and open defacement or destruction of images. Yet those who preached iconoclasm in this context were doing more than repeating the Genevan reformer's views on images and materiality. Calvin was openly and determinedly hostile to the presence of images in churches and to the attendant superstition that surrounded them. His views were publicly expressed in biblical commentaries, in catechism and in preaching, but Calvin stopped short of defending popular iconoclasm.[20] The prohibition of graven images contained in the Decalogue was, for Calvin, the second commandment, and as valid in the sixteenth century Church as it had been when dictated to Moses. The defence of images by the medieval Catholic Church, he argued, was grounded upon a slim evidential basis, which could not conceal the fact that religious images were contrary to the law of God. Veneration of images in Christian churches was no more than pagan survival, and the proliferation of such artefacts further diminished their credibility as books for the laity or embodiments of doctrinal truth. The word of God, rather than the materiality of images, was the only appropriate tool of religious instruction. The human mind was 'a perpetual forge of idols', and one that needed to be purged.[21]

The argument against images was crisp and clear, but in terms of action, Calvin made clear that it was incumbent upon the magistrate rather than the populace to cleanse the churches. This part of the message was perhaps less attractive to those who were attempting to purge the Church of false religion and reform its devotional and liturgical practices. Calvin's letters to the French Protestant congregations in the mid-sixteenth century counselled care and moderation, but it was the more confrontational and destructive language of his earlier writings, including the 1543 *Treatise on Relics*, that seemed to be more compelling in the context of confessional strife.[22] Responding to outbreaks of iconoclasm and destruction in France in the early 1560s, Calvin sought to distance himself, asserting that he had never approved of such actions.[23] From the summer of 1561 onward, isolated instances of destruction gave way to more general and determined efforts to cleanse the churches of Languedoc, Gascony and Dauphiné, the majority seemingly the work of local believers, work in which the reformed clergy and consistories claimed to have had no involvement.[24] Yet even if there was no formal sponsorship for iconoclasm, it is hard to see such destruction as anything other than an expression of discontent and opposition to Catholicism, or a visible expression of reformed belief. The destruction of images allowed the physical enactment of God's law, but it also, if unpunished by divine intervention (or that of the saints), validated the reformed interpretation of that law. The fact that images did not defend themselves, bleed or bring divine vengeance upon the iconoclasts was a striking visual demonstration of their simple materiality, but also lent support to those who opposed images, and fuelled scepticism and hostility among those who felt captive to the Catholic Church and misled by its practices.

THE AFTERMATH OF ICONOCLASM

Just as theology and practice had co-inhered in the presence of images, so reformed theology and practice combined in their destruction. Iconoclasm was a tangible sign of change, a tool for evangelism and an opportunity for congregations to take religious reform into their own hands. It is tempting to see the destruction of images and the purging of false religion as the end of the story, but the polarity between true and false in the rhetoric and polemic did not always match experience on the ground. As we have seen, it was possible for 'popular' action to exceed (or transgress) the hopes of the theologians, but it is also possible to identify compromises and continuities in the relationship between the Reformation and the religious image, and instances in which reformers were willing to work with, rather than against, traditional pieties.

The process of Lutheran reform in Nuremberg is a prime example. Bridget Heal's study of the cult of the Virgin and the continuing presence of Marian imagery in the city reveals how, despite the Lutheran rejection of traditional theology that emphasized the role of Mary as a divine intercessor, some aspects of traditional Marian piety survived. Luther's criticism of images was very much a criticism of the viewer as much as the object; it was the nature of seeing that dictated whether an image was an idol, not its simple existence. It was, in this schema, still possible to see a positive benefit deriving from religious art and sculpture, as long as the believer was able to view these material objects appropriately. There was also a personal sense of ownership to consider; most of the Marian paintings and statues in Nuremberg churches had been donated by members of the city's ruling elite, who were, as a result, perhaps less likely to demand their destruction. Alongside these pragmatic reasons for survival, though, ran a more interventionist approach. Rather than demanding the removal of images, Protestant writers and preachers attempted to remodel their meaning, turning the position of the Virgin from that of a powerful intercessor into a model of faith, obedience, humility and domestic virtue. A virgin and child portrait from the workshop of Cranach was part of the town hall collection, and several pre-Reformation feast days continued to be observed. Any person who spoke against the honour of the Virgin was to be punished. But this was no failure of the part of the civic authorities to suppress a cult; rather the Reformation in Nuremberg proceeded on the basis that, imbued with a new message, old images and devotions might become a potent vehicle for the dissemination of change. Mary's position as the mother of God was not questioned, but honour was due to the Virgin because of the favour that God had shown to her, and not because of her own merit. Mary as mother could be transformed into a model of maternity and care within the godly household, but this new message would need to be communicated to the faithful effectively. This was, in some respects, a calculated risk. Without iconoclasm and humiliation, there was no potent symbol of the impotence of images. If the meaning attributed to an object was constructed as much in the heart and mind of the viewer, rather than in the wishes of the city authorities, it could not be guaranteed that the 'reformed' Mary was actually what churchgoers saw, or chose to see, in the surviving statuary and imagery.[25]

Traditional imagery also survived in other forms. Despite the iconoclastic impulse, it is clear that Protestant printed images were deeply rooted in the iconography and visual traditions of the culture of late medieval Christianity. The idea of 'reformed' images might seem inherently contradictory, but the engagement between the Reformation and the visual arts was more complex than we might expect.[26] Despite the warnings of the Strasbourg painter Heinrich Vogtherr that 'in a few years there will scarcely be found anyone working as a painter or sculptor', the fate of the image was not sealed. Art, and artists, were pressed into the service of the Reformation, adopting a new vocabulary while adapting the old for pious or didactic purposes. Lucas Cranach, an early convert to the Reformation, was responsible for the production of a torrent of anti-papal and anti-Catholic imagery, but also a series of Lutheran painted altarpieces depicting biblical figures, the risen Christ and the 'proper' celebration of the sacraments. The celebration of communion, around a table, and in both kinds, might well take place in front of a dramatic visual representation of that same commemoration of the Last Supper. Luther argued in 1530 that these depictions of biblical events and sacraments should be there 'for the eyes to behold, so that the heart can think upon it and the eyes too, by reading, might praise and give thanks to God'. It was entirely appropriate that the evangelical theology of justification be conveyed in art as well as in the spoken and written word.[27] The altarpiece fashioned for the church of SS Peter and Paul in Weimar depicted a series of scenes from the life of Christ, all of which invited the audience to reflect upon the giving, rather than earning, of divine grace.[28] Art mirrored the new reality, but also positioned that reality firmly in the gaze of the believer. In some cases, the loss of images from churches was accompanied by a greater exposure to them in the private sphere, with print copies of evangelical sermons often accompanied by visual images. The rejection of cultic images in churches was not necessarily paralleled by a decisive shift away from the visual in printed texts, as sermons and devotional works continued to use images to hammer home the message. A visual image that imparted a reformed message was a powerful polemical tool, as long as the message was appropriately understood and internalized.[29] The traditional divide between the visual world of late medieval Catholicism and the didactic word of Protestantism was more permeable than we might think.[30]

It is hard to ignore the theatricality and performative function that underpinned acts of iconoclasm, and therefore the capacity for the moment of removal or destruction to fulfil a powerful polemical and persuasive function. Yet some of the theatricality,

Fig. 13: Lucas
Cranach,
*Christus
am Kreuz,*
Altarpiece,
Church of
SS Peter and
Paul, Weimar,
1555

gesturing and physical spaces involved in the smashing apart of superstitions involved a verbal and visual language that was very much part of pre-Reformation culture. Scribner's study of carnival and the Reformation has shown the way in which the traditional observance of carnival in the German cities might be accompanied, or appropriated, in the service of the Reformation, by acts of iconoclasm. Such instances were more common in the 1520s and 1530s and perhaps reflected a desire to test the limits of tolerance on the part of the civic authorities, or exploit the ongoing potential for carnival to become an acceptable flashpoint for rival ideas and ideologies.[31] The visual and verbal vocabulary deployed in iconoclasm was often, itself, borrowed from past generations.

The legacy of iconoclasm was also ambiguous and evolving. While in many cases the ease with which images and other material objects were removed from churches was presented as evidence of their impotence and illegitimacy, in other cases the space left behind could impart an equally striking message. *The fantasie of idolatrie*, a polemical work commissioned by Thomas Cromwell, mocked and denounced the proliferation of sacred places on the English landscape and those who ran 'hyther and thyther' to access the sacred in these locations and objects: 'Thus were we poore soules, Begyled with Idolles,' the text ran, 'with fayned myracles and lyes, By the devyll and his docters, The Pope and his Procters, That with such have blerid our eyes.'[32]

Such rhetoric justified destruction, but it was harder to control its legacy. When the shrine of Thomas Becket in Canterbury Cathedral was destroyed in 1538, the marble that remained in situ served as a testament to the scale of the shrine and to the work of destruction. It is worth reflecting at this point on the extent to which physical disappearance equated with mental eradication. In 1553, Sheriff Robert Broddis of York indicated that he wished to be buried at the foot of St William's tomb, suggesting that the memory, if not the bones, of the saint had survived beyond the predations of the 1530s and 1540s.[33] The suppression of the English monastic houses in the 1530s created the same problem of visual and culture memory, and the renegotiation of relationships between people and place. The 'Bare ruin'd choirs where late the sweet birds sang' had the potential to remain part of the English cultural and literary landscape well beyond their formal use as houses of prayer.[34] At Hailes, for example, after the dispatching of the blood relic the remains of the shrine were also removed in order that it might not become a focus of veneration. Yet even those individuals whose iconoclasm extended only as far as removing redundant materials and objects from the former monastic buildings have been seen as complicit in the work of reform and, as a result, capable of internalizing the evangelical message. Ethan Shagan's analysis of the dissolution of Hailes Abbey in Gloucestershire concluded that individuals who plundered lead and other items from the dissolved monasteries were engaged (intentionally or otherwise) in acts of iconoclasm and sacrilege that would embed the underlying justificatory theology in their hearts and minds. By viewing the monastic buildings as an appropriate source of wood, lead and stone, those who plundered the sites were both preaching and enacting a message directed against the whole notion of sacred space that had underpinned the physical and mental position of monasteries.[35] In this reading, the remnants of images, empty plinths and ruined buildings were not evidence of the survival of Catholic devotion on a reformed topography, or the less than total achievement of iconoclasm, but rather symbols of the triumph of Protestantism over popery, and monuments that warned of the feigned superstition and idolatry of traditional religion.[36]

The removal or destruction of material objects had the capacity to cement a new theology and understanding in the minds of those who either witnessed the destruction, to embed a new meaning in old symbols and to present a blank canvas onto which could be imprinted the message of reform. By removing altars from churches, and positioning the pulpit as the focal point, it was possible to present a critical judgement on the theology of the Mass, while at the same time offering a clear reminder that the preaching of the word of God was the prime function of the Christian congregation and its pastors. The whitewashing of the walls of churches, obscuring the richly decorated scenes of the lives of the saints removed these heroes of the medieval Church from the physical sight of the believer, but also facilitated the dissemination of the key reformed tenets of faith by creating a blank canvas onto which could be painted biblical texts, the words of the Decalogue, the Lord's Prayer or the Creed. The preaching of the word of God, in this scheme, resonated around a church that was visually marked with these same words.

The sense of the physical church as a sacred space was not completely eradicated, but the parameters and function of that space were ideologically and materially transformed. Sensory understandings and uses of the sacred that had created the material culture of holiness of late medieval religion, not only their physical manifestations, were subject to the iconoclastic fervour of the reformers. Incense, candles, bells, processions, imagery which had served as channels for the communication of the sacred were rejected, but this is not to say that no sense of the sacred survived. Reformed places of worship, purged, it was argued, of idolatry, were not 'un-sacred', or, indeed, 'un-sensory' in their function. More than seeing, hearing mattered: the sound of the word of God being preached, the sound of the Psalms being sung, emerged as – and created – physical and cultural understandings and delineations. Bells continued to be rung to call the faithful to church, and the whitewashed walls of the churches continued to be illuminated by glass windows. Some church organs survived, often with a more secular concert-giving function, but occasionally to support congregational hymn-singing.[37] Henri Lefebvre described the late medieval landscape as 'haunted by the church', which had provided the multitudinous points of engagement with the holy to which Reformation theologians objected.[38] However, the 'reformed' landscape continued to be haunted by some of the same ghosts, physically, but also in the sense that the Protestant churches, purged of idols, were still 'positioned in the same forcefield of sacrality' as the Catholic Church.[39] The real division over images and the sense-able aspects of religion, Scribner has argued, was epistemological as much as confessional; it was a question over the extent to which knowledge of the divine might be achieved through material objects, or whether these were idols that clouded the mind of man against the word of God.[40] The assault on idolatry did not prevent the survival of some of the most potent images through which Christian belief was represented and propagated, and it was, in many respects, still possible to gaze, devoutly, upon the material in post-Reformation Europe.

4

THE REFORMATION, AUTHORITY AND RADICALISM

SOLA SCRIPTURA

The principle of *sola scriptura*, as we saw in Chapter 1, was a cornerstone of evangelical theology, but it was one that did not necessarily guarantee unity and consensus. The assertion that Scripture was the ultimate source of authority in matters of doctrine and Christian life carried with it the ambition to put the word of God in the hands of the entire community of Christian believers, the ploughboys of Tyndale's promise. But as vernacular Scripture proliferated, so did its interpretation; the permanence and perspicuity of the Word of God became subject to the vocabulary and vicissitudes of polemical debate and pastoral concern. Division and debate opened up over the central components of Reformation thought, soteriology, the theology of the sacraments, the nature of the Church and the very understanding of authority itself. The fault lines lay, more often than not, in questions about what *sola scriptura* meant in practice, the authority of the Word and the location of the authority to interpret Scripture. In the exegesis of the written Word, where was the believer to perceive the precise meaning of God's promise? When sacred text was transmitted in the vernacular, at what cost and profit were the decisions of the translator made? Where there was dissent and difference, at whose instance was the dividing line between truth and falsehood drawn? What was the role of believer, preacher, church or magistrate in the dissemination of the Word and the definition of its meaning? Such questions, often driven by practical necessity, revealed both the intrinsic simplicity of a faith that was grounded in Scripture alone, and the scale of the ambiguity around exactly what that might mean in practice.

'CAPTIVE TO THE WORD OF GOD'

Martin Luther declared at the Diet of Worms in 1521 that his conscience was captive to the Word of God, and that unless he could be shown to be wrong by that same Word of God, his mind could not be changed. 'I am sure that the word of God is with me and not with them,' Luther wrote, protesting that where the defenders of the Roman Catholic Church could argue only from its own tradition, Scripture was on the side of the evangelicals.[1] In this sense, as Alec Ryrie has argued, early modern Protestantism was a 'fundamentalist movement', one which accepted a single authority, Scripture, in the determination of doctrine, and which pronounced the authority of the biblical text to be absolute.[2] But that single authority, as the debates of the Reformation exposed, was capable of exhibiting alarming ambiguity and disconcerting silence on key issues, sometimes doctrinal, sometimes in deliberations over the nature of the godly community, Christian society and the structures of authority in Church and state. The unmediated reading of the sacred text had the potential to produce a cacophony of interpretations, as the multiplicity of radical forms of reformation in the first half of the sixteenth century demonstrated. Luther's defence of the equality of a Christian priesthood that was shared by all members of the Christian community, and the right of all Christians to 'test and judge what is right or wrong in matters of faith', did not guarantee individual interpretations either authority or legitimacy. Rather the reading of Scripture by the faithful was to be undertaken within the constraints of the Christian community, in which resided the administration of the sacraments and the Word.[3]

PATRISTIC AUTHORITY

Equally troubling, however, was the apparent absence of clarity (or indeed a simple absence) of Scriptural mandate on key issues. In the defence of, for example, infant baptism, or the theology of the Trinity, the leaders of the magisterial reformation turned to textual authorities outside the canonical books of the Bible, particularly the writings of the Fathers of the Church, whose chronological proximity to the purity of the apostolic Church imbued their words with a persuasive voice. The legitimacy of the theologies articulated in patristic writings was asserted on the basis of their apparent conformity with the biblical text in a way that suggested a coinherence between Scripture and patristic writing, but also justified the rejection of particular Fathers and texts which sat outside this consensus.[4] In the 1549 disputation in Oxford on the subject of the Eucharist, the Italian Protestant and newly appointed Regius Professor of Divinity, Peter Martyr Vermigli, declared his intention to draw upon the testimony of the Fathers in his iconoclastic assault on the theology of the Mass:

> Truly I will not reject the Fathers, on the contrary, I attribute a great deal to them when they speak according to the Scriptures. I have cited them as you have heard, and perhaps lingered too much in that line, not that I depend upon them, but because I see many addicted to them in a superstitious way, who are forever crying: the Fathers, the Fathers! Thinking that they are always against us. I wished to show such people that they make most of all for us.[5]

Martyr's point here was twofold, and reflective of a broader sense of the value of the patristic inheritance in sixteenth-century Protestantism. The ability to find evidence of support for evangelical theology within the writings of the Fathers demonstrated that such ideas were far from novel (a response to the accusation 'Where was your church before Luther?'), but also wrested possession of patristic texts from the hands of Catholic polemicists. Evangelicals were far from unwilling to shift the debate onto the patristic territory that was claimed by their opponents. As a result, arguments were not simply constructed around an oppositional sense of Scripture vs tradition, but in a way which allowed the use of that effective weapon in the polemical armoury: proving your opponent wrong from the words of his own authorities. As the Elizabethan bishop John Jewel challenged his Catholic opponents who defended their faith on the basis of its antiquity and continuity, '[A]nd as for their religion, if it be of so long continuance as they would have men ween it is, why do they not prove it so by the examples of the primitive church and by the fathers and the councils of old times?'[6] Jewel's assertion here was not that the primitive Church was the ultimate authority in matters of doctrinal debate, but rather that the very authorities that were claimed by his opponents were singularly silent on the very matter upon which they were asserted as arbiters.

In much the same way, Catholic theologians and polemicists were willing to confront the Reformation on the basis of the biblical text. By and large, protagonists on both sides of the confessional divide were in agreement over the primacy of Scripture in the identification of doctrinal authority. The more divisive issue was the relationship between Scripture, the Fathers and the tradition and history of the Church in the definition of doctrine and practice. The evangelical argument that the authority of the Fathers as exegetes and commentators derived from the extent to which their arguments could be shown to be in accordance with that same scriptural text was polemically attractive but rather circular. Such circularity provided Catholic polemicists with a point of entry into the debate, and supported the assertion that the custodian of truth and veracity in biblical interpretation had to be the institutional Church rather than the private person. If the true church, as defined in evangelical writing, was to be recognized in its possession of the Word of God, how did that Word come into being? As Gillian Evans has commented, 'It is a supreme irony that it was at the time when *Scriptura sola* became a reforming slogan that it became unprecedentedly difficult to point unequivocally to the Sacred Page and say, "That is Holy Scripture".'[7] The challenge stretched beyond the matter of interpretation and into more basic, material questions over the reliability of manuscripts, the relationship between the Latin Vulgate and biblical texts in their original languages, and decisions about acceptable vocabulary in vernacular bibles. The application of humanist philological learning to the study of the sacred text was far from neutral; such efforts were a manifestation of the apparent presumptuousness of those who sought to undermine the interpretative authority of the Church by challenging both the lessons and the language of Scripture.[8]

Catholic polemicists took to the defence of the argument that the authority, and indeed very existence, of the canonical text of Scripture came through its recognition as such by the Church. As John Rastell argued against Thomas Cooper, '[I]f you know it by the scriptures, what persuaded you these scriptures to be true?'[9] The intrinsic authority of the Bible was beyond doubt, but for Rastell, the Word of God in Scripture was, as it had been for earlier Catholic polemicists, insufficient and ambiguous. The process of revelation had not come to an end with the apostolic Church, the argument ran, and it was through the gift of the Holy Spirit that the preservation of truth in the Church was assured. In the traditions of the Church, and in its public faith, consistency of faith and the inspiration of the spirit presented a solid defence against the dangerous multiplicity of interpretations and beliefs that characterized heresy and dissent from the early Church to the Reformation.[10] As Gillian Evans noted, the acceptance of the canon of Scripture as authentic Christian witness by the community of the Church changed the relationship between Church and Scripture to one in which the role of the Church was that of stewardship. The preservation of the sacred text, and its dissemination, remained closely connected with the Christian community of the Church. To assert obedience only to God, and the Word of God in Scripture, not only challenged the interpretative authority of the Church, but also threatened to undermine the sacramental nature of the ecclesiastical institution.[11] As a result, there was something polemically persuasive in the articulation of an opposition between *sola scriptura* and *sola ecclesia* that asserted the existence of an almost unbridgeable gulf between the Catholic and evangelical standpoint. However, such an approach relied upon an ability to pit Scripture and tradition against one another as alternative sources of authority. Beneath the caricature, such a model was largely meaningless; both were part of an ongoing process of divine revelation, and to use one to test the veracity of the other was intellectually pointless and pastorally dangerous. Disputes over authority in matters of theology frequently lay in the matter of its transmission and articulation rather than in the extent to which its roots could be seen in Scripture or tradition.[12] The extent to which this interconnection of Church and Scripture was understood was evident at the (ultimately abortive) Colloquy of Ratisbon in 1541, in the assertion that

> the unity of the church consists in this association [*consociatio*] under one head through the same Gospel and the same ministry [...] so that there should be one consenting church, God has always passed on the same Gospel through the fathers and prophets and afterwards through Christ and the apostles.[13]

'ONE CONSENTING CHURCH'

The key question of the extent to which doctrinal authority lay in Scripture alone, Scripture interpreted or the combined voice of Scripture and tradition was not the invention of the Reformation, but it was enlivened further by the rhetoric and priorities of church and state in the sixteenth century.[14] In his foreword to the 1516 Greek and Latin New Testament, Desiderius Erasmus articulated a strident argument for the free availability of the text of Scripture to all who wished for it:

> I absolutely dissent from those people who don't want the holy scriptures to be read in translation by the unlearned, as if, forsooth, Christ taught such complex doctrine that hardly anyone outside a handful of theologians could understand it, or as if the chief strength of the Christian religion lay in people's ignorance of it.

The Gospel was no longer mediated through the traditions and theologians of the Church, and encounters with God took place through the eyes and the mind of the individual reader.[15] In this sense, access to vernacular Scripture was part of the rejection of the authority of the separate sacramental priesthood, and a rallying cry for the role of the individual in articulating a personal relationship with God. However, Luther's *Biblia Deutsch* not only presented the word of God in a language that made it accessible to the 'common man', but also provided that same audience with a framework for the reading and interpretation of the sacred text. At one level, vernacular Scripture offered free and unconstrained access to the work of God, but as the full force of the multiplicity of interpretations unleashed by this freedom became apparent in the mid-1520s, Luther and others sought to shape the way in which the laity approached and engaged with the biblical text. Luther appended prefaces to the translated books of the Bible, encouraged readers to make connections between the Old and New Testament and hammered home those aspects of evangelical theology that he regarded as woven into the Gospels and Epistles. The rhetoric of Scripture alone continued to shape debate and controversy, but the extent to which vernacular bibles provided an access to the sacred text that was entirely divorced from any institutional framework should not be overestimated. Where the authority of the Bible was articulated most strongly, the vexed question of authority in the context of exegesis remained.

As Peter Marshall has noted, the most revolutionary aspect of Luther's approach was 'his insistence that all traditions must be tested against scripture, and that beyond the explicit mandates of the Bible lay a great vista of Christian liberty'. The full extent of this iconoclastic approach to Scripture and authority was evident in the assault on four of the seven sacraments in Luther's treatise on the *Babylonian Captivity of the Church*, in which only baptism, the Eucharist and marriage were presented as grounded in Scripture. Luther's assault on the sacraments provoked a determined defence, not least in the *Assertio Septem Sacramentorum*, published in the name of Henry VIII in summer 1521.[16] Criticisms of Luther's stance were anchored in the argument that Scripture was insufficient as a touchstone for all matters of doctrine, and that the oral tradition of the apostolic Church, and a broader understanding of *scriptura sacra* that extended beyond the two testaments, embodied the Gospel of Christ, uttered, but not recorded, by the evangelists. From a different direction, Luther's position came under fire from those who argued that this desire to test every tradition by Scripture had an even broader reach than Luther had envisaged, turning the criticism of doctrine and practice that appeared non-scriptural against the institutional churches of the magisterial reformation, and demanding a more radical approach to the application of the *sola scriptura* principle. Just as Luther had declared at Worms that his conscience was captive to the Word of God, so the radical preacher Thomas Müntzer asserted that his model of a Christian church and society was anchored in the visible Word of God. The debate over authority was conducted not only between Catholic and Protestant, but also within Protestantism, where conflicting ideas about church, state and Scripture fanned the flames of conflict, separatism and persecution.

RELIGIOUS RADICALISM

My son, hear the instruction of your mother; open your ears to hear the words of my mouth. Behold, I go today the way of the prophets, apostles and martyrs, and drink of the cup of which they all have drank. I go, I say, the way which Christ Jesus, the eternal word of the Father, full of grace and truth, the Shepherd of the sheep, who is the Life, Himself went, and who went this way and not another [...] This way was travelled by the dead under the altar, who cry, saying: Lord, Almighty God, when will you avenge the blood that has been shed? This is the way in which walked the twenty-four elders, who stand before the throne of God, and cast their crowns and harps before the throne of the Lamb [...] My son, if you desire to enter into the regions of the holy world and into the inheritance of the saints, follow after them; search the Scriptures, and it shall show you their ways. The angel who spoke to the prophet said: A holy city has been built, and set upon a broad field, and is full of all good things; the entrance thereof is narrow, and set in a dangerous place to fall, like as if there were a fire on the right hand, and on the left deep water, and only one path between them both, even between the fire and the water. See, my son, this way has no retreats; there are no roundabout or crooked little paths; whosoever departs to the right or to the left inherits death. Therefore, my child, do not regard the great number, nor walk in their ways. But where you hear of a poor, simple, cast-off little flock, which is despised and rejected by the world, join them; for where you hear of the cross, there is Christ. Flee the shadow of this world; become united with God; fear Him alone, keep His commandments, observe all His words, write them on the table of your heart, bind them upon your forehead, speak day and night of His law and you will be a pleasant tree and a sprout in the courts of the Lord, a beloved plant growing up in Zion. Take the fear of the Lord to be your father, and wisdom shall be the mother of your understanding. Do not be afraid of people, forsake your life rather than depart from the Truth.

Fig. 14: Jan Luiken, etching showing Anna Jansz on the way
to her execution. In the *Martyrs Mirror*, 1685

These words of Anna Jansz, addressed to her infant son, became a
rallying cry for Anabaptist radicals, resonant with the language of
Scripture and articulating an eschatological expectation.[17] At the
age of twenty-four, Anna and her husband had been baptized by
Maynaart von Emden, a Münsterite Anabaptist preacher, whose
sermons, like Anna's song, were heavily laden with apocalyptic
hope and expectation. Anna's husband fled to England when
violence was unleashed against the Amsterdam Anabaptists; Anna
followed in 1536, but returned to the Netherlands in 1538, with
her fifteen-month-old son, Isaiah.[18] Shortly after her return, Anna
and her companion were arrested, imprisoned and sentenced to
death by drowning, a common penalty for Anabaptists who had
rejected infant baptism and been rebaptized as adults. On the way
to her death, Anna appealed to the crowd to care for her son, and
a local baker stepped forward. Anna had composed a letter for her

son, which was to become part of the narrative of her martyrdom, a story that was told and retold in the following decades.

In 1562, a small collection of stories and letters that recorded the experience and theology of the persecuted Anabaptist churches in the Netherlands, *Het Offer des Heeren* (The Sacrifice of the Lord), appeared from the press of a Dutch printer. Its pages described the suffering, persecution and witness of twenty-two Anabaptists, including Anna Jansz. By the end of the century this small pocket book had run to eleven editions of increasing size. By the late seventeenth century, the eleven different increasingly larger editions had grown into the substantial text that we now know as the *Martyrs Mirror*. The first martyr narrative was that of Stephen, described in the Acts of the Apostles. The second martyr, Michael Sattler, was a leader of the Swiss Brethren, who had played a key role in the drafting of the Schleitheim Confession and was executed in 1527 in Rottenburg am Neckar. Sattler was taken to the square, where the executioner was ordered to 'first cut out his tongue, and then forge him fast to a wagon and there with glowing iron tongs twice tear pieces from his body, then on the way to the site of execution five times more as above and then burn his body to powder as an arch-heretic'.[19] Anna Jansz's execution narrative followed. These, then, were the 'poor, simple, cast-off little flock which is despised and rejected by the world' that Anna had described to her son in her testament, those who were persecuted for their beliefs and whose suffering and martyrdoms stretched as an unbroken chain between the church of Christ described in the Acts of the Apostles and the confessional strife of the Reformation.[20]

'[N]o moderate Reformer, however liberal by temperament,' wrote the late A. G. Dickens, 'dared to refrain from showing his dislike of Anabaptism.'[21] But fear of Anabaptism was not articulated only by the voices of the moderate Reformation; anxiety about manifestations of religious radicalism contributed to what has been described by Carter Lindberg as 'a kind of perverse early ecumenicalism' in which magisterial reformation and Roman Catholicism found a common enemy.[22] In order to understand what was meant by Anabaptism, or religious radicalism, and what it represented in relation to the authority of the institutional churches, it is worth recognizing that the terminology itself is far from unproblematic. The origin of the label 'radical' in the context of the religious climate of the sixteenth century is associated with the work of Weber, Troeltsch and others who first encouraged the categorization of evangelical ideas and movements into institutional churches and sects. The representation of religious radicalism has continued to be shaped by this schematic sense, even if the boundaries have become rather more blurred.[23] G. H. Williams's study of 'radical' groups as a valid form of historical enquiry encouraged this trend, not least because it provided subsequent scholars with a recognizable intellectual apparatus. Williams assumed the existence of a clear distinction between the 'magisterial' and the 'radical' reformers, a distinction that certainly makes sense in the context of the language used in preaching and polemic against those who opposed the 'magisterial' reformation, but has been found to be less satisfactory as a general descriptor of belief. For Williams, the 'moderate' Reformation was magisterial, controlled by secular governments, embodying primarily the Lutheran, reformed and Anglican confessions. The magisterial reformation was anchored in confessions of faith that acted as the custodians of orthodoxy, alliance with secular powers, the assertion of the authority of the clergy and a clearly defined sacramental theology and practice. Christian piety originated not in the subjective judgement and experience of the individual, but in the teaching authority of the institution.[24] Religious radicalism focused less upon liturgical celebrations and priesthood, and more upon individual piety and its social expression. In Williams's model, radicalism was tripartite, comprising Anabaptism, spiritualism and evangelical rationalism, the embodiment of a set of opinions that were sometimes inconsistent and divisive. Radicalism was distinct from the magisterial reformation, and guided by its own interpretations of Scripture, grace and social action. This amounted to more than simply a form of magisterial reformation, but was instead a set of shared core beliefs outside which there existed some diversity. While Anabaptism was defined by a core belief about the errors of infant baptism, the expression of those core radical beliefs was rather more chameleonic in colour.[25]

The challenge to Williams's model articulated by Dickens, among others, is focused upon the extent to which radical beliefs might be better described as a 'highly fissiparous tendency' than as a reformation, particularly given the failure of radicalism to assert and implement control over a functioning society for a recognizable period of time. Dickens was prepared to accept that cruelty had been visited upon these radicals by both Catholic and Protestant, but suggested that there was a real danger in distorting the narrative of the Reformation by according radicals a greater influence than they in reality possessed. But alternative terminologies are not necessarily any more accurate in their use or intention. The phrase 'left wing of the reformation', coined by Roland Bainton, makes some sense in the context of modern Western political language and helps to integrate the radicals into the broader picture of reformation by identifying a spectrum of belief, rather than two forms of Protestantism separated by clear blue water. From the terminology of 'left wing' we can take away a sense that these individuals and groups were more militant, or at least unconventional in their character. But the language still assumes some kind of consensus among the radicals, and encourages us to view early modern Christianity in a rather linear manner, with the authority of the papacy at one end, radicalism at the other, and Lutheranism, Calvinism and other forms of magisterial reformation arranged at intervals in between. In this model, radicalism emerges as a variant form of Protestantism, rather than a distinctive and therefore dangerous alternative to the institutional churches. In this already complicated mix (in Dickens's phrase, a whirlpool) sits Anabaptism. It is vital to recognize that the representation of radicals as dissenters and deviants from the confessional structures of the institutional churches owes something to the vocabulary that was used by magisterial reformers to denounce their opponents. The label 'anabaptist' provided a convenient shorthand for a multiplicity of beliefs and actions, but also prioritized opposition to infant baptism as the main dogma and danger of radical dissent. Any term that is used to label one's opponents is likely to be informed by a stance that is sceptical, judgemental or outright polemical.[26] There are likely differences between self-identification and oppositional labelling, and identities that are defined by doctrinal statements, social action or both.

A closer analysis of not just radical theology, but the social context in which it operated, has raised questions about the scale of the radical 'problem' and the extent to which the radicals truly spoke with a collective voice. But the work of Claus-Pater Clasen, Hans-Jurgen Goertz and others has also done much to encourage further reflection upon the social and economic background of the radicals, and the often complicated relationship between belief, community and secular authority. Goertz's conviction that there was no 'collective Anabaptism' certainly does not blunt the impact that the study of radicalism has had upon our understanding of the sixteenth-century Reformation. The tendency to focus upon points of theological principle has been eroded by a broader willingness to think about the nature of belief as it was lived out in the individual, family and community. Evidence of plurality and conflict in the radical reformation raises questions about such issues in the context of the magisterial reformation, and the extent to which the comparison between the two is either helpful or schematically defensible.[27] In this sense, the challenge that radicalism posed to authority lies not only in the nature of radicalism, but also in the perception of radicalism on the part of the institutional churches, who used that same perception to justify opposition and persecution. The vehemence of hostility that both the Protestant and Catholic churches exhibited and enacted against radicals and Anabaptist sects is conspicuous. In William Monter's estimate, these groups accounted for 2,000 of the 3,000 heretics that were condemned and executed between 1520 and 1565.[28] As well as being numerically significant, the willingness of magisterial reformers to persecute religious radicalism both changed the colour of radicalism by creating a history of martyrdom that provided a focal point for shared identity, and impacted upon the historical narrative of Protestantism in which the reformed churches were presented as the 'poor simple cast-off little flock' that made up Anna Jansz's church of Christ. Radicalism presented a challenge that was a matter of doctrine, a potential threat to the social order, an implicit and explicit interrogation of the authority of the institutional churches and a counter-narrative of history.

INFANT BAPTISM

In matters of doctrine, the most controversial and visible hallmark of Anabaptism was the rejection of infant baptism. The first article of the *Schleitheim Confession of Faith* (1527), in which Sattler had played a pivotal role, asserted:

> [Adult] Baptism shall be given to all those who have learned repentance
> and amendment of life, and who believe truly that their sins are taken
> away by Christ [...] This excludes all infant baptism, the highest and
> chief abomination of the Pope.[29]

The rejection of paedobaptism was a clear challenge to Catholic sacramental theology, which presented infant baptism as the means by which the stain of original sin was wiped away. For Luther, Melanchthon and other magisterial reformers, the baptism of infants had a permanent effect, obviating the need for the elaborate penitential structures of medieval Catholicism.[30] But for both Catholic and magisterial Protestant, infant baptism was an inviolable principle. On this issue, we can see the origins of 'perverse ecumenism' described by Lindberg; Catholic and Lutheran were united against the Anabaptist stance, even if the precise nature of their opposition was not identical.

The rejection of infant baptism, or a decision to seek rebaptism as an adult, was part of the accusations brought against Anna Jansz. But it was a point of faith that had already acquired a clear ancestry. In 1524, William Reublin, a priest in Zollikon, preached openly against infant baptism, and persuaded several of his flock to refuse to present their children to be baptized. Thomas Müntzer dismissed the baptism of infants as 'a clumsy monkey business', a form of fictitious faith that had been the ruin of the Church. The outward sign of baptism, he complained, had obscured the inner essence, and the baptism of infants had no scriptural basis. Furthermore, infant baptism had effectively eroded the catechumenate, and allowed access to the sacraments to those who lacked any formal instruction.[31] The reformation of baptism was a critical part of Müntzer's theology, in a way in which it was not for Luther, Zwingli, Melanchthon or Bucer.

The Zurich evangelical Conrad Grebel expressed his sympathy with Müntzer's view on baptism, indicating that he had read two of Müntzer's works and shared his opposition to 'ritualistic and anti-Christian customs of baptism'. Although initially favourably inclined toward Zwingli and the Zurich Reformation, Grebel and others claimed that they had come to recognize that they had been misled by the superficial faith of Zwingli and Luther, and, informed by Scripture, intended to take matters into their own hands. Hiding the Word of God and intermingling it with the words of men would not produce reform. Such sentiments led to Grebel's arrest and imprisonment in October 1525.

Grebel managed to escape confinement, but his friend and companion Felix Mantz was condemned to death in Zurich on 5 January 1527, the first victim of the city council's edict that imposed a sentence of death by drowning upon those guilty of adult baptism.[32] Mantz claimed that his intention was that all should follow in the footsteps of Christ, but Zwingli denounced his refusal to recede from his error and caprice. Mantz became not only the first victim of the Zurich council's mandate, but also the first Swiss Anabaptist to be put to death by other Protestants. Mantz presented a challenge to magisterial reformation in which doctrine and discipline were intricately entwined.

On the matter of infant baptism, Zwingli and the Zurich council were not prepared to compromise; neither were they prepared to concede that a model of reformation predicated upon an appeal to the authority of Scripture alone allowed the free interpretation of the sacred text, or justified open dissent on doctrine. Luther and Melanchthon condemned the Anabaptist insistence upon credobaptism as a manifestation of the same Donatist heresy that had been condemned by Augustine, and repeated efforts were made in the 1520s and 1530s by magisterial reformers, and the Catholic Church, to suppress such beliefs.[33] Dissent over the sacrament of baptism has been described as an 'enormous embarrassment' to the magisterial reformation, not only because radical dissent attempted to undermine Lutheran sacramental theology, but also because the argument over baptism threatened to open up a fault line within the Reformation that played into the hands of Catholic controversialists who contrasted the lack of internal unity within Protestantism with the unbroken authority and teachings of the papal Church. Indeed the Strasbourg reformer Martin Bucer expressed a willingness to consider tolerating the Anabaptist stance on paedobaptism if this would contribute to the preservation of the unity of the Church.[34] A decade after the execution of Mantz, Endres Keller, a member of a prominent

Rothenberg family, repeated the same arguments that had been used by Mantz, Grebel and their companions: '[I]nfant baptism cannot be defended from Scripture even if Luther and the pope say so.'[35] Such a statement laid bare the nature of the Anabaptist threat to secular authority, magisterial Protestantism and the integrity of the Christian community.

ANTICLERICALISM

The centrality of credobaptism in Anabaptism threw into sharp relief the consequences of the evangelical rhetoric of anticlericalism that permeated polemic discourse in the 1520s and beyond. Anticlerical language was dominated by references to clerical immorality, greed and incontinence on a personal and institutional level, intended to justify reformation. Whether or not such polemical anticlericalism either reflected or shaped the attitudes of lay men to their priests, the evangelical lexicon was readily adopted by the proponents of more radical reform.[36] As Gunter Vogler has suggested, anticlericalism could be a transitory unifier in a multifaceted Reformation, helping to turn particular grievances into general complaints and provide a social context for doctrinal criticism. However, the heterogeneity of early evangelicalism became apparent as its proponents, and those who gave vent to such anticlerical statements, argued for different, even competing, applications of the rhetoric of reform.[37] Anticlericalism often found its more energetic expression in the denunciations of the Catholic clergy by evangelicals who had once been among their number, those such as Luther, Müntzer and Sattler, who in words and action turned against the Catholic clerical estate. Reformation anticlericalism tapped into pre-existing strands in lay piety and social action, not least, as Peter Blickle has pointed out, concerted local attempts to undermine the privileges and power of the clergy.[38] Siegfried Hoyer has identified anticlericalism as one of the most important driving forces behind the actions of the German peasants in the mid-1520s; the demand for the free preaching of the Gospel carried with it a clear anticlerical sentiment, reflected in the demands for lay appointment of pastors and the right to refuse the payment of tithes to individual clergy or to ecclesiastical landlords.[39]

However, the common ground occupied by the rejection of Catholic sacerdotalism did not make it any easier to build a shared understanding of a reformed ministry. By the 1560s there is evidence of lay criticism of the Lutheran clergy that used much the same language as Luther and his circle had used against the Catholic clergy. Lutheran pastors were privileged, a burden on their community, with a tendency to interfere in the lives of their flock and exploit the disciplinary mechanisms of the Church to extract obedience and money from their congregations. Such clergy may well have been trained, committed evangelists, dedicated to the religious and moral reform of their congregations, but they were also often outsiders, better educated than their flock, and inhabitants of a rather different theological and intellectual world.[40] In Stromberg, visitors reported that several Anabaptists claimed to have fallen away from the Lutheran Church on the basis that the immoral and adulterous conduct of their pastor had persuaded them that he could not have possessed the Holy Spirit.[41] But in the heated context of the 1520s, the language of radical anticlericalism, flavoured with a radical social agenda, was more militant. Justification by faith alone mandated a reconfiguration of the relationship between priest and people, and encouraged swift and militant protest and agitation in defence of the 'gospel'.[42] 'The countertype to the ordained priest' was less the Lutheran pastor, and more the 'new layman, who has been seized by the spirit of God and needs no human being to mediate his salvation'.[43] An institutional church that was defined by a clerical hierarchy was rejected in favour of what Karlstadt described as 'the assembly of God-fearing spirits who live in the will of God', a community of faith formed by the congregation of the laity.[44]

The greatest threat to this community of faith, it was argued, came from the clergy. Thomas Münzter's *Prague Manifesto* alleged that the clergy shared collectively in the corruption of faith in the post-apostolic Church. The 'pitch smeared' priests and false monks had no interest in the extirpation of this false faith from the root, but rather gobbled, guzzled and plagued the poor folk. The clergy were, uniformly, the devil's priests.[45] The solution to this crisis was simple: 'the laymen must become our prelates and pastors'.[46] The Thuringian Anabaptist Hans Hut, who died in prison in Augsburg, lamented the way in which the magisterial

Fig. 15: Artist unknown, *Andreas Karlstadt*, 1541–2

reformers had 'torn the pope, the monks, and the parsons from their thrones', yet failed to reform, but instead went 'whoring again with the woman of Babylon'.[47] Melchior Rinck alleged that despite the initial promise of spiritual renewal, Luther had 'become a devil, and the true Antichrist'. Lutherans and papists were equally repugnant, because both insisted upon infant baptism which was tantamount to sacrificing children to the devil. When interrogated in 1563, the Hutterite Paul Glock proclaimed that 'you, on the other hand, Lutherans and popish priests together with your godless congregations, are worse and more godless from day to day, following your baptism [...] It is manifest that both of you,

Lutherans and papists, are wrong, and not a church of Christ but a church of the devil.' The issue for Glock was not just baptism, but the fact that Lutheranism and Catholicism were little more than an assembly of fornicators, adulterers, drunkards, usurers, in whom the devil does his work.[48] This identification of the failings of Catholic and Lutheran clergy as one and the same was likewise evident in the rhetoric of the Münster Anabaptists, and particularly in the promise to obliterate both Catholic and Protestant clergy in the city.[49]

SEPARATISM

In the imperial city of Münster, anticlericalism blended with social grievance and a potent apocalypticism to found an Anabaptist kingdom, which would prepare the way for the imminent second coming of Christ. Inspired by the eschatological prophecies of Melchior Hoffman and further radicalized by the influence of Dutch Anabaptists, the community in Münster attempted to purge the city of the godless. An attempted compromise between Catholics and evangelicals in the city had been brokered by Landgrave Philip of Hesse in February 1533, which allowed the cathedral and cloisters to remain Catholic, while the rest of city adopted an evangelical position. The city council began the 'purification' of the city, removing altars and images, and levying fines upon citizens who attempted to participate in Catholic rites. But even this uneasy coexistence was unsettled by the opening of a fracture within the evangelical faction over the question of infant baptism. A public disputation was held, without reaching a conclusion, but the council instructed that baptism was not to be used in a manner that contravened imperial law. The moderate stance of the council was not popular, and Rothmann and his supporters were silenced only briefly. In January 1534, Anabaptist leaders started rebaptizing adults in their congregations, and with the arrival of Dutch Anabaptist prophets later in the month, the debate over 'child washing' started to merge with a more sweeping language of apocalypticism. Rumours that the prince-bishop intended to suppress Anabaptism by force led its adherents to take up arms in defence of the city. Members of the Catholic community and

moderate evangelicals in Münster fled, and those who remained
prepared to build the New Jerusalem in the city. Under the rule
of van Leiden, adult baptism was enforced in the city, polygamy
for men licensed and the money economy abolished. Those who
resisted either fled or faced execution. The Anabaptist kingdom of
Münster defended its position for sixteen months under siege by
the forces of the prince-bishop. The city fell on 23 June 1535, with
most of the men in the city dead, and Jan van Leiden was executed
in the city in January 1536.

In polemical terms, the events in Münster were the logical
extension of the scriptural literalism, personal inspiration and
credobaptism of the Anabaptist radicals. When antagonism toward

Fig. 16: Erhard Schoen, *Tropper stormer byen pinse*, Siege of Munster, 1534

the clergy was used to justify a refusal to pay tithes, this was not just a financial protest but an action that was fundamentally divisive. The protest against infant baptism was a challenge to the position of the institutional churches as the custodian in doctrinal truth; the protest against tithes and oaths an active non-participation in communal religious life which threatened the very foundations of the *corpus Christianum*.[50] Indeed this very union of Church and state ran contrary to the Anabaptist stance that the governance of the Church should lie in the hands of the congregation, rather than the magistrate.[51] A mutually reinforcing relationship between secular and ecclesiastical power was anchored in the assumption that religious uniformity was a precondition of political stability, and secular support was necessary in order to ensure religious conformity. With both of these assumptions rejected, the impossibility of accommodating Anabaptism within the structural schema of the magisterial churches was evident. Even without open physical expression, radical or Anabaptist separatism was a form of sedition.[52] What is less clear is the extent to which this was an intended consequence of religious radicalism; as Peachey has observed, there is a difference between disobedience that was predicated upon the desire to follow individual spiritual conviction, and a more deliberate intent to propose an alternative model of the *corpus Christianum*.[53] And how well constructed was the relationship between Church and state in Luther's own thought? The vigorous persecution of radicalism, Sohm suggests, grew out of the medieval notion of the Christian state, rather than anything that was specific to the Lutheran understanding of the Church.[54] This offers an insight into why Catholic and magisterial Protestant spoke with one voice on Anabaptism, but does not quite address Peachey's question about the extent to which the secular consequences of the Anabaptist approach to Scripture and inspiration lay in the heart of the believer or the eye of the beholder.

'RASH AND LEWD PREACHERS?'

In this respect, the condemnation of the Anabaptists in Johannes Sleidan's *Commentaries on Religion and State under Charles V* provide a useful illustration of the anxieties and opposition aroused by a radical theology that carried with it the threat of social and political disorder. Sleidan's work represented the most substantial attempt to narrate a Protestant history of the first half-century of the Reformation, construct a confessional identity and defend the authority of the evangelical churches. In 1544, the Strasbourg reformer Martin Bucer approached Landgrave Philip of Hesse to seek his support for such a history of the Reformation and charged Johannes Sleidan, a lawyer, diplomat and historian, to undertake the task. The authoritative narrative would include among its sources not just biblical and patristic texts, but the records of secular institutions. Sleidan combined the theological and political contexts of the Reformation in order to produce a history that was not simply a history of salvation.[55] The organization of the text was chronological rather than biblical or martyrological, and references to extra-scriptural sources abounded. However, Sleidan was also at pains to downplay any evidence of dissent and division within the Reformation; the Colloquy of Marburg emerges from the narrative as a success, there is no mention of Calvinism, and religious radicals and Anabaptists are cast in a determinedly negative light. Sleidan used Luther's call for secular support for reform in the 1520s to argue that the authority of princes and magistrates was the most appropriate means by which to ensure uniformity and reconciliation between conflicting ideas. Sleidan's account of Thomas Müntzer was blunt in its condemnation of the threat that religious radicalism posed to this model of magisterial Protestantism:

> A great occasion of this terrible warre came by rashe & lewd preachers, wherof Thomas Muncer was principall: who leaving of the preaching of the Gospell, set forth a new kind of Doctrine in Alstet a towne of the Dukes of Saxonie [...] He said, he was commanded of God to distroy all wicked Princes, and substitute new in their places. He taughte moreover, that all thinges should be common, & al men of like fredom & dignitie. Wherupon the common people leaving their daily labor, toke such things as they neded of others & had store, even against their wils [...] [and were defeated in battle].[56]

For Sleidan, the Anabaptist threat was a theological, social and political challenge to authority, and to the stability and survival of the Christian body politic. Disobedience and nonconformity might be doctrinally destructive, but its connections with the rejection of magisterial authority made the Anabaptist threat look all the more dangerous. The simple act of interrupting a sermon presented a challenge to the authority of the institutions of Church and state, even before such oppositional behaviour became associated, at least in linguistic terms, with demonic activity.[57] The lack of firm unity in matters of doctrine among radicals and Anabaptists encouraged the polemical prioritization of the material threat that they posed, the depiction of Anabaptist leaders as divided and disordered and the focusing of the magisterial response upon the core issue of paedobaptism. By the second half of the sixteenth century, the Dutch

Anabaptists had become, primarily, a pacifist group, but those that dwelt in Habsburg lands, southern Germany and Switzerland were persecuted virtually out of existence. Here, the combination of religious and political anxiety and the growing threat of the Ottoman Turks on the frontiers of Europe made separatism and division seem all the more dangerous. A set of religious convictions that undermined religious uniformity, disregarded obedience to secular and ecclesiastical authority, and liberated followers from the mutual obligations that maintained Christian society might well look more dangerous in the eyes of its opponents than it was in reality, but this was the essence of the Anabaptist 'problem'. Radicalism grew out of the challenge to authority presented by the Reformation, but ultimately presented too great a challenge to the authority of that same evangelical impetus.

5

THE REFORMATION, WOMEN AND MARRIAGE

THE ANGELS LAUGH AND THE DEVILS WEEP

On 16 June 1525, Luther wrote to his good friend George Spalatin with news of a personal matter that had a truly iconoclastic meaning:

> I have stopped the mouths of my calumniators with Catharine von Bora. I have made myself so cheap and despised by this marriage that I expect the angels laugh and the devils weep thereat. The world and its wise men have not yet seen how pious and sacred is marriage, but they consider it impious and devilish in me. It pleases me, however, to have my marriage condemned by those who are ignorant of God. Farewell and pray for me.[1]

Luther had been released from his monastic vows some eight years previously, and his excommunication and papal condemnation would clearly have implied a separation from the Church and its canonical demands. He had written a stridently polemical assault on monasticism and its demands, *The Judgement of Martin Luther on Monastic Vows*, early in 1522, and had made clear his opposition to both the mandatory celibacy of the secular clergy and the vows of chastity, poverty and obedience made by the regulars. Such man-made promises, he asserted, were nothing more that false faith and idolatry. Still unmarried at the age of 40, Luther was well aware of the extent to which marriage had been the subject of abuse and ridicule among his contemporaries, and argued stridently for the need to reform marriage and re-establish its God-given position as the central pillar of family life and Christian society. 'What we would speak most of is the fact that the estate of marriage has universally fallen into such awful disrepute' Luther complained in 1522. 'There are many pagan books which treat of nothing but the depravity of womankind and the unhappiness of the estate of marriage, such that some have thought that even if wisdom itself were a woman one should not marry.'[2] Yet in the years preceding his own marriage, Luther showed no personal intent to commit to that path; in 1521 he told Spalatin that he would not accept a wife forced upon him, and in 1524 was blunt in the assertion that 'hitherto I have not been, and am not now, inclined to take a wife' given the precarious circumstances in which he lived.

Luther's close friend and colleague Philip Melanchthon described his marriage to Katherine von Bora as 'unexpected', unannounced and attended by only a handful of friends.[3] Katherine, aged 26 at the time, had been born into a landed gentry family in Saxony, and had entered the Cistercian house at Nimbschen in 1515. In 1523, she had been part of a group of a dozen nuns released from the cloister by the efforts of Leonhard Koppe, whose actions Luther compared to the labours of Moses in delivering Israel from the bondage of Egypt.[4] Some of the women returned to their families, but in April, nine of them arrived in Wittenberg, without financial or family support. Katherine's original ambition to marry Jerome Baumgartner was thwarted, leaving her with no formal status, financial means or position in the city. Luther had presented a strident defence of those who had chosen to abandon the cloister, *Why nuns may, in all Godliness, leave the Convents*, but words alone would not solve the practical problem presented by Katherine's continued presence. Luther tried, and failed, to arrange a marriage for her, and by May had decided to take Katherine as his wife. The marriage was presented as in accordance with the wishes of his father, but it was not preceded by a period of formal courtship, and, by Luther's account, was entered into for practical and pragmatic reasons. 'God has willed and caused my act,' he

Fig. 17: Lucas
Cranach the Elder,
Katharina von Bora,
1526

wrote, 'for I neither love my wife nor burn for her but esteem her highly'.[5]

Luther's esteem for his wife was not shared by all. Philip Melanchthon referred to the union as 'reckless', the Duke of Saxony expressed his horror that Luther would act on the desires of the flesh and so exclude himself from the wedding feast of Christ, and Erasmus mocked the shift from tragedy to comedy in Luther's life and the direction of the Reformation. Henry VIII denounced the union between a monk and a nun as incest, a charge repeated by Thomas More on multiple occasions as a means of exploiting Luther's apparent lack of self-control as a judgement upon his faith.[6] The Catholic controversialist Johannes Cochlaeus used the same analogy; whatever the justification that Luther used for his actions, there was no escaping the fact that the marriage of a monk and a nun was incest by the law of God:

> A nun married to a monk; a damned woman to a damned man; an infamous woman to an infamous man; clearly so that this might be a work worth the trouble of performing, and equal might be easily joined to equal, and St Paul might lie when he said 'They have damnation, because they have made their first faith void.'

In a similar vein, Jerome Dungersheim denounced the marriage of Luther, and other Protestant clergy, as 'pretensed' unions, and Simon Lemnius depicted Luther and Katherine among other incestuous and licentious former religious in his *Monachopornomachia*. A satirical image in which Protestant pigs were depicted entering a church included caricatures of Luther and his wife as the 'biggest pigs of all'.[7]

For all the comment that his marriage provoked, Luther was not the first of the Catholic-turned-evangelical clergy to marry, and like many of his companions, he regarded clerical marriage with some ambivalence. The appearance of married clergy on the landscape of parish ministry was, undoubtedly, a sign of the transformative potential of the early Reformation, and a signal of the break that some individuals were prepared to make with the Catholic past. But these first clerical marriages, despite the polemical commentary that accompanied them, did not guarantee the future of the married priesthood, and did not answer a growing range of questions about marriage, within or outwith the ministry, in the reformed churches. And this was not, of course, the first time that clerical marriage and clerical celibacy had been debated within the Latin Church.[8] But those clergy who chose to take wives were still participating – either implicitly or explicitly – in discussions about the nature and function of the priesthood, the relationship between priest and people, male and female, that often seemed to have rather unpredictable outcomes. Marriage was, for Luther and for others, an intensely personal matter but one that was also open and public. It had the potential to send a signal (perhaps not always an accurate one) about attitudes to the disciplines of

Catholicism, sympathy with evangelicalism and the place of the pastor within his congregational community. As Beth Plummer has observed, the debates over clerical marriage and clerical celibacy in the early sixteenth century, for the first time, were accompanied by a sudden and apparent shift in conduct and practice. Arguments about whether clergy should be allowed to marry were conducted against the backdrop of a growing number of priests and former religious who had taken matters into their own hands and entered into marriages.[9]

Debate over clerical celibacy and marriage had been energized by the marriage of several evangelical leaders in the 1520s, including Philip Melanchthon (although his marriage was not in violation of holy orders), Justus Jonas, Johannes Bugenhagen, Andreas Karlstadt, Martin Bucer, Wenceslas Linck, Thomas Müntzer, Wolfgang Capito, Matthias Zell, Ulrich Zwingli, Ludwig Cellarius and Johannes Oecolampadius. Not all of these unions were unproblematic, and scandalous marriages fuelled hostile caricatures of clerical marriage. Johannes Apel, appointed canon of Wurzburg Cathedral by the bishop, entered into a clandestine affair with a nun shortly after his appointment. She left the cloister, and the two married in 1523. However, the marriage was declared null by Apel's bishops, who imposed penance and ordered Apel to return his wife to the cloister. Apel was open in his opposition to the ruling, and his written defence of his actions, *Defensio Johannis Apelli ad Episcopum Herbipolensem pro suo Coniugio*, was printed in Wittenberg in 1523, with a preface by Martin Luther. Apel's refusal to accept the authority of the bishops led to his arrest and imprisonment, an accusation of heresy and excommunication.[10] The marriage of the Strasbourg preacher and historian Caspar Hedio in 1524 was similarly controversial, not least because Hedio addressed the objections presented by his new brother-in-law by declaring that the law of celibacy was not the law of God, and arguing that there was no scriptural authority for the prohibition of clerical marriage.[11] The protracted nature of cases against individual priests who married in the first years of the Reformation, amply documented by Beth Plummer, expose the complexity of the interactions between polemical and confessional arguments, practical expediency and personal preference. Cases such as these, heard in the courts, would have exacerbated the concerns of lay observers that their priests had entered into invalid marriages, and exposed the precarious status of clerical marriages and the contested nature of authority in such cases.[12]

LUTHER ON MARRIAGE

Luther's assertion that his own marriage was enough to make the 'angels laugh and the devils weep' was not entirely divorced from the tension that existed in other areas of his thought between the requirements of salvation and the demands and pleasure of physical existence. Marriage was, in the Catholic tradition, a sacrament, but one which did not always sit easily alongside the promotion of celibacy as a higher path to holiness. Reflecting upon his own childhood perception of marriage, Luther observed the connections made between marriage and a sense of impiety or impurity, to the extent that 'I thought I could not think about married life without sin.' To lead a life that was 'holy and acceptable to God' was to live celibate.[13] This was not necessarily a personalized caricature born of hindsight; in a 1494 catechism, the presentation of the third deadly sin, impurity, was accompanied by a discussion 'how the laity sin in the marital duty'. The purpose of marriage was, in this text, the fulfilment of the human need to procreate. Where pleasure entered into the equation, so did sin. Self-control within marriage, as within other areas of life, was a necessary step along the path to virtue.[14] In definitions of holiness and piety, married life was a poor third to widowhood or virginity. Luther's early writings on marriage exhibit the ongoing influence of such attitudes, but with the sense that the stance of the Church had somehow served to entrench the notion that the purpose of marriage was not companionship, but as an outlet for lust. Marriage, he argued in a 1519 sermon, *On the Estate of Marriage*, had fallen into disrepute, where once it had been the generous and fruitful gift of God to mankind. The purpose of marriage was both procreation and support, and love within marriage 'the greatest and purest of all loves'. Marriage embodied the union of the will of God and man, and a man and woman who were committed to bearing and raising children fulfilled a vocation that brought greater spiritual reward than simple adherence to the demands of the Church. Marriage,

Luther wrote, 'does not consist of sleeping with a woman – anybody can do that – but of keeping house and bringing up children'.[15] The sacramental nature of marriage meant that the expression of lust in intercourse within marriage was not offensive to God; borrowing from Augustine, Luther reflected upon the benefits of marriage as a remedy for sin, but also as a covenant of fidelity and an expression of love.[16]

In the *Sermon on the Estate of Marriage,* Luther declared that '[I]n the case of Adam, God creates for him a unique, special kind of wife out of his own flesh. He brings her to him, he gives her to him, and Adam agrees to accept her. Therefore, that is what marriage is.'[17] Marriage was part of the early narrative of creation, and God's relationship with mankind, Luther argued, had been recognized as such by the Fathers and doctors of the Church who presented it as a means by which God confers grace, as a covenant of fidelity and as a gift from God that enabled procreation and the raising of children.[18] Marriage was an outward and spiritual sign of the 'greatest, holiest, worthiest, and noblest thing that has ever existed or ever will exist: the union of the divine and the human natures in Christ'.[19] It was in this sense that marriage was indeed an 'estate', and one that preceded both the Church and secular government. Those who married, but failed to recognize marriage as an estate, Luther claimed, were no better than pagans, and part of the reason why marriage had, in his own age, fallen into such disrepute. Those who criticized and disparaged marriage all too often did so on the basis that the work of marriage was singularly unappealing; the care of children, providing and caring for a spouse were the 'bitterness and drudgery married life involves', and nothing short of imprisonment. 'The godless world,' Luther complained, 'is moved neither by God's ordinance nor by the sweet nature of little children who are produced in marriage; it sees only the shortcomings and hardships in marriage – it does not see the great treasure and benefit that is in it.' No wonder then, that some were attracted to the free and quiet existence of the unmarried state, choosing to lead the life of a priest or a nun in order to avoid the obligations and commitments of family life.[20]

However, marriage was also a remedy for sin, and a preservative against the failings of chastity and the difficulty of celibate life. Instituted in the perfection of creation, the covenant of marriage had come to provide a necessary protection against the corruption of the flesh by sin and temptation. The sin of Adam could be confined by a life of chastity, virginity or marriage, but within marriage there still existed a 'shameful desire', albeit one that God did not acknowledge as sin. Indeed the 'destructive flood' of human sexuality was contained only by marriage, and those who chose to ignore it did so at their peril.[21] Paul's Epistle to the Corinthians opened with what has become an infamous statement in defence of chastity: 'it is not good for a man to touch a woman' (1 Cor. 7.1), but the later assertion that it would be 'better to marry than to burn' (1 Cor. 7.9) was to become the touchstone of defences of clerical marriage. The Pauline epistle referred to both marriage and celibacy as holy and gifts from God (1 Cor. 7.14, 34), and in the face of the potentially short time before the second coming, suggested that it would be better for the married to remain married, and the unmarried to refrain from marriage. Sexual relations within marriage did not defile, but they did distract the faithful from prayer (1 Cor. 7.5, 32, 34). However Paul counselled married men and women to withhold themselves from each only on a temporary basis and only with the mutual consent of both parties.[22] The gift of continence had not been given to all, and therefore marriage was the appropriate remedy for those who might otherwise 'burn with passion' (1 Cor. 7.9). This apparently ambivalent attitude to marriage, in which it appeared to serve as remedy for fornication rather than a positive good, was, as Brown suggests, 'a fatal legacy' for the future, raising the spectre that a married Christian might be only '"half" a Christian'.[23] Whether the letter is read as a commendation of sexual asceticism, as evidence of the Christological foundations of celibacy, or as confirmation that God had, in marriage, provided a remedy for fornication, it is immediately apparent why Paul's correspondence with the Church in Corinth should assume such a prominent place in subsequent debate.[24]

Demonstrable evidence that this was the case was to be found in Scripture, but also in the conduct of those who chose to remain unmarried, believing celibacy to be the path to salvation, but who could not contain their desires. Perpetual chastity, Luther argued, was not something that could be willed or chosen by man, but a gift from God. For those to whom the gift was not given, marriage was the God-given remedy. Chastity and marriage were equal in the eyes of God, with marriage the appropriate path for the many, and the gift of chastity offered only to the few. The dangers inherent in assuming that chastity lay within the powers of those who promised or vowed such a life were all too apparent in the conduct of a supposedly celibate Catholic priesthood whose members were driven to concubinage and worse by their compelled chastity. The rejection of marriage, he suggested, was a devilish deceit, intended to open the door further to sin by encouraging mankind to reject the very remedy that God had provided in marriage.[25] There was a clear contradiction, he suggested, in presenting marriage as a holy thing, a sacrament of the Church, while in the same breath demanding that the priesthood remain unmarried in order to uphold and preserve the purity of their ministrations.[26] It would be far better for the preachers of the gospel to be married men than impure priests.

Luther's views had echoes in the works of Zwingli, Calvin and Bullinger. Calvin's *Institutes of the Christian Religion* defended the scriptural basis of marriage as companionship ('It is not good that man should be alone': Gen. 2.18), and rejected any argument that godly marriage was in any way inferior to priestly celibacy or monastic chastity. The gift of continence was rare, but for the majority, marriage was the best remedy for the sin of lust. To suggest otherwise was 'intolerably presumptuous'.[27] The energetic defence of the gift of marriage laid the foundation for Heinrich Bullinger's *Christian Matrimony* (1540) in which marriage was represented as part of God's pre-lapsarian creation, a holy state, pleasing to God, and one that should be embraced with confidence rather than seen as somehow second best. Marriage was given for the purposes of procreation, for comfort and companionship, and as a remedy for fornication, and no vows or promises invented by men could change that purpose.

Marriage, then, was the will of God for his people. When Luther argued against the compulsory celibacy of the priesthood in his address *To the Christian Nobility of the German Nation*, it was on the basis that every man, priest or layman should be free to choose whether or not to marry.[28] In the *Babylonish Captivity of the Church*, however, the focus of the debate shifted to the sacramental nature of marriage. The presence of valid marriage outside the Christian tradition, Luther argued, demonstrated that marriage could not be a sign or channel of grace, but existed rather as an image or allegory of the relationship between man and God.[29] Marriage was a divine ordinance 'which it is not our prerogative to hinder or ignore'. It was no more possible to refrain from marriage than from the basic impulse to breathe, and the natural state for man, ordained by God. To reject marriage was to reject God's gift and to stand against nature. The impediments to marriage that filled the pages of the penitentials and books of canon law were, on that basis, constructed on foundations that lay beyond the words of Scripture. The freedom of the Gospel was an enduring freedom that left 'every man free to marry or not to marry'.[30]

Luther's most substantial treatment of marriage, *Vom Ehelichen Leben* (*The Estate of Marriage*), presented a radically different theology of marriage, distanced from the sacramental understanding of marriage within the Roman Catholic, and to some extent Augustinian, tradition. The treatise was structured around three key questions: who can marry, who can divorce (and on what grounds), and how to live within the godly estate of Christian marriage. Marriage, he argued, was the means through which mankind fulfilled the mandate of God in Genesis 1.26-8. As part of God's creation, marriage was available to all, and the decision to marry required no formal justification. Rather it was the law of celibacy that distorted the original ordinance, and which need only be observed by a small proportion of the faithful, namely the impotent, the castrated and those who were able to live a life of celibacy without temptation.[31] Yet it was still incumbent upon the Christian to take seriously the obligations of marriage, and upon pastors to provide adequate instruction to their flock. Where there was contempt for marriage, Luther agued, this arose from 'the fact that no one has either preached or heard what marriage is'. It was vital, therefore, that marriage be understood for what it was, an estate commanded by God, not a sacrament under the authority of the Church, but a worldly estate which lay under the governance of the secular authorities.

Marriage was, for Luther and other religious who opted to leave the cloister and marry in breach of their vows and promises, an intensely personal matter, but also a topic that carried a substantial practical and pastoral importance.[32] A sense of the immutability of the natural order and the will of God was one of the building blocks of Luther's vehement rejection of priestly celibacy and monastic chastity, and a language that was repeated in the polemic and formularies of the early Reformation. Promises of perpetual celibacy, he argued, both endangered souls and encouraged public scandal. The law of celibacy was unjust, but even if its legitimacy were unchallenged, the consequences of enforced celibacy were surely enough to dissuade good people from tolerating an act that had destroyed innumerable souls.[33] The discipline of clerical continence in the Catholic tradition was argued to be motivated not by the cure of souls, but by the financial benefit that it brought to the Church. Writing *Against the Spiritual Estate of the Pope and the Bishops Falsely So Called* (1522), Luther alleged that the income of the bishops was substantially enhanced by what amounted to a tax on clerical concubinage; here was evidence that obligatory clerical celibacy was neither feasible nor desirable.[34] Its consequences were destructive in personal terms, in economic terms and in terms of the distortion of the divine and natural order that it implied and required. A rejection of marriage brought with it the rejection of social responsibility and obligation towards fellow men.

Yet despite the existence of what MacCulloch describes as a 'barrage of rhetoric about the importance of family and the role of the father as its head', there was little that was overtly new in Reformation ideas about marriage and family. The shift in emphasis – and it was one that was substantial – came in the articulation of what were largely familiar ideas about family and household in a manner that undermined virginity and celibacy.[35] Here was a highly visible sign of institutional and theological change. In the marriage of evangelical clergy, as Ozment has shown, 'theology and practice corresponded [...] successfully' and with implications that extended far beyond the union of the individual priest and spouse. The desacramentalization of marriage, hand in hand with the argument that clerical office was not an impediment to marriage, had a transformative effect upon attitudes to marriage, family and the priesthood.[36] While Bainton's assertion that Luther 'got married in order to testify to his faith' may be a little simplistic, his more general observation that in doing so, Luther 'actually founded a home and did more than any other person to determine the tone of German domestic relations for the next four centuries' should encourage us to think about the extent to which the godly (clerical) household became a model for Christian life in post-Reformation Europe.[37] In marriage, the companionship and community of a shared life turned the household into the godly family. Liberated from the sense that salvation might be earned, it was possible for the Christian spouse to accept God's gift of marriage and to focus physical, economic and spiritual activity upon the needs of others.[38] The raising of children carried particular responsibilities, responsibilities that were incumbent upon both parents, the 'patres et matres familias', a father and mother who were 'apostles, bishops and priests to their children', and whose duty it was to instruct the young in the message of the Gospel. The role of the *hausvater* as the head of the household, responsible for the spiritual instruction of the family, was articulated clearly in Luther's short and long catechisms, but it is clear that the duty to provide a Christian education was incumbent upon both parents, not just fathers.[39]

Yet in many cases, women are absent from Luther's biographical tradition, despite being increasingly evident in the consideration of the social and cultural impact of the Reformation. Steven Ozment's assertion that the impact of the Reformation upon women was largely positive remains influential, but grew out of Luther's polemical writings against monasticism and clerical celibacy, alongside some of the more pastoral works on marriage and the godly household. Outside the pages of the printed text, the place of women in post-Reformation society starts to look rather more complicated, as Roper, Wiesner-Hanks, Schorn-Schutte and others have demonstrated with some force. There are dangers in assuming that the positive vocabulary that was used to promote marriage was necessarily intended to extol the virtues and the abilities of women, or indeed that the emphasis that was placed upon the role of women as mothers in the godly household was in any sense contributing to a broadening of their influence and standing in the wider community.[40] The text of Scripture might point to examples of godly women, but it did not present male and female as physical or spiritual equals, or assert that women were to be encouraged to exercise a prominent role in evangelization and the dissemination of the Reformation.

Luther was predictably blunt in his assertion that the bodies of women were made for bearing and rearing children, and that their minds lacked the strength of men. His commentaries on Genesis made clear that Eve had been created inferior to Adam, and that as a consequence of temptation, women had become subordinate to men, lesser but distinct beings, as the moon was to the sun.[41] Luther's position was consistent with that expressed in medieval commentaries from Jerome onwards that attributed to Eve, and to her female descendants, a susceptibility to temptation and to sin that marked women out as subservient to men. The celebration of marriage as God's gift to humanity did not necessarily undermine this assumption. Neither did the rhetorical prioritization of marriage expressed in the polemical denigration of the celibate state have much to offer cloistered men and women, or indeed those who were simply unmarried and who resented the destruction of their way of life by the iconoclasm of the Reformation. Margaretha Blarer, the unmarried sister of the Constance reformer Ambrosius Blarer, for example, was accused by Martin Bucer of being 'masterless' without a husband. The narrative of the liberation of Katherine von Bora and her companions from their confinement in the convent was a powerful piece of propaganda, but it was not one that conveyed a positive message to those women (and men) for whom religious life had been a conscious and fruitful choice. Catholic clergy, and male religious, could become pastors in the reformed churches, but for women religious there was no such opportunity.

'MARRIED TO CHRIST': CLOISTERED WOMEN AND THE REFORMATION

Cloistered women were among the first to encounter the Reformation. The appeal of the liberation motif lay in the assumption that the medieval Church had forced women, even children, to embrace an ascetic existence that might be either demanding or luxurious, but which either way amounted to a rejection of what it meant to be female and a denial of any position in family and society. Nuns were women who brought no benefit to their families, and were committed instead to a lifetime of spiritually and materially worthless activities, which made no meaningful contribution to society. In theory, the contribution of these women to society came through their commitment to the labour of prayer, but in evangelical polemic convent life prevented women from marrying, bearing children and honouring their responsibilities as wives and mothers in a godly household.[42] But an analysis of the extent to which this freedom to marry and bear children was welcomed with open arms paints a rather mixed picture. As Merry Wiesner has pointed out, the Protestant prioritization of marriage and family had the potential to impose an alternative form of confinement upon women, tying them to the home and preventing the articulation of a distinctive or communal form of spirituality in an all-female context.[43] Protestant family life did not necessarily present women with the freedom to exercise their physical desires within the framework provided by godly marriage, but simply created a different, but ultimately still restrictive set of obligations and requirements that left women no more free than in convent life. Religious debate and discussion, particularly in the urban environment, was a masculine conversation, and one from which women were, by and large, excluded.[44] In this sense, there was a loss of female voice. Communal female religious life was not necessarily the imposition of chastity and obedience upon the unwilling, but rather presented opportunities for an awareness and articulation of a physical and spiritual identity among women. Ulrike Strasser's analysis of the experience of women, and women religious, in post-Tridentine Munich makes a similar point from a different context, suggesting that 'the enduring emancipatory potential of the Catholic ideal of virginity [...] could enable women to utilize the space of the convent and their virginal bodies for their own purposes'.[45]

Convent life, as Amy Leonard has shown, presented an opportunity for a form of self-assertion through obedience and asceticism.[46] At the point at which the Strasbourg religious houses were instructed to close, there were some 200 cloistered women in the city. Three houses survived, largely, Leonard argues, because they had already undergone a process of internal reformation and regeneration. As a result, their members were better placed to resist the demands of the council and to map out a new form of existence in the reformed city. These female religious houses were able to maintain much of their original way of life and devotional activity within their walls, while presenting an outward face and function that rendered them useful in the reformed city as teachers and moral guides who prepared the young women of Strasbourg for their vital function as 'nails in the wall' of the godly family and household. Convent life was maintained not only by the surviving generation of nuns, but by new members of the community recruited from among those who objected to the model of married life that lay before them.[47]

The convent communities were able to build upon a well formed collective identity; there was a clear sense of conventual community at work, which had led many of the nuns to enter the convents in the final years before their closure. Several were financially secure, and may well have recognized that, as nuns, they would have more control over their lives within the convent than outside its walls. Convent life constructed a particular female identity that was simultaneously assertive and powerless. The nuns clearly prized and asserted their autonomy, but when necessary were prepared to argue that, as women, they were intellectually weak and unable to understand evangelical theology or use new prayers and liturgies in German. They tolerated rather than appreciated weekly Lutheran sermons, were prepared to relinquish their habits and claimed to be willing to cease outwardly their traditional Eucharistic observance while receiving priests into the convent to celebrate the sacraments. In this way of life, they posed no threat to the city. Indeed the Dominican nuns presented themselves as an important component of urban society, partly through prayer, but also through care for the poor and the needy, through religious instruction and through the creation of a way of life that, in many ways, seemed to meet the demands of the reformed family and household. Contribution to community and society was prioritized over confessional opposition and polemical exchange.

The experience of the Dominican nuns of Strasbourg is not representative of the impact of the evangelical assault on monasticism and convent life, but in the focused interrogation of the experiences of cloistered women at such tumultuous moments we can get a glimpse of the multiple forces that impacted upon their decisions and actions. It is worth noting that female religious were more likely to resist the suppression of monasticism than their male counterparts.[48] In the territory of Duke Ernst of Brunswick, male religious houses closed without protest, but almost without exception convent women refused to engage with the process of reformation. In Medingen, a hole was made in the convent wall through which Lutheran preachers attempted to persuade the community to relinquish their position. Caritas Pirckheimer, Abbess of St Clara's convent in Nuremberg, mounted one of the most infamous defences of cloistered life in response to the demands of the city council in Nuremberg, and refused to leave her convent until her death. Members of the Nuremberg council attempted to persuade Pirckheimer and her companions to leave, and ordered that the nuns be denied the services of Catholic priests and access to sacraments. Lutheran preachers delivered sermons to the nuns four times each week. Members of the urban community mocked the women religious, threw stones over the walls of the convent and refused to sell food to the nuns. Three families forcibly removed their daughters from the convent, 'soaked in the abundance of the wine of anguish, and sang compline in tears'. But after confiscating the land of the community the council left the remaining nuns to live out their lives alone.[49]

With the dissolution of the English religious houses, cloistered women found themselves in a more precarious financial position, which perhaps informed the decision of some former religious to continue to live together in community. Without family support, there were few alternatives, but the survival of female communal religious life was in part shaped by a nostalgia for the convent community, and the experience and independence that it provided. Claire Cross's analysis of the wills of the nuns expelled from the convents highlights both that sense of nostalgia and, 'among some bolder souls', a desire to see the restoration of conventual life. Carthusian and Cistercian monks, and Cistercian nuns, maintained what Cross describes as a 'shared sense of community' long after the structures of monasticism had been dismantled. Marilyn Oliva's examination of the experience of nuns in Norfolk after the dissolution paints a similar picture, and Joan Greatrex sees evidence of that same commitment to community life among the former Benedictine nuns of Winchester, who continued to live together after the suppression of their house. After the suppression of Syon Abbey, groups of nuns continued to live together either out of necessity or in hope of restoration.[50]

For those ex-religious who did not endeavour to maintain the common life and who did not have family support, one

Fig. 18: Caritas Pirckheimer, *Nürnberg Königstraße*, 1900

other option remained: marriage. Beth Plummer has charted the presence of former nuns among the wives of evangelical clergy in the 1520s, calculating that these women made up around 10 per cent of clerical wives in this period. There is little evidence that nuns were entering into marriage before 1523, with the notable exception of Martin Bucer's wife, Elizabeth Silberstein. Laymen who married dispossessed nuns tended to have evangelical sympathies themselves and were generally drawn from lower social ranks, perhaps reflecting the difficulty faced by these women in presenting a dowry, which would generally have been given to the convent to which they were admitted. Where nuns who entered into marriage provided an explanation for their actions, this tended to revolve around the argument that marriage was a godly institution, superior to a vowed and cloistered life that lacked any scriptural warrant. Women defended their rejection of religious life on the basis that they had either been compelled to enter a convent by their family, or that they had been persuaded by Scripture and evangelical preaching that there was an error, even an arrogance, in making vows that lay in the gift of God alone. As Plummer notes, men who argued in favour of clerical marriage tended to make the subtly different argument that in vows of chastity, monastics had denied themselves the God-given remedy for lust and fornication, and that marriage was the more appropriate course of action.[51]

All too often, women religious who left their convents disappeared from view, but it is still possible to catch occasional glimpses into the views of the dispossessed nuns. Ursula von Munsterburg's account of her own actions deployed the language of evangelical theology and polemic to defend her decision to abandon religious life; vows of poverty, chastity and obedience were unjust and without merit, 'a road which bypasses God', Eucharistic devotion was misdirected, and the cult of the Virgin a form of idolatry. Convent life brought no spiritual benefit, but was rather a detriment to the soul. 'We are married to Christ and to seek to be saved by another is adultery.' Martha Elizabeth Zitterin wrote a series of letters to her mother explaining her decision to leave the convent in Erfurt. The letters were printed and used as propaganda against the religious life, although none of the five editions made clear that Martha had later returned to the convent. What is striking is the diversity of female responses to the suppression of religious houses. For all the determination of the nuns of St Clara to defend their position, Caritas Pirckheimer noted that it was the women of the city who were most vocal and violent in their opposition to the survival of the convent.[52] At Schlettstadt in Alsace, a group of women used force to enter a convent of Dominican nuns in order to 'turn them to the Gospel' and persuade them to renounce their vows. The Abbess of Oberwesel convent composed a written tract against the Reformation, printed in 1550. But in Ulm, it was female opposition to evangelical reform manifested in the defence of images that preserved aspects of traditional piety into the late 1520s. Beneath the polemical rhetoric and language of liberation, the response of nuns to the Reformation was intensely personal and often unpredictable.

THE CULT OF THE VIRGIN MARY: THE REFORMATION OF A ROLE MODEL

The position of Mary as the embodiment of virginity, obedience and motherhood had, for centuries, presented a model of womanhood that stood in sharp contrast to the disobedience and sin of Eve. In Mary, there was a focus for female devotional activity and for the cultivation of the virtues of humility and obedience. But Mary was an almost unattainable role model, and the celebration of her role in the redemption of mankind did not go hand in hand with a more positive attitude to female morality or spirituality. Indeed, the most vociferous criticisms of women often came from the pens of those most committed in their devotion to the Virgin. Neither was the cult of Mary as mother of God instrumental in articulating a more confident or expressive female piety; Mary as a model of obedience and humility might, if anything, be far less empowering.[53] The membership of the Marian guilds and confraternities was almost exclusively male, making it less clear that the primary appeal of the cult of the Virgin was as a role model for women. However, Heal's study of Marian devotion in Nuremberg warns of the dangers of generalization on this score; in Nuremberg, the cult of Mary as mother provided a central component in female piety and spirituality. Motherhood, rather than virginity, perhaps resonated more clearly with the needs and anxieties of the young women of Nuremberg, albeit the motherhood enacted by Mary was protective and intercessory. Such a multiplicity of meanings inherent in the cult ensured that on the eve of the Reformation, the popular cult of the Virgin was vibrant, and supported by an ever proliferating range of devotional practices, relics and images. Mary was, as Bridget Heal has demonstrated, 'the most frequently depicted, described, and invoked saint in Germany'. Most churches had at least one altar dedicated to the Virgin, often richly decorated and supported, and Marian pilgrimage shrines, confraternities and prayers made the veneration of Mary a universal phenomenon.[54]

Universal did not mean uniform, however, and the richness of Marian devotion lay in its diversity and ability to adapt to the needs of the community and locality. This same diversity is apparent in the commemoration and veneration of the Virgin in post-Reformation Europe. Predictably, the differences are most evident in the positioning of Mary in the devotional and confessional framework of early modern Catholicism or Protestantism, but beneath this rather polarized model lay a range of practices and beliefs that communicated a more variegated message. As Heal demonstrates, the blunt assertion that the 'most obvious characteristic of the picture of Mary in the Protestant Reformation was its critique and rejection of what it took to be the excesses of medieval devotion and teaching' is based upon the language of polemical exchange, rather than personal piety and pastoral necessity. The vehement condemnation of the cult of the saints and the cult of the Virgin as idolatry, false religion and Antichristian superstition may well have encouraged and informed the iconoclastic impulse that led to the destruction of shrines and images, but it is clear that it did not eradicate Mary entirely from the devotional landscape.[55] The rejection of Mariolatry in Reformation Germany did not necessarily imply or demand the rejection of the Virgin as role model.

Luther was strident in his opposition to those aspects of the cult that seemed to detract from the redemptive suffering of Christ, but was still convinced that in Mary there stood an example of obedience, humility and trust in the will of God. Luther's sermon on the nativity of the Virgin in 1522 accepted that there was good reason to honour Mary, but only as far as Scripture allowed. Mary had received God's grace, but had not earned it by her works. Mary was 'gifted or graced more than other women' and deserving of honour because she had been honoured by God.

However to treat Mary as a goddess 'as the priests and monks pretend we should' was to dishonour her son, turning 'fables into examples' and encouraging the faithful to invest time and effort running to pilgrimage sites rather than rushing to meet the needs of their neighbour.[56] Perhaps in order to avoid such an error, the presentation of Mary as the embodiment of the virtue of virginity gave way to her elevation as a model of marriage and motherhood, in which the Holy Family presented a striking example for the Christian household. Mary was to be honoured not in hymns and prayers, but as a reminder of God's grace and, in the words of the Magnificat, God's mercy upon the humble, and the promise that the proud would be scattered in the imagination of their hearts. Where her sister, Elizabeth, had remained at home, pious but confined by the old law, Mary's actions symbolized the church of Christ and the freedom of the Gospel.[57] For such reasons, it was possible for Mary to occupy a pastoral and physical space in Lutheran piety, as Marian imagery and statuary remained visible in churches, even if the role of the mother of God as intercessor and patron had been subjected to the hammers of intellectual iconoclasm. In Nuremberg, material objects that had been the locus for Marian devotion were also the product and outworking of civic pride; where their central message was undermined by a new soteriology, it was still possible to overlay new meanings and interpretations.[58] In other cases, the attack on the intercessory position of the Virgin delivered a fatal blow against the material cult. Georg Hauer, defending the cult of the Virgin from Protestant polemical assault in 1523, complained bitterly that the consequence of Luther's sermons had been iconoclasm, violence and open assertions that Mary was 'a woman like any other'. Most alarming of all, such words and actions came not from men, but from women, whose conduct was the antithesis of the qualities exhibited by Mary as the obedient servant of God. Like the suppression of convent life, the suppression or remodelling of the cult of the Virgin was the product of a potent mix of theological debate, the attitudes of civic government and the personal response of the community. The position of the Virgin in post-Reformation Germany raises as many questions as it answers, and exposes the range of ideas and anxieties that existed beneath the bold statements.

WOMEN AS EVANGELISTS

Beth Plummer's reference to pastors' wives as 'partners in his calamities' reflects the anxieties that existed over clerical marriages in the early years of the Reformation, but also raises questions about the extent to which clergy wives were active participants in the activities of their husbands. Marriage to a priest was hardly a 'convenience', and the voices of the women involved are all too often inaudible. Alongside the weaknesses of the sources, debates about the role and agency of women in determining and enacting their religious affiliations position clerical wives in a contested theological and domestic space. The interactions between Martin Luther and Katherine von Bora are well documented, but perhaps less than representative of the decisions and actions of women whose personal experience of the Reformation was also highly public and polemical. If the marriage of a priest or a monk was an act of rebellion against the disciplines of the Church, so it was for the woman who chose to enter into such a marriage. However, although the defence of married clergy was taken up in print and pulpit, Plummer notes that the decisions taken by the first generations of clergy wives lacked such a clear point of reference and had more to do with an assessment of the concerns of the moment than with debates over the legality of the union.[59] For all the polemical debate that surrounded clerical marriage, much of it composed by married clergy, clerical marriage is only rarely described by the women involved.[60]

The most obvious exception to this generalization is Katherine Schutz Zell, who was outspoken in her defence of clerical marriage and in her assertion that an obligation was placed upon all believers, not just men, to disseminate the Gospel. In this respect, her views and actions did not entirely coincide with assumptions about the type of women who would make appropriate wives for evangelical clergy; Katherine was far from silent and obedient, and presented herself very much as an equal partner in her marriage and its 'calamities'.[61] As a child, she had committed to a life of virginity within the family home, but by her own account she was both active in her faith and anxious about her own salvation. After hearing Matthias Zell preaching in Strasbourg in 1521, Katherine was persuaded that salvation came through faith, not works, and that her works of piety were without worth or value. Late in 1523, she married Matthias, an act which she believed to be the first occasion on which a 'respectable' woman, rather than a concubine, had married a priest in the city. Certainly the accusation that priests' wives were no better than concubines was a commonplace in polemical writing against the marriage of priests, and many of the first generation of clergy wives in Germany were indeed women who had been housekeepers to clergy, or concubines. In the mid-1520s, evangelical leaders and councils were inclined to insist that clergy marry their concubines or face further sanctions as legislation was passed against concubinage. As clerical immorality was presented as a justification for reform, priests and their concubines had little to lose by entering into marriage.[62] But for Katherine Zell, the key question was the defence of the principle of clerical marriage, and her commitment to evangelicalism. Strasbourg was still in the early stages of its Reformation, and Katherine felt compelled to write to the bishop to defend her marriage, arguing from Scripture that there was no proper impediment to the marriage of priests. Early in September 1524, Katherine published the *Apologia*, a small treatise on clerical marriage, accompanied by her original letter to the bishop. Marriage, she argued, was a holy vocation, not a poor second to a life of celibacy. It was also a remedy for fornication, given by God to humanity for the avoidance of precisely the kind of immoral activity that Katherine claimed to see in the streets of Strasbourg. The celibate clergy of the city might cultivate an image of holiness, but that sense of virtue was based upon an erroneous understanding of Scripture and the assumption that salvation came through adherence to the laws of man rather than the grace of Christ alone.

From the outset, Katherine was clear that the pamphlet outlined the basis of her own dissent from the traditions and disciplines of the Church; her husband, she claimed, was untroubled by the hostile and slanderous comments of those who rejected clerical marriage, but she asserted that she had an obligation and a right to defend herself, a right that was firmly rooted in Scripture. It was a Christian duty to suffer for the sake of truth rather than remain silent in the face of error and falsehood, 'for that silence is half a confession that the lies are true'. Zell's text was punctuated with references to biblical texts, allegory and the pamphlets and sermons of Catholic propagandists who had been swift to condemn the Strasbourg Reformation, including Murner and Cochlaeus, who 'deafen the people with their prattle'. Clerical marriage, she argued, was so clearly rooted in Scripture that 'children and fools can read and understand', but those who defended clerical celibacy had no basis for their beliefs other than self-interest and financial gain. A married priest was an honourable citizen, taking marriage as a free gift from God, Zell suggested, but a concubinary priest was a member of the 'harlotry guild' lining the coffers of the Church with the taxes that they paid for the privilege. Incontinent clergy lacked the moral authority to speak out against adultery and fornication from the pulpit, and marriage had fallen into disrepute. The Roman clergy made martyrs out of married clergy, but 'the unchaste chastity of celibacy, the sin-flowing harlotry of Sodom and Noah's age, they do not punish and have never punished, but instead they protect it'. The rejection of marriage, God's gift and covenant, came at a financial, moral and social cost.[63]

Here we are left with a clear sense of how Katherine Zell viewed her role and calling. The role of the clerical wife was to support her husband, but as an equal, not one who was subservient to his wishes. Katherine had read and reflected upon the text of Scripture, but was also aware of the doctrinal and pastoral controversies that had erupted in the early years of the Reformation. Her request to Johannes Cochlaeus that he provide her with a translation of his Latin work gives a sense of the limitations of her learning, but also the limitless sense of her own authority to engage in debate. Katherine defined for herself a position that brought with it an obligation to speak out against injustice and error, and to support those who suffered in the defence of truth. Perhaps the best documented intervention in this fashion is to be found in Katherine's letter of consolation addressed to the women of Kentzingen who faced persecution for their evangelical beliefs. A group of men from the town, including the pastor, sought refuge in Strasbourg, where they lodged with Katherine and Matthias Zell. Echoing the sentiments of the Strasbourg evangelical theologian Martin Bucer, Katherine spoke of her role in providing a visible model of reformed marriage, anchored in mutual support and companionship.[64] But her sense that she was a partner not just in marriage but in ministry made Katherine's presence all the more controversial.

Martin Bucer expressed some concern that Katherine was using her own reading and interpretation of controversial issues to shape her husband's stance on the presence of godparents at baptism, but as McKee has pointed out, much of the hostile commentary on Katherine's involvement in her husband's work came not from his peers but from the second generation of reformed clergy in the city. The role of the clerical wife, and the role of women in shaping the Reformation, was challenged not only from outside, but also from within early evangelicalism.

The assertive voice of Katherine Zell was being heard in the same city in which three convents were saved from secularization and continued to defend themselves against the demands of the city council. The persistence of convent life in Strasbourg demonstrates the potential for women to establish a position for themselves in circumstances in which civic and ecclesiastical authorities were prepared to compromise and look the other way. But female response to religious reformation was not something upon which it was always possible to compromise. Frau Voglin was condemned by the city council in Nuremberg after taking it upon herself to preach in the hospital church in the city.[65] The council in Memmingen attempted to impose limits upon the discussion of matters of religion among women at the city wells, and female preachers, often inspired by more radical forms of evangelicalism, were ejected from Zwickau and other cities.[66] It is worth noting at this point that the involvement of women in preaching had been a defining feature (at least in the eyes of the medieval Church) in a range of heresies. Many Lollard women demonstrated an ability to memorize large sections of the Bible and apply that knowledge in defence of their own position.[67] Like Cathars and Waldensians, English Lollardy seemed to offer women outlets for religious activity that were either absent from, or simply more attractive than, those presented by the institutional Church. Women participated in heresy as readers, teachers and preachers, although as Margaret Aston notes, the evidence of whether women ever fulfilled the role of priests is inconclusive.[68] The response of religious women, and evangelical women, to the Reformation was in part a response to novelty, uncertainty and context, but it was a response that was not entirely divorced from the web of ideas and relationships with the Church and belief that had been negotiated by women in the centuries before.

CONCLUSION

Any assessment of female responses to the Reformation is predicated upon the assumption that at some level there is something 'different' about women, a difference that may be imagined or constructed, but still invites investigation in any reflection upon the nature of Reformation society and culture. In tangible, archaeological terms, the evidence of the last 150,000 years demonstrates that the physiological make-up of male and female bodies has remained largely constant. But if human biology is little changed, the way in which we have attempted to make sense of that biology, to articulate emotion and thought, and to negotiate our relationships with family, friends and neighbours, has demonstrated a greater degree of plasticity. And within the Christian tradition, the vocabulary of that understanding, language and expression has been deeply anchored in the attitudes and pronouncements of the institutional churches.[69] In its rejection of celibacy and virginity as a higher form of life, and assertion of the value and benefits of Christian marriage, the Protestant Reformation created a fundamental shift in the dynamics of human relationships, intruding into an intensely individual context where theology, sexuality and emotion collided.

In some respects, little had changed. Pre-Christian ideas about women found their way into the writings of Augustine, in which the relationship between women, sexuality and the Fall was presented as evidence of the danger that was embodied in the daughters of Eve. The influence of Augustine in Roman Catholic moral theology was substantial, and Reformation ideas about women and marriage were laid out beneath this shadow. In that sense the parameters of the debate remained the same. But Luther's reflections upon the Gospel, sin and salvation required a recalibration of the Augustinian tradition. Human sin, particularly sexual sin, he argued, had its roots in a failure to appreciate the justifying grace of God. A failure to perceive the grace of God encouraged not love but objectification of women, and herein lay the difference between *Hurenleibe* and *Brautliebe*, the motivation of the whore and of the bride. In marriage, men and women were simultaneously sinners and saints, but it was married life that enabled the couple to live and learn in faith.[70] In this model, marriage and family were presented as the remedy for sin to the point where Steven Ozment went as far as to suggest that Luther 'placed the home at the center of the universe'.[71] In post-Reformation Europe, we are told, marriage was 'the fundamental unit of society and a microcosm of social order'.[72] The image of the godly household provided the connection between faith and practice, giving physical and visible expression to Luther's ideas about virginity, sexuality and sin.

But we need to be careful here; the Reformation did not invent the family. Devotion to the Holy Family was a vibrant part of late medieval Christianity, the piety of the *Devotio Moderna* emphasized the positive relationship between married couples and God, and the bond between man and woman in marriage was honoured as sacred. Marriage was an instrument of sanctification, a channel of grace modelled on the marriage of Christ the bridegroom, who took the Church as his bride.[73] Protestant rhetoric which asserted with confidence the role of the husband and father in the Christian household was deeply rooted in this tradition. The vehement rejection of the value of virginity and sacerdotal celibacy set family and household within a different context, but the common language in Catholic and Protestant pastoral writing is indicative of their shared roots. Similarly, the positioning of women as morally, intellectually and physically inferior to men in Luther's message exemplifies the extent to which Reformation attitudes to the female sex did not entirely overwrite tradition. The assault on clerical celibacy was a visible act of doctrinal iconoclasm, but not one that immediately overturned embedded assumptions about women, sex and sin. Evangelical thought was informed by an ingrained understanding of women as (medically) cooler, moister, weaker and less rational, physically designed for childbearing and dominated by reproduction. Women who married, who submitted to the authority of their husbands and who bore children were behaving in a way that was natural, moral and ordered. However, the pessimistic tone adopted in much later sixteenth- and seventeenth-century Protestant literature on marriage suggests that this model was not always well received. Frequent references to the duty of obedience and the feminine vices of pride, vanity and lust carry with them the implicit sense that marriage and morality remained pressing concerns.[74] The idea of Gospel freedom, imbued with evangelical optimism, might have made Protestantism an attractive choice for women, but we should not overestimate the extent to which it was a genuine choice, or the extent to which the reformed household genuinely changed the position of women in Reformation society. As we have seen, female responses to the Reformation were personal and pragmatic, with variety the only constant. Shifts in soteriological principles were not abstract intellectual ideas, but part of an ongoing conversation between doctrine, discipline and deed that had begun long before the Reformation, and did not end with it.

6

THE REFORMATION
AND THE SUPERNATURAL

FIRES IN THE SKY

'On 28 December [1561], between five and seven of the early morning, people saw a very dreadful fire-sign in the sky, between East and North. It was such a terrible sight that no people living at that time had ever seen such a thing. [They] saw nothing but the sky burning, and under the flames pure blood was running.' The Mansfeld chronicler thus described the celestial fire that was observed on Holy Innocents' Day, a wonder that was reported in chronicles, broadsides and printed treatises. In Frankfurt an der Oder, it was claimed that the sky opened like an eye, with a black figure or cloud appearing, which poured out red fire and flames that resembled a spear. Such 'strange' or 'wonderful' sights in which the sky was filled with blood, lights, water or figures were widely documented in Reformation Europe, shaping and shaped by a range of beliefs about the relationship between the natural and the supernatural, wonders and providences. Portents and prodigies might, simultaneously, be evidence of God's continued attempts to call mankind to repentance, the 'ruses' of the devil, the fruits of a superstitious imagination or simply the particularities of nature. Even if, as was commonly asserted, the age of miracles had passed, such events act as a reminder of the extent to which the supernatural continued to occupy a contested space in post-Reformation culture.[1]

The relationship between religion and the broader supernatural in Reformation Europe has become a much more complex field of study in recent decades. The scholarship of Max Weber continues to cast a long shadow over more recent writing, but in the re-evaluation of some of the fundamental assumptions that underpinned older studies, we have arrived at a more satisfying and nuanced understanding of the early modern supernatural, even if it is one that is more complex and challenging as a result. The gradual erosion of Weber's conclusions has been informed by consideration of the relationship between popular and elite belief and culture, the permeability of the boundary between official and unofficial religion, and a much more comprehensive, and perhaps less judgemental, understanding of the nature of belief about magic in this period. Where older histories tended to assume that there existed an identifiable and enforceable boundary between magic and religion, encouraged by the gradual but inexorable rise of reformed religion, and an accompanying decline in the beliefs and potency of the magical and preternatural, more recent scholarship has encouraged a questioning of both the meaning and value of commonplace vocabulary and labels, and the plausibility of the assumed trajectory of belief from superstition to religion to secularization and a scientific worldview. As a result, the pre-modern world has ceased to be seen as a world dominated by ignorance and magic, a world in which a lack of awareness of the potency of natural forces encouraged acceptance of an animated universe which lay at the mercy of a diverse range of supernatural forces.

The effect of this recalibration of the medieval supernatural has been significant in its own right, but has carried in its wake an implicit challenge to the assumption that the superstitious mindset of the pre-modern world was somehow made to surrender to the self-evident perspicuity and truth of the Gospel, and eventually to the new scientific worldview. In much the same vein, the challenge to the teleological assumption that medieval magic gave way to reformed religion, and the accompanying sense that magic and religion presented two alternative approaches to a universe that was inhabited and animated by numinous beings, has been called into question by the work of historians and anthropologists who challenge the very basic assumption upon which such ideas were constructed.[2]

MAX WEBER AND THE 'DISENCHANTMENT OF THE WORLD'

'The fate of our times,' Weber asserted, 'is characterized by rationalization and intellectualization and, above all, by the disenchantment of the world.'[3] The 'disenchantment' of the world was the cornerstone of modernity, especially Protestant modernity. That, at least, is the simple summary of the rhetorical position with which most recent studies of the relationship between religion, reformation and the supernatural continue to open. But to distil Weber's work into a single assertion is to neglect the broad and complex landscape against which his approach was played out, and the range of processes and social interactions and models to which it was applied. The architecture of the argument was a monument to a particular confessional outlook informed by nineteenth-century German intellectualism, but Weber's model of rationalism, achieved by disenchantment, still acts as a gateway to more recent debates over the decline of magic and its relationship to the redefinition of religious belief and the continued existence of a sacralized view of the world.

Weber's image of rationalism and disenchantment was predicated upon the rejection of a model of salvation that was centred upon sacramental mediation as a consequence of the Reformation. For salvation to depend upon the mediatory actions of humans was to diminish its nature and function to a form of magic, by asserting the potential for human actions and words to dictate the mind of God. In contrast, the 'religious virtuoso can make himself sure of his state of grace either in that he feels himself to be the vessel of the Holy Spirit or the tool of divine will'. The route to salvation lay not in sacramental magic, but in faith and in subjugation to the will of God.[4] Once deprived of its soteriological function, human action was, at the most basic level, secularized. Specific religious actions, commitments and rituals lost meaning and function, and came to be categorized not only as inessential, but as irrational. The monastic vocation and ideal of retreat from the world gave way to a sense that human action was located within the world, formed by rationality rather than any attempt to know and influence the mind of God. Linguistic changes reinforced this shift. Vocation or calling (Beruf) ceased to be a task required by God and came to mean a profession or livelihood.[5] Human action no longer sought to influence spirits and supernatural beings through ritualized action, but rather turned to an intellectualized worldview in which God was less visible in the operations of the world. The emergence of what might best be described as a rational religiosity undermined the material immanence of the holy, and encouraged (or was encouraged by) iconoclasm, the rejection of objects that were argued to act as *loci* of divine or supernatural power. Via this desacralization came modernization, in a teleological narrative of the transition of Western Christendom from superstition to modernity. 'That great historic process in the development of religions, the elimination of magic from the world, which had begun with the old Hebrew prophets and in conjunction with Hellenistic scientific thought, had repudiated all magical means to salvation as superstition and sin, came here to its logical conclusion.'[6]

The basic argument that Europe moved from a cosmology that was dominated by magic and religion to one that was was mechanistic, even secular, between 1500 and 1800 still holds traction, but comes under pressure from evidence and argument that disputes both this chronology and the sense of completeness that the 'disenchantment' hypothesis implied. That sense that the age of enchantment had passed can certainly be heard in comments from those who observed the transformative process described by Weber. The English jurist and scholar John Selden, for example, observed that 'There never was a merry world since the fairies left off dancing and the parson left conjuring.' But assertions of a 'paradigmatic' change in mental and intellectual attitudes can seem less compelling when such language is not rooted in a sense of why and how such a shift might occur.[7] A greater sensitivity to the richness of ideas and experience that lies beneath the surface of this 'disenchantment' has produced a more nuanced and in some ways sympathetic analysis of belief in early modern Europe, and the relationship between religious reformation and the supernatural. The publication of Keith Thomas's magisterial volume *Religion and the Decline of Magic* in 1971 encouraged scholars to attempt just such a careful examination, and continues to exercise a potent influence over the histories of belief. Magic, Thomas argued, filled the gap left on those occasions upon which man lacked the means to exert control over his environment. As the search for such control continued, other mental and intellectual systems – science – eventually diminished the need for such magic.[8] But in the late medieval period, where Thomas begins his analysis, the unpredictable and uncontrollable challenges of the environment both made misfortune potentially catastrophic and encouraged the desire to identify its cause and the means by which it might be alleviated. The rhetoric of the Church denounced magic and superstition and forms of deviance, but Thomas demonstrated that such beliefs were not marginal but rather central to the general worldview and to the intricacies of daily life. Magic relied upon rituals that echoed rather than contradicted religion, and which could therefore be adjusted to meet the needs of a changing theological and environmental climate. This was more than just a form of credulous survival; the relationship between magic and religion was navigated in the particular and the general, but gravitated around a central belief in the coherence and cohesiveness of the supernatural.

The difference between a prayer and a spell was defined with clarity and determination by the Church, but, as Thomas demonstrated, that clarity was not always apparent in the hearts and minds of the faithful. The centrality of Eucharistic devotion to the devotional life of the late medieval Church, and the articulation of a clear and determined exegesis of the miracle of transubstantiation inculcated a vibrant popular piety, but one in which elements of the magical were attributed to both the priest and the consecrated elements. The physical and linguistic separation of priest and people tended to encourage the sense that the operative factor in the consecration was the recitation of the required words by the priest, which imbued the sacrament with an almost mechanical efficacy. Churchmen were at pains to make clear that there was an unbridgeable chasm between the Eucharistic miracle and the spoken words of magic, but the emphasis placed by the connection between word and transformation meant that this distinction was readily eroded.[9] The hopeful anticipation of miraculous cures and saintly interventions provided one means by which the operations of the natural world might be known and contained, but natural magic and astrology could fulfil a similar purpose. 'St Agatha's letters' provided protection from fire, and 'relics for rain and certain other superstitious usages for avoiding of weeds growing in corn' were listed among the inventory of the Abbey of Bury St Edmunds at its dissolution. Church bells inscribed with the names of saints had the potential to ward off storms and tempests.[10] So apparent were the connections between magic and religion, Thomas concluded, that magic was a 'corpus of parasitic belief' rooted in that potent combination of anxiety and ritual in the devotional practices of the Church.

As Catherine Rider has noted, any discussion of the influence of religion upon magic needs to be set within the broader context of the influence of magic upon religion. Pastoral manuals reveal the extent to which attitudes towards magic reflected a changing natural and intellectual environment; in the fifth century, St Augustine condemned amulets as magic, but by the late medieval period it was possible for churchmen to defend the wearing of herbs and stones to cure illness because their power was 'part of the natural world, put here by God himself'.[11] Drawing upon the writings of Augustine, Aquinas and Buchard of Worms, Euan Cameron has reflected upon the diversity of a 'densely populated universe' and its cosmology that defied 'Christian-Aristotelian-Thomist categories of God, people, angels, and demons'.[12] Magical practices often borrowed from religious ritual, with those who defended practices such as lot casting or the interpretation of dreams laying claim to biblical precedent and therefore legitimacy. Even where the pastoral steer provided by theologians was clear, it is possible to see a deepening fissure between the views of churchmen and the beliefs of their flock, whether over magic or the broad range of numinous beings that were believed to inhabit and animate the universe.[13] As the theologian and conciliarist Jean Gerson summarized the popular sin, 'what do I care as to who heals me ... let it be God or the devil, just so long as I get what I want'.[14] A rough consensus might exist over the position of the line between 'pious but unofficial religious activities and unacceptable magic', but the line was not just fine but permeable.[15] Perhaps for this reason, magic emerges from Rider's work as a topic that was not typically a major concern for either the medieval clergy or laity because the distinction was too complex to enforce. By the sixteenth and seventeenth centuries, however, accusations of harmful magic between quarrelling neighbours appear much more frequently in the court records, particularly in the context of accusations of witchcraft. Rider's evaluation of this shift contains echoes of Keith Thomas's commentary on the 'magic of the medieval church'. Before the Reformation, the scepticism of the Church, and the apparent protection that it offered against harmful magic, may well have limited the involvement of the courts in disputes over magic. Magic had never occupied an entirely neutral ground, but the evangelical assault upon the effectiveness and legitimacy of ecclesiastical ritual and sacramental, while in theory an attack on magic, had the potential to make magic appear more dangerous. The very term 'magic' was far from impartial, and the tendency for it to be used derogatively to condemn the views of others exemplifies the problems that arise from such a multiplicity of meanings. As Cameron notes, even the 'pixies and fairies of the folklorists' became part of a clearly delineated struggle between God and the Devil.[16]

Evidence of a blurred boundary between magic and religion does not in itself present a challenge to the Weber model of disenchantment. Indeed Thomas's work supported the contention that the Reformation was a part of this recalibration of attitudes to the animated universe. As Thomas contended, 'The notion that the universe was subject to immutable natural laws killed the concept of miracles, weakened the belief in the physical efficiency of prayer, and diminished faith in the possibility of direct divine inspiration.'[17] But why did this change in attitudes occur? Thomas conceded that it was one thing to demonstrate that magical beliefs had declined in significance, but quite another to understand why and how. If, as Thomas had suggested, the appeal of magic lay in its ability to provide a solution to the challenges of life, then an amelioration of these conditions as a result of changes in weather, medical knowledge and institutional charity might provide a practical answer to the question of decline.

With a suitably broad brush approach, such an argument might appear convincing, but the more detailed analysis presented by Thomas highlighted the flaws in such assumptions. The strides taken in the fields of medicine and natural science do not map readily onto changes taking place in attitudes to magic and religion. The decline of magic was apparent before medical knowledge and understanding had advanced enough to provide a coherent and widely available alternative to the local cunning man or folk healer, and the rhetoric of the Reformation against the superstition of the medieval Church pre-dated these developments in natural science. Questioning of the miraculous that resided in the relics of the saints pre-dated the Reformation, but a broader hostility to non-Christian sacred time and place was evident even earlier, as the post-apostolic Church negotiated its relationships with paganism and its system of the sacred. The interpenetration of the material and the spiritual was a complex web to unravel, but this process of unravelling did not begin with the doctrinal changes of the sixteenth century alone. As Walsham's impressive study of the relationship between the Reformation and the landscape has demonstrated, trends within late medieval Catholicism frequently prefigured later Protestant scepticism of the sacred significance of particular physical locations. Such attitudes were evident not only in overt dissent, for example in the arguments of Lollard heretics, but also within the writings of orthodox humanists.[18] Tensions within the presentation of superstition and magic as a theological and pastoral problem for the medieval Church provided the foundations for Renaissance humanists and Reformation polemicists to challenge the sanctioned practices of Roman Catholicism. The debate over superstition was not new in the sixteenth century, but was enlivened by the rhetoric of Erasmus and, in Cameron's assessment, particularly Martin Luther, who 'brought to the issues raised by superstition, as to everything else, a mind of extraordinary vigour and originality'.[19]

Religion and the Decline of Magic posed as many questions as it answered, but the inadequacies of the vocabulary used to draw distinctions between magic, religion and science highlighted in Thomas's work continue to shape studies of the mental world of early modern European, and indeed other pre-modern societies.[20] A more sensitive approach to the structures of medieval religion and the negotiated impact of religious change has certainly encouraged further reflection upon the form and image of superstition in Reformation Europe. Increasingly, the dichotomy between the 'superstitious' Middle Ages and 'rational' European modernity is seen as potent but ill-conceived.[21] Superstition and ignorance are far from identical; as Cameron notes, superstitions occupy a variety of spaces that range from the idiosyncratic to the alternative cosmology, and for the same reason defy definition and compartmentalization. Some are local in their origins and meaning, others global; some derive from folklore and others from within Christianity.[22] The term 'superstition' was a weapon in polemical debate as much as an objective term. Key to this is the realization that definitions of superstition emerged from the same discursive processes in which the term was applied often as part of the process intended to denounce and undermine a contested set of beliefs.[23]

Kathleen Kamerick's examination of superstition in late medieval England provides a cogent exploration of the practical consequences of rhetorical criticism, reflecting upon the pastoral obligations that accompanied calls for the eradication of superstition. The meaning and location of superstition was often ambiguous, potentially a 'fearful portal allowing the devil's entry into human affairs', but also a problem which the English clergy were less inclined (or were perceived as being less inclined) to engage. The efforts of theologians and pastors who were exercised by the danger of superstition were often frustrated by its imprecise and pliant meaning. The concomitant diversity of practices and problems that fell under the umbrella of superstition in the late Middle Ages provided a vocabulary of complaint and condemnation that elided into the debates and polemic of the Reformation. Lollard critics of the medieval English Church, and Protestant reformers of the sixteenth century exploited the capricious and capacious term 'superstition' to argue that a heavily sacramentalized Catholic devotion was indicative of the extent to which the Church had compromised with magic. But that same language of superstition was also used against critics of Catholicism in the sixteenth century. Thomas More launched an energetic defence of traditional piety against accusations of superstition, but also recognized the polemical capital in turning these accusations against his evangelical opponents. Superstition was not, on the face of it, a new problem in the sixteenth century, but its ongoing metamorphosis certainly enlivened polemical and pastoral debate.

Within that debate, there exists substantial evidence of intersection and overlap between Catholic and evangelical writing on superstition and magic. Lutheran criticism of ecclesiastical rituals that opened the door to demonic corruption, for example, had their roots in the discussions of magic and superstition in Augustine, Lombard and Aquinas. As Bob Scribner noted, Catholic and Protestant shared 'the cosmological belief that the natural world was dependent for its subsistence on the sustaining power of the supernatural', which could intervene to interrupt natural processes and which inserted itself into the space and time of nature. For all the rigidity of rhetoric and debate, both inhabited the same mental world, and the energetic denunciation of purgatory, saints and miracles in evangelical theology and polemic did not bring about a sudden or complete 'disenchantment'. Sacred time, places and objects continued to shape interactions with the sacred, and sacrality was remodelled rather than rejected.[24] Polemical and pastoral writing on both sides of the confessional divide held out the possibility that a ritual might be 'vain' or 'superstitious', but precisely which devotional activities fell into that category was more hotly contested. But the shared roots of ecclesiastical opposition to superstition could still support and sustain a more confident reclassification and recategorization of the supernatural in early modern religious dialogue and discourse. At a general level, tensions over what was nominally common ground are visible in the polemical exchanges over the cult of the saints in Reformation Europe. The Council of Trent, while defending the theological underpinnings of saints cults, demanded that some of the devotional practices that had proliferated around the cult be suppressed or reformed. Some of these concerns were shared by evangelical theologians and propagandists, but emerged in the pages of hostile polemic as a justification for iconoclasm and suppression, not reform.[25] Sacramentals occupied similarly contested ground. The legitimacy and value of holy water, salt and crosses, for example, had not been questioned by the medieval Latin Church, although some of the abuses associated with these objects had been the subject of criticism and inquiry. That same sense that the sacramental might be open to abuse is evident in evangelical writing, but in the pages of anti-Catholic polemic, such abuses were evidence that a more root and branch reform was necessary in order to suppress the use of objects and rituals that were the word of the devil, intended to deceive the faithful.[26]

For all the common ground that existed in the assertion that it was possible to separate the natural from the supernatural and preternatural, the precise meaning and application of these terms was far more contested and heterogeneous. Miracles, worked by God, exceeded that which was possible within nature and were, by implication, properly supernatural. However, the category of preternatural was far more fluid. Such wonders might appear to be supernatural, their causes hidden from the imperfect eyes of man, but were more often natural, and the work of created beings. Increasingly, in the pages of polemical theology, such wonders came to acquire a more sinister interpretation, as the work of the devil and his minions.[27] The words of Peter Martyr, that 'the devil had only two "bridles": one was the will of God the other the boundary of nature', resonated in a distinctly polarized worldview. The accompanying 'ideological squeeze' on wonder-workers had implications for natural philosophy, ideas about the miraculous, and the broader nature of the licit and illicit supernatural.[28] The nature of the debate over the miraculous supernatural in Reformation Europe exhibited some cosmological continuity with late medieval attitudes, but at the core of the argument the differences are more readily visible than the similarities. The demonization of opposition both exemplified and deepened divisions in a debate that was not simply about categories of the supernatural, but rather demanded a broader reconsideration of the capacity of sinful man to access the supernatural independently of God's grace. If grace could no longer be conferred through rituals, images and other material objects, such things were neither desirable nor even neutral, but dangerous and demonic.[29] No wonder then that the lexicon of Weber's 'disenchantment' drew upon the language of Reformation debate, and its social consequences.

But to attack the doctrines and the devotional practices of the medieval Church as superstitious was not the same as to articulate a worldview that was entirely desacralized, or secularized. The latter might well be argued to be a feature of the modern intellectual landscape, but this is not the same as the disenchantment, or desacralization that Weber associated with Protestantism.[30] Evangelical cosmology did not exclude the possibility that the supernatural might exert an influence over the natural world, not least because a theology that was constructed around an energetic assertion of the sovereignty of God could not curtail the outworkings of that sovereignty. Some of the evidence for this sacralized universe comes from the survival of pre-Reformation devotions and beliefs, but in other cases it is possible to see the emergence of distinctively Protestant actions, objects and beliefs. The reformation of the supernatural has the potential to engage in iconoclasm and destruction, but in parish life the process was often one of negotiation and adaptation.

Such an approach has been recognized in the proliferation of the plural term 'reformations' in recent scholarship, and explored in different ways in the work of Shagan, Walsham and Scribner. Carlos Eire's recent book, *Reformations*, grows out of an acceptance of a model of multiple reformations, and an emphasis upon the interrelatedness of all forms of reformation, rather than confessional division and conflict. The approach is not new; 40 years ago Jean Delumeau argued that the emergence of Protestantism and the reformation of Catholicism initiated by the Council of Trent did not run in parallel, but rather interacted in a process of 'Christianization'. Difference and division was evident, but Delumeau argued that Catholic and Protestant reformers shared a sense that the focus of their labours should be the continued presence of an ill-informed, semi-pagan, popular religion, and the desire to impose upon this unpromising landscape a Christo-centric and morally disciplined faith inculcated by preaching and catechism.[31] In Eire's study, the picture is more complex, with the energy for reform coming not from a single sense of Christian evangelism, but from the multiple incompatibilities that characterized religious life and reformation in early modern Europe. The common ground that might be seen to emerge over catechism and social discipline is far less evident in the stance of Catholic and Protestant on clerical marriage and mendicancy.[32] The efforts of the two Christian religions seem similar in such areas as intensive catechization or 'social disciplining' but dramatically different in their attitudes toward begging and clerical marriage.

Responses to the redrawing of the physical and mental cosmologies were varied, and the impact of the Reformation often patchwork rather than uniform. The continued existence of a Catholic community, as Walsham charts in the English context, could ensure both the survival of traditional sacred sites and the construction of new material and topographical features that commemorated the steadfastness and survival of the old religion. The persecution of Catholic and Protestant dissenters in post-Reformation England created alternative sacred spaces, often removed and remote from the ecclesiastical architecture of the institutional Church. Attempts to suppress belief in the healing powers of holy wells and streams were accompanied by the emergence of new locations that were, if not sanctified, at least sacralized by the preaching of the Gospel by separatists and dissenters. The energetic evangelical polemic against a religious culture that was too focused upon the spiritual significance of material objects and physical landmarks might come to serve as a catalogue of those very places that it sought to condemn, preserving the memory albeit through mockery of its meaning. The history of the holy thorn at Glastonbury serves as an example of the way in which a sacred object could be subject to the vicissitudes of religious reform and polemical controversy, revered and denounced in almost equal measure. Its ability to restore itself after destruction gives a sense of the capacity for old myths to be reborn in the heat of controversy and opposition. In all this, the natural world remained a source of spiritual support and access to the sacred. For all that the idea of 'disenchantment' encourages us to think about the destructive power of science wielded against the superstitions of traditional Christianity, natural science was often the preserve of churchmen, and knowledge of the landscape and environment was a path to the knowledge of God. As a result, the narrative of the landscape did not end with desacralization, but rather told a story in which humanity first imbued the material with a sense of the sacred, then sought to break apart that link by physical and verbal iconoclasm, before restoring that sense of the sacral to God's creation.

This assertion of a post-Reformation sacralized mental world is most commonly associated with the groundbreaking work of Bob Scribner, which did much to energize scholarly challenge to the 'incombustible Weber'.[33] Scribner's extensive work on the interactions between German Lutheranism and popular culture exposed the extent to which the outcome of the iconoclastic

Fig. 19: Ruins of Glastonbury Abbey

rhetoric of the Reformation was a process of modification rather than transformation. The context in which Weber wrote provided an inducement to see the 'disenchantment' of Europe as a key component of progress in the economy of European thought and finance, but Scribner argued that the initial radicalism of Reformation thought on saints, images, pilgrimage and sacred objects was not, in the event, a defining characteristic of post-Reformation religion and devotional practice. 'The world of Luther and the reformation,' he suggested, '[was a] world of highly charged sacrality.' Catholic sacramentalism gave way to a more loosely defined form of sacrality, but did not represent a paradigm shift from a 'sacramental to a secularised world'.[34] It was this mental world that supported, even encouraged, the development of a Protestant supernatural in which the language of traditional piety was reformed rather than rejected.

The relics of medieval saints were often reported to be immune to the flames, and incombustibility was an integral part of the miracles associated with the consecrated host. Perhaps we should not be surprised, then, that this same immunity to destruction by fire was attributed to objects associated with Martin Luther. Pictures of Luther repeatedly refused to succumb to the flames. The house in which Luther was born survived a number of conflagrations, and when the Augustinian house in Magdeburg was destroyed by fire in 1631, the cell that had once been occupied by Luther remained undamaged.[35] Such exploitation of the verbal and visual language of the cult of the saints as propaganda for the Reformation may well have encouraged a more tolerant attitude towards the continued presence of the sacred in material objects and physical locations. Scott Dixon's work on post-Reformation Brandenburg-Ansbach contributes to the multifaceted image of Lutheran piety that characterizes recent scholarship. Images, it appears were still present, in use and revered in post-Reformation Germany; in Langenzenn, parishioners continued to gather at sites of traditional devotion and leave wax dolls and chickens as offerings. The Reformation did not 'overthrow these charms', thus perpetuating the belief that the material had the potential to act as a vehicle of sacred power. The peasantry continued to invoke the name of Christ and the Virgin in spells and verses, trusting that the power of God and the saints could still be summoned for human aid, as a cure for illness, to protect crops and livestock and to preserve the welfare of the parish community.[36]

In England, Rogationtide customs did not cease with the Reformation, but maintained a liturgical presence and practical function in which song, sermon and prayer defined the physical and devotional boundaries of the parish.[37] The royal commissioners for the dissolution of the monasteries in England in the 1530s presented Thomas Cromwell with lists of the 'the roten bones that be called reliques' discovered in the religious houses, which were then collected in the Tower of London, or in Cromwell's wardrobe of beds in Westminster. Those that were destroyed in public spectacles of humiliation turned relics into mere remains, in a powerful display of desacralization and reformation of belief and memory.[38] But polemic and propaganda can conceal the underlying reality. Some 30 years after the Cromwellian visitors did their work, Bishop John Jewel lamented the 'wilderness of superstition' that had been allowed to spring up in the 'darkness of the Marian times'. Their roots lay in the survival of traditional objects that had been rescued from the iconoclasm of the 1530s and preserved by pious believers, but also in the transfer of sacred significance from the destroyed material object to the place where it had once stood.

The same process is evident in the construction of memory around the ruins of English monasteries after the dissolution. The suppression of the religious life in England was an institutional and material break with the past, and imparted a potent theological and political message. But the ruins of monasteries cast a shadow on the surrounding landscape, shaping the memory of the past and directing attention to the present. The breezes that blew through Donne's 'ruin'd abbeys', and the sweet birds of Shakespeare's 'bare ruin'd choirs' imposed the invisible past upon the visible landscape. The destructive language and impulses of the 1530s forced a reimagining of the relationship between the ruins and the local community, and a renegotiation of the interactions between the sacred and the profane as the physical remains of medieval monastic architecture found their way into private hands and homes.[39] In the midst of such turmoil, the location of sacrilege and sacrality was far from obvious. Just as the cult of the incombustible Luther both complemented and contradicted the doctrinal impulses of the early Reformation, so the desire of those who watched the martyrdoms of English evangelicals in the reign of Mary Tudor to gather the 'burnt bones of these stynkyng martyrs' from the fire seemed to undermine the condemnation of the cult of the saints as idolatry that had been voiced by those who died for their commitment to the Reformation.[40] Yet were these remains identical in form and meaning to the relics of the saints of the medieval Church? Were they memorials, examples and mnemonics of a new understanding of sainthood or miracle-working material objects in which resided the divine? Divorced from the rhetorical certainties of Reformation polemic (a rhetoric that fuelled Weber's conviction that post-Reformation culture was, in this sense, disenchanted), the boundary between symbolic and sacral meaning remained pervious and pliable.

The continued presence of saints and relics on the Protestant religious landscape was an indication of the extent to which the relationship between the Reformation and the supernatural was driven by context and open to a process of negotiation and the layering of belief, rather than by suppression and denial. To deride relics and other devotional objects and the materiality of traditional religion did not necessarily remove the vocabulary of relic or miracle from the lexicon of belief. Jean Calvin denounced the cult of relics as a 'filthy pollution the which ought in no wise to be suffered in the church', but the enduring energy of polemic directed against relics in post-Reformation culture turned relics into an indicator of confessional allegiance, reforming rather than rejecting their spiritual and physical meaning. Relics and saints possessed multiple meanings, and the link between material object and metaphor continued to be debated and contested.[41] Relics and shrines have lost some of their ritual significance as objects to be viewed and touched, but sacred objects and places still sustained a supernatural significance. As Walsham has noted, it was possible for not just bones, but books, to acquire a sacred significance, to the point where book covers were almost indistinguishable from reliquaries. Books that lay on the altar, close to the species, could be 'receptacles of numinous power', and, like images of Luther in Reformation Germany, acquired a reputation for immunity to the flames.[42] But to label a book as a relic was to perpetuate the language of traditional devotion while at the same time allowing it to occupy a rather different space. Relics became objects of mockery and later curiosity, but never quite disappeared, materially or metaphorically. Wrapped in legends and traditions that were intertwined in social memory, the persistence of that memory of the relic contributed to the survival of ideas about sacrality that inhered in material objects.[43]

Evangelical denunciation of medieval Catholic materialism did not carry with it the total rejection of sacred objects. Indeed material objects were building blocks in the construction of a confessional identity amid doctrinal conflict, and remained a vital part of memory and history. Reformed religious culture continued to be shaped by the material of traditional devotion, and diverse interactions between survival, manipulation, transposition and construction of the sacred.[44] With this in mind, Daniel Woolf suggests that by the late seventeenth century, most Protestants were willing to approach popular Catholicism with an air of 'benign amusement'. Medieval relics gradually lost their status as idolatrous objects and became a focus for antiquarian curiosity, items of interest that could still be examined, touched and valued, but no longer venerated.[45] The boundary between that interest and respect and veneration was not always rigidly drawn, and even if they were no longer objects of popular public devotion, relics retained a cultural significance that was not entirely divorced from their sacred meaning.

If the relics of the saints raised questions about the status of the holy dead, the debate over ghosts and ghostly apparitions in the early modern period grew out of a desire to explain and reform the 'untimely dead'. Medieval ghost lore was heterogeneous and fluid, with interactions with the dead acting as a prism of the needs and concerns of the living, and their cultural, personal and doctrinal priorities. The Protestant abolition of purgatory was a tangible but not entirely watertight statement that there could be no beneficial soteriological relationship between the living and the dead. In this model, the souls of the dead lay beyond the reach of the prayers of the living, and the affairs of the living lay beyond the influence of the dead. A geography of the afterlife in which purgatory had no place swept away provision for the suffering souls in purgatory and created a culture that had no place for the wandering dead. Sharing the certainties of evangelical polemic, Keith Thomas describes a belief in ghosts as 'a shibboleth which distinguished Protestant from Catholic'.[46] Exemplifying the reformed stance on such matters, the English evangelical Robert Wisdom was blunt in his assertion that the 'sowles departed do not come again and play boo peape with us'.[47] Reginald Scot concluded that the Reformation had suppressed the widely held belief in apparitions.[48] The rejection of purgatory undermined the very existence of ghosts, Scribner argues, and ghosts had little reverence for the confessional conflicts of early modern religion. Indeed their continued presence on the religious and cultural stage placed them beyond the reach of such doctrinal certainties.[49] The purgatorial dead did not exist, yet continued to be seen.

As a result, the early modern ghost became the focus for a vibrant if recursive debate about the theology and geography of the afterlife, the nature of death and the interpretation of apparitions. Ghost stories were traditionally syncretic, a melting pot in which were mixed theological assumptions about the origins and role of the medieval ghost, and more pragmatic and pastoral concerns created by the search for comfort and security. Into this potent mix came a combination of Protestant views of divine providence and the presence of the supernatural in the world of nature. Ghosts infiltrated literature and language, as arbiters and creators of tensions and conflicts, as the void left by the abolition of purgatory became a space in which ghosts were still able to exist.[50] Little was said about the clearing of haunted places, presumably because there was little to discuss; there were no such things as ghosts. However, as time went on, it became obvious that the ghosts themselves were oblivious to official opinion and 'continued to come and go at their own sweet will'.[51] As John Bossy has observed, the ghosts of the deceased who visited their living relatives were not real, but personal, and inhabiting a space that was mental rather than material.[52] The restless dead continued to occupy a devotional and emotional space, created by and creating a religious culture that was complex and contradictory.

Within this multifaceted culture, reports of ghosts were hard to suppress. As Bishop Pilkington of Durham complained to Archbishop Parker in 1564, sightings of ghosts 'be so common here, and none of authority that will gainsay it, but rather believe and confirm it, that every one believes it'. In the same year, Bishop Grindal complained that the persistence of sightings of ghosts was the fruit, but also the cause, of popish superstitions.[53] On the face of it, the post-Reformation ghost story suggests that there is an oversimplistic undercurrent to the arguments of Keith Thomas and others that ghosts 'presented no problems' to Protestant reformers.[54] Rhetorically, this was the case, and the very basic assertion that ghosts were not, in any sense, real, was not undermined by the continued reports of such apparitions. If ghosts seemed to appear, the simple explanation was that they were not ghosts at all. Zachary Jones's 1605 translation of the *Livres des Spectres* simply expunged Le Loyer's evidence for the reality of ghosts, ending the discussion with a blunt statement, 'Finis'.[55] The 'marvellous tales' of ghosts and apparitions were argued to be anchored in the superstitions beloved of old women, who constructed the ghost from the sounds of nocturnal animals. If not the fruit of superstition, ghosts were dismissed as frauds and deceptions. In an attempt to resolve the infamous case of the ghost of Mother Leakey, the commissioners concluded that the appearance of the ghost was a fiction, invented for financial gain.[56] But while such accusations offered a practical explanation for ghost sightings, it was certainly not a neutral one. The ghost may have lost its association with purgatory, but it was not devoid of supernatural meaning. Ghostly apparitions inhabited an intellectual world in which devils and demons came to occupy an ever more central position in the language of controversy, and 'thinking with demons' provided a means by which theologians, jurists and pastors could interpret and shape human experience, ghosts included.[57] Ghosts, and those who perceived them, blended the old and the new in order to accommodate the continued presence of the ghost in post-Reformation Europe. Here, as in other categories, the supernatural was not rejected, but reformed and reinterpreted in a discursive process of linguistic and cultural exchange.

On this basis, there is a plausibility in Alexandra Walsham's observation that the linear model of disenchantment proposed in Weber's work might be better presented as a series of cycles of desacralization and resacralization.[58] Such cycles were fuelled by an increasingly complicated and diverse dialogue over the supernatural, evident both in the printed word and the pastoral environment. This might, on occasion, be a simple clash between evangelical optimism and the needs and beliefs of the faithful, but the position of the supernatural in Reformation Europe was consciously constructed to a much greater degree than this model suggests. The sacralized universe was not destroyed as readily as statues, images and the material culture of traditional religion, not least because the continued potential for the supernatural to intrude into the world of the profane was an integral part of post-Reformation religious culture. As Walsham demonstrates, providentialism was not only part of the evangelical mainstream, but also part of a set of assumptions that enjoyed near universal acceptance. Opposition to the material, miraculous and magical aspects of traditional piety did not denude the sacral universe of its moral and theological meaning. The relationship between the Reformation and the 'superstitions' of the past that it sought to suppress was adaptive and syncretistic, and God's judgement continued to be evinced in portents and prodigies, as the needs of the present were interwoven with the framework of the past. Transformation was possible, but was neither rapid nor unidirectional. If new attitudes were built on traditional foundations, those same foundations were just as likely to become invested with the values superimposed upon them. In Lutheran *Wunderzeichenbuch*, wonders, and the written record of such events, testified to God's continued presence in the natural world, divine judgement upon the sinful depravity of mankind, and the interventionist nature of that judgement. The roots of the wonderbook lay in the fifteenth century, but the continued existence of a semiotic universe in which strange events imparted a message to mankind turned the genre into a weapon of evangelical propaganda. Lutheran wonders were not synonymous with Catholic miracle, and the *Wunderzeichenbuch* were not identical to late medieval and early modern miracle collections that documented the intercession of saints at shrines and other sacred places. But collections of providences and *Wunderzeichenbuch*, and their evolution, exemplified the role that traditional forms and new contexts played in shaping the representation and understanding of the supernatural.[59] Religion, magic and the supernatural were as much in the eye of the beholder in post-Reformation Europe as they had been in the centuries before, and the very capaciousness of such terminology fuelled not only polemical debate and pastoral controversy, but also imposed limits upon the eradication of superstition and 'enchantment'.

Epilogue

What happened in the past cannot be changed, but what is remembered of the past and how it is remembered can, with the passage of time, indeed change. Remembrance makes the past present. While the past itself is unalterable, the presence of the past in the present is alterable. In view of 2017, the point is not to tell a different history, but to tell that history differently.

From Conflict to Communion: Lutheran-Catholic Common Commemoration of the Reformation in 2017[1]

What was the Protestant Reformation? As we look back on the 2017 celebration of the 500th anniversary of the event, what was it that was being commemorated, and what does this tell us about the mark that the Reformation has left upon the European landscape? For a scholarly discipline that has become increasingly sceptical of the 'grand narrative' approach to the past, questioning in its attitude to the 'great men of history' and increasingly sensitive to the problems of labels and identities, the very idea of 'Reformation 500' can be disconcerting. The relationship between memory and commemoration is complex in any context. The decision to mark an anniversary, and what form that commemoration will take imbues it with a modern meaning, and a meaning that has the potential to infiltrate the memory of the past. Our priorities can all too readily mould the priorities of the past. Where the event that is commemorated is intricately tied to such personal considerations as faith, the relationship between past and present, history and memory, becomes all the harder to disentangle.[2]

The events of what has been declared the 'Luther decade' give some sense of the scale of the endeavour, and the energy with which Luther's legacy is being debated in the first years of the twenty-first century. As the authors of *From Conflict to Communion* note, Lutherans and Catholics share good reasons to reflect upon and retell their histories. Despite the furore over the 1517 anniversary, recent research has taught us that the Reformation certainly did not end with the death of Luther, and almost as certainly did not begin in 1517. Modern ecumenism has shifted the focus of debate over the Reformation in a direction that encourages a search for common ground rather than the hardening of division and difference. Expositions of Reformation theology have taken their place alongside more general reflections upon the political, cultural and social context in which these ideas were expressed, moulded and reformed. The 'long Reformation' positions events and ideas within a much broader chronological context, seeing the roots of reform in the Middle Ages, and its consequences stretching well into the eighteenth century. The Reformation presented a real and destructive opposition to the unity of Western Christendom, but it was a unity that existed, and was sustained, by the tension between vitality and vulnerability of the Latin Church.[3] The *corpus Christianum* of the medieval period was not monolithic, but rather accommodated different theological opinions, attitudes and devotional practices. The Reformation emerged out of this situation, not from outside it.

The very idea of 'the Reformation' feels too simplistic a label for such a complex series of processes and events. More and more, as we have seen, there is a value in thinking in terms of 'reformations' rather than a single reformation, and reflecting upon what 'reformation' meant to those who shaped and were shaped by it. The Latin *reformatio* carried the implicit meaning of a return to the better times of the past, rather than a determination to open a schism between past and present. It was not a term that Luther used repeatedly to describe his own actions and intentions, but it became a label that was applied, sometimes with ruthless efficiency, to religious change in early modern Europe. The label 'Reformation', a creation of eighteenth-century German scholarship, implied (and to some extent created) something that was identifiable, clear in its content and positive in its outcomes. One of the core themes that has emerged throughout this survey is the extent to which the language of reformation does an injustice to the complexity and diversity of the ideas and beliefs that sit under its shadow. Certainly, the 'Reformation' continues to act as a convenient shorthand on book jackets, in school and university teaching and in the articulation of something that was celebrated in 2017. But below the surface, the Reformation exists as multiple local or national processes, as a set of beliefs tied to one individual, as something that had a multiplicity of meanings for the literate and illiterate, for clergy and laity, for men and women, for culture, society and community. The label 'Reformation' certainly imbues these events and processes with an impressive degree of unity and coherence, but is it possible that this can be traced to a single event in Wittenberg in October 1517?

If 'Reformation' has become something of a loaded term, so too has 'Protestant'. Like many of the words used to describe belief in early modern Europe (papist, superstitious, radical and Puritan among them), 'Protestant' has a historical meaning that is culturally defined. In its first decades, 'Protestant' carried with it a strong political association with the Schmalkaldic League, and a rhetoric of protest against the piety but also the power and princes of the Catholic Church. 'Lutheran' was little better; it was, like *reformatio*, a term that Luther seemed unwilling to embrace. And what did it mean? Fidelity to the core theological principles that underpinned Luther's criticisms of traditional religion, an acceptance of justification by faith as an explanation of man's relationship with God, or a more rudimentary anti-papalism under which sat a range of competing ideas and solutions? Perhaps the answer lies somewhere in the common ground between these ideas, but it is still hard to escape the fact that 'Lutheran' and 'Protestant' were essentially labels applied by opponents, and that such labels have the potential to shape the events and ideas that they described. To talk and write about 'Lutherans' was to prioritize the role of Luther in the unfolding of reform; to use the label 'Protestants' was to imply unity and consensus among the diverse group of uneasy bedfellows that make up the 'Protestant Reformations'. The use of more familiar terms such as Hussite,

Antinomian or Manichee to describe Luther and his early followers was intended to position them as the latest in a long line of heretics who had challenged the medieval Church, worthy of censure and suppression. In this sense, the connotations were damningly negative, but the use of such language to describe those who sympathized with Luther had the effect of providing a somewhat inchoate group with an identity and purpose, as well as a history. In answer to the question 'Where was your church before Luther?', the answer could be (as we saw in the case of Anna Jansz in a different context) that the existence of such a church was evident within the historical narrative that the Catholic Church claimed as its own.

The statement in *Conflict to Communion* observes that 'while the past itself is unalterable, the presence of the past in the present is alterable. In view of 2017, the point is not to tell a different history, but to tell that history differently.' Here lies both the challenge and importance in reflecting upon what we can learn from the commemorations. The presence of the past in the present is indeed unalterable; the consequences of the religious divisions of the early modern period are still evident in the modern world. Whether they would be either recognizable to or accepted by those individuals whose name they bear is another matter, but the intended or unintended consequences are deeply embedded in the modern world.[4] The impact of these ideas is evident in our physical landscape, whether in the ruined abbeys and empty niches in which statues once stood, or the monuments to the Reformation in Wittenberg, Geneva and elsewhere that honour its leaders and identify its ancestry.[5] It is there in our language, which still resonates with the phrasing of sixteenth-century translators of the Bible, and authors of printed sermon collections.[6] It exists in the pluralism of modern Christianity and in the energetic debates about the relationship between Church and state in the early twenty-first century. It is cited in debates over toleration, secularism and equality. The history of the Reformation is ubiquitous, at least in the eyes of those who choose to perceive it. But in that perception, there is the risk that history is changed. It is almost axiomatic that we will 'tell that history differently', because the present has an inbuilt capacity to modify the past. It is one thing to observe that the celebrations

Fig. 20: Martin Luther Memorial in Worms, depicting
Luther surrounded by John Wycliffe, Jan Hus and Girolamo Savonarola

that attended the Luther anniversaries of 1617, 1717 and 1817 were shaped by their context and moulded to meet the needs of the time, but quite another to assume that 2017 was any different. If we seek to present a history of the Reformation and its impact upon modernity, we, too, intrude on that history. Would the Luther that was commemorated in 2017 be recognizable to Luther the 'renegade friar'?

The image of Luther's hammer driving the nail of the 95 Theses into the door of the church is iconic, a sign which has a characteristic in common with the thing it signifies, but is not identical with it. Luther's protest has become sufficiently ingrained in communal memory that it has acquired an almost mythical status, and one that has been remodelled and re-formed by successive generations for half a millennium. That re-forming of the Reformation leaves us with a story that is made up of multiple stories, spoken in multiple voices. If the Reformation did indeed 'impel the human mind to new courses', then the lack of a single narrative of its events and achievements is to be celebrated.[7] The new courses mapped out in modern scholarship, not least in the cascade of books, articles, conferences and commemorations of 2017, have raised diverse questions and presented even more diverse answers. This lack of consensus in the response should be seen as evidence that the questions are worthwhile. If the underlying conclusion of this book is that the Reformation is still more complex than we might imagine, shaped by context and conflict, discursive interactions and diversities of opinion, that is not because we have failed to understand, but because we continue to try.

Further Reading

Althaus, P., *The Theology of Martin Luther*, trans. R. C. Schultz (Philadelphia: Fortress, 1966).

Arnold, M., 'De l'hérétique Allemand au témoin œcumenique de Jesus-Christ: La biographie de Martin Luther au XXe siècle, a la croisée des ecoles historiographiques Françaises et Allemandes', *Revue d'Allemagne* 334 (2001): 395–412.

Aston, M., 'English Ruins and English History: The Dissolution and the Sense of the Past', *Journal of the Warburg and Courtauld Institutes* 36 (1973): 231–55.

——, 'Lollard Women Priests?', *Journal of Ecclesiastical History* 31, no. 4 (1980): 441–61.

——, *Lollards and Reformers: Images and Literacy in Late Medieval Religion* (London: Hambledon, 1984).

——, *The King's Bedpost: Reformation and Iconography in a Tudor Portrait* (Cambridge: Cambridge University Press, 1993).

——, 'Gods, Saints and Reformers: Portraiture and Protestant England', in L. Ghent (ed.), *Albion's Classicism* (London: Yale University Press, 1995), pp. 181–220.

Bachmann, M., ed., *Lutherische und neue Paulusperspektive: Beiträge zu einem Schlüsselproblem der gegenwärtigen exegetischen Diskussion* (Tübingen: Mohr Siebeck, 2005).

Backus, I., *Historical Method and Confessional Identity in the Era of the Reformation (1378–1615)* (Leiden: Brill, 2003).

Bagchi, D., *Luther's Earliest Opponents: Catholic Controversialists, 1518–1525* (Minneapolis, MN: Fortress, 1991).

Bagchi, D. and Steinmetz, D., eds, *The Cambridge Companion to Reformation Theology* (Cambridge: Cambridge University Press, 2006).

Bailey, M., *Fearful Spirits: The Boundaries of Superstition in Late Medieval Europe* (Ithaca, NY: Cornell University Press, 2013).

Bainton, R. H., *Women of the Reformation in Germany and Italy* (Minneapolis, MN: Fortress, 1971).

——, *Here I Stand: A Life of Martin Luther* (Peabody, MA: Hendrickson, 2009).

Balserak, J., *John Calvin as Sixteenth Century Prophet* (Oxford: Oxford University Press, 2014).

Bast, R. J., *The Reformation of Faith in the Context of Late Medieval Theology and Piety* (Leiden: Brill, 2004).

Bast, R. J. and Gow, A. C., eds, *Continuity and Change: The Harvest of Late Medieval and Reformation History. Essays Presented to Heiko A. Oberman on His 70th Birthday* (Leiden: Brill, 2000).

Bath, J. '"In the Divells likeness", interpretation and confusion in popular ghosts belief', in J. Bath and J. Newton (eds), *Early Modern Ghosts* (Durham: Centre for Seventeenth-Century Studies, 2002), pp. 70–8.

Bauckham, R., *Tudor Apocalypse. Sixteenth Century Apocalypticism, Millenarianism, and the English Reformation from John Bale to John Foxe and Thomas Brightman*, Courtenay Library of Reformation Classics, vol. 8 (Oxford: Sutton Courtenay Press, 1978).

Beilin, E., ed., *The Examinations of Anne Askew* (Oxford: Oxford University Press, 1996).

Bennett, G., 'Ghost and Witch in the Sixteenth and Seventeenth Centuries', *Folklore* 96 (1986): 3–14.

Benrath, G., *Reformierte Kirchengeschichtsschreibung an der Universitat Heidelbert im 16. Und 17. Jahrhundert* (Speyer: Zechnersche Buchdruckerei, 1963).

Benson, P. J., *The Invention of the Renaissance Woman* (Pittsburgh: Penn State University Press, 1992).

Berg, G., *Leopold von Ranke als akademischer Lehrer: Studien zu seinen Vorlesungen und seinem Geschichtsdenken* (Göttingen: Vandenhoeck & Ruprecht, 1968), pp. 109–13.

Bernard, G., *The Late Medieval English Church: Vitality and Vulnerability Before the Break with Rome* (New Haven, CT: Yale University Press, 2012).

Biel, B., *Exposition of the Canon of the Mass* (1495).

Blickle, P., *Die Gemeindereformation: Die Menschen des 16. Jahrhunderts auf dem Weg zum Heil* (Munich: Oldenbourg, 1985).

Bossy, J., *Christianity in the West 1400–1700* (Oxford: Oxford University Press, 1985).

Further Reading

Brady, T., *Communities, Politics, and Reformation in Early Modern Europe* (Leiden: Brill, 1998).

——, 'Confessionalization: The Career of a Concept', in J. M. Headley, H. J. Hillerbrand and A. J. Papalas (eds), *Confessionalization in Europe, 1555–1700: Essays in Honor and Memory of Bodo Nischan* (Burlington, VT: Ashgate, 2004), pp. 1–20.

Brecht, M., *Martin Luther*, trans. James L. Schaaf, 3 vols (Philadelphia: Fortress, 1985).

Brevicoxa, J., 'A *Treatise on Faith, the Church, the Roman Pontiff, and the General Council*', trans. in *Forerunners of the Reformation*, ed. H. A. Oberman (Philadelphia: Fortress, 1981).

Brown, C., *Singing the Gospel: Lutheran Hymns and the Success of the Reformation* (Cambridge, MA: Harvard University Press, 2005).

Brown, P., *The Body and Society: Men, Women and Sexual Renunciation* (New York: Columbia University Press, 1988).

Brown, T., *The Fate of the Dead: A Study in Folk-Eschatology in the West Country after the Reformation* (Ipswich: D. S. Brewer, 1979).

Brundage, J., *Law, Sex and Christian Society in Medieval Europe* (Chicago: University of Chicago Press, 1990).

Budd, J., 'Rethinking iconoclasm in early modern England: The case of the Cheapside cross', *Journal of Early Modern History* 4, nos 3–4 (2000): 371–404.

Bultmann, C., Leppin, V. and Lindner, A., eds, *Luther und das monastische Erbe* (Tübingen: Mohr Siebeck, 2007).

Burghartz, S., 'Ordering Discourse and Society: Moral Politics, Marriage, and Fornication during the Reformation and Confessionalisation Process in Germany and Switzerland', in H. Roodenburg and O. Spierenburg (eds), *Social Control in Europe Volume 1: 1500–1800* (Columbus: Ohio State University Press, 2004), pp. 78–98.

Burschel, P., *Sterben und Unsterblichkeit: Zur Kultur des Martyriums in der frühen Neuzeit*, Ancien Régime, Aufklärung und Revolution 35 (Munich: Oldenbourg, 2004).

Calendar of State Papers Relating To English Affairs in the Archives of Venice, Volume 3, 1520–1526, ed. R. Brown (London, 1869), 121 n.208, *British History Online*, http://www.british-history.ac.uk/cal-state-papers/venice/vol3 (accessed 4 May 2018).

Calvin, J., *Ioannis Calvini opera quae supersunt omnia*, ed. G. Baum, E. Cunitz and E. Reuss, 59 vols, Corpus Reformatorum 29–87 (Brunswick: Schwetschke, 1863–1900).

——, *Institutes of the Christian Religion*, trans. F. Battles (Philadelphia: Library of Christian Classics, 1960; Louisville, KY: Westminster John Knox Press, 2001).

——, *John Calvin: Selections From His Writings*, ed. John Dillenberger (Garden City, NY: Doubleday Anchor, 1971).

Cameron, E., *The European Reformation* (Oxford: Oxford University Press, 1991).

——, *Enchanted Europe: Superstition, Reason and Religion 1350–1750* (Oxford: Oxford University Press, 2010).

——, 'Primitivism, Patristics and Polemnic in Protestant Visions of Early Christianity', in K. Van Liere, S. Ditchfield and H. Louthan (eds), *Sacred History: Uses of the Christian Past in the Renaissance World* (Oxford: Oxford University Press, 2010), pp. 27–51.

Carlson, E., 'Clerical Marriage and the English Reformation', *Journal of British Studies* 31 (1992): 1–31.

——, *Marriage and the English Reformation* (Oxford: Clarendon Press, 1994).

Carroll, A. J., 'Disenchantment, Rationality, and the Modernity of Max Weber', *Forum Philosophicum* 16, no. 1 (2001): 117–37.

Chrisman, M. U., 'Women and the Reformation in Strasbourg 1490–1530', *Archiv fur Reformationsgeschichte* 63 (1972): 143–68.

——, *Lay Culture, Learned Culture: Books and Social Change in Strasbourg, 1480–1599* (New Haven, CT: Yale University Press, 1982).

Christensen, C., *Art and the Reformation in Germany* (Athens: Ohio University Press, 1979).

Clark, E., ed., *St Augustine on Marriage and Sexuality* (Washington, DC: Catholic University of America Press, 1996).

Clark, S., 'The rational witchfinder: conscience, demonological naturalism and popular superstition', in S. Pumfrey and P. Rossi (eds), *Science, Culture and Popular Belief in Renaissance Europe* (Manchester: Manchester University Press, 1992), pp. 222–48.

——, *Thinking with Demons: The Idea of Witchcraft in Early Modern Europe* (Oxford: Oxford University Press, 1997).

——, *Vanities of the Eye: Vision in Early Modern European Culture* (Oxford: Oxford University Press, 2007).

Clasen, C.-P., *Anabaptism, a Social History* (Ithaca, NY: Cornell University Press, 1972).

Cochlaeus, J., *Commentaria de actis et scriptis Martini Lutheri ex ordine ab Anno Domini MDXVII usque ad Annum MDXLVI inclusive, fideliter conscripta* (Mainz: Franz Behem, 1549).

Cohen, D. W., *The Combing of History* (Chicago: University of Chicago Press, 1994).

Cole, R., 'Pamphlet Woodcuts in the Communication Process of Reformation Germany', in K. Sessions and P. N. Bebb (eds), *Pietas et Societas: New Trends in Reformation Social History* (Kirksville, MO: Sixteenth Century Journal Publishers, 1985).

——, 'The Use of Reformation Woodcuts by Sixteenth-Century Printers as a Mediator Between the Elite and Popular Cultures', *Journal of Popular Culture* 21, no. 3 (1987): 111–30.

Collinson, P., *The Elizabethan Puritan Movement* (London: Jonathan Cape, 1967).

——, 'A Comment: Concerning the Name Puritan', *Journal of Ecclesiastical History* 10 (1980): 483–8.

——, *English Puritanism* (London: Historical Association, 1983).

——, *From Iconoclasm to Iconophobia: The Cultural Impact of the Second English Reformation* (Reading: University of Reading Press, 1986).

——, 'Ecclesiastical Vitriol: Religious Satire in the 1590s and the Invention of Puritanism', in J. Guy (ed.), *The Reign of Elizabeth I* (Cambridge: Cambridge University Press, 1995).

Congar, Y.-M., *Tradition and Traditions: An Historical and a Theological Essay* (London: Burns and Oates, 1966).

Corby, P., *Seeing Beyond the Word: Visual Arts and the Calvinist Tradition* (Grand Rapids, MI, and Cambridge: W. B. Eerdmans, 1999).

Coster, W. and Spicer, A., eds, *Sacred Space in Early Modern Europe* (Cambridge: Cambridge University Press, 2005).

Coupe, W. A., *German Political Satires from the Reformation to the Second World War*, 3 vols (White Plains, NY: Kraus International Publications, 1993).

Cressy, D., *Birth, Marriage and Death* (Oxford: Oxford University Press, 1997).

Crick, J. and Walsham, A., *The Uses of Script and Print 1300–1700* (Cambridge: Cambridge University Press, 2003).

Cross, C., 'Community Solidarity among Yorkshire Religious after the Dissolution', in J. Loade (ed.), *Monastic Studies: The Continuity of Tradition* (Bangor: Headstart History, 1990), pp. 245–54.

Crouzet, D., *Les guerriers de Dieu. La violence au temps des troubles de religion, vers 1525–vers 1610* (Seyssel: Champ Vallon, 1990).

Crowther, K., 'From Seven Sins to Lutheran Devils: Sin and Social Order in an Age of Confessionalization', in P. Gilli (ed.), *Les pathologies du pouvoir* (Leiden: Brill, 2016), pp. 481–520.

Daniell, D., *William Tyndale: A Biography* (New Haven and London: Yale University Press, 1994).

——, *The Bible in English*: *History and Influence* (New Haven, CT: Yale University Press, 2003).

Davis, N. Z., 'City women and religious change', in *Society and Culture in Early Modern France* (Stanford, CA: Stanford University Press, 1975).

de Boer, W. and Göttler, C., eds, *Religion and the Senses in Early Modern Europe* (Leiden: Brill, 2012).

Delumeau, J., *Catholicism between Luther and Voltaire: A New View of the Counter-Reformation* (London: Burns and Oates, 1977).

Depperman, K., 'The Anabaptists and the State Churches', in K. von Greyerz (ed.), *Religion and Society in Early Modern Europe, 1500–1800* (London: German Historical Institute, 1984).

Dickens, A. G., 'The Radical Reformation', *Past and Present* 27 (1964): 123–5.

——, *Reformation and Society in Sixteenth Century Europe* (New York: Harcourt, 1966).

——, *Ranke as a Reformation Historian* (Reading: University of Reading Press, 1980).

Dickens, A. G. and Tonkin, J., *The Reformation in Historical Thought* (Cambridge, MA: Harvard University Press, 1985).

Dillenberger, J., *Images and Relics: Theological Perceptions and Visual Images in Sixteenth-Century Europe* (New York: Oxford University Press, 1999).

Dixon, C. S., *The Reformation and Rural Society: The Parishes of Brandenburg-Ansbach-Kulmbach, 1528–1603* (Cambridge: Cambridge University Press, 2002).

——, *Contesting the Reformation* (Oxford: Wiley Blackwell, 2012).

Dixon, C. S., Freist, D. and Greengrass, M., eds, *Living with Religious Diversity in Early Modern Europe* (Farnham: Ashgate, 2009).

Dixon, C. S. and Schorn-Schutte, L., *The Protestant Clergy of Early Modern Europe* (Basingstoke: Macmillan, 2003).

Douglass, J. D., 'Women and the Continental Reformation', in R. R. Ruether, *Religion and Sexism: Images of Woman in the Jewish and Christian Traditions* (New York: Simon & Schuster, 1974).

Driedger, M., 'Anabaptism and Religious Radicalism', in A. Ryrie (ed.), *The European Reformations* (Basingstoke: Macmillan, 2006), pp. 212–32.

Driver, M., *The Image in Print: Book Illustration in Late Medieval England and its Sources* (London: British Library, 2004).

Düfel, H., *Luthers Stellung zur Marienverehrung* (Göttingen: Vandenhoeck u. Ruprecht, 1968).

Duffy, E., *Stripping of the Altars: Traditional Religion in England c.1400– c.1580* (New Haven, CT, and London: Yale University Press, 1993).

Duke, A., *Reformation and Revolt in the Low Countries* (London: Hambledon, 1996).

Dülmen, R. van, 'The Reformation and the modern age', in C. S. Dixon (ed.), *The German Reformation: The Essential Readings* (Oxford: Oxford University Press, 1999), pp. 196–221.

Dykema, P. A. and Oberman, H. A., eds, *Anticlericalism in Late Medieval and Early Modern Europe* (Leiden: Brill, 1993).

Edwards, J. and Truman, R., *Reforming Catholicism in the England of Mary Tudor: The Achievement of Friar Bartolomé Carranza* (Aldershot and Burlington, VT: Ashgate, 2005).

Edwards, K., *Leonarde's Ghost: Popular Piety and 'The Appearance of a Spirit' in 1628*, ed. and trans. in collaboration with S. Speakman Sutch (Kirksville, MO: Truman State University Press, 2008).

Edwards, M., *Printing, Propaganda, and Martin Luther* (Berkeley: University of California Press, 1994).

Eire, C. M. N., *War Against the Idols: The Reformation of Worship from Erasmus to Calvin* (Cambridge: Cambridge University Press, 1986).

——, 'Incombustible Weber: How the Protestant Reformation Really Disenchanted the World', in A. Sterk and N. Caputo (eds), *Historians, Religion, and the Challenge of Objectivity* (Ithaca, NY: Cornell University Press, 2014), ch. 8.

——, *Reformations: The Early Modern World* (New Haven, CT: Yale University Press, 2016).

Eisenstein, E., *The Printing Press as an Agent of Change: Communications and Cultural Transformations in Early Modern Europe* (Cambridge: Cambridge University Press, 1979).

——, 'An Unacknowledged Revolution Revisited', *American Historical Review* 107, no. 1 (2002): 87–105.

——, *The Printing Revolution in Early Modern Europe*, 2nd edn (Cambridge: Cambridge University Press, 2005).

Erasmus, D., *Opera Omnia Desiderii Erasmi Roterodami* (Amsterdam: North-Holland, 1969–).

——, 'Two Forewords to the Latin Translation of the New Testament', in *The Praise of Folly and Other Writings*, trans. R. M. Adams (New York: Norton, 1989).

Evans, G. R., *Problems of Authority in the Reformation Debates* (Cambridge: Cambridge University Press, 1992).

Fairfield, L. P., *John Bale: Mythmaker for the English Reformation* (West Lafayette, IN: Purdue University Press, 1976).

Febvre, L., and Martin, H.-J., *L'apparition du livre* (Paris: A. Michel, 1958).

——, *The Coming of the Book: The Impact of Printing, 1450–1800*, 3rd edn (London: Verso, 2000).

Fentress, F. and Wickham, C., *Social Memory* (Oxford: Oxford University Press, 1992).

Finucane, R. C., *Miracles and Pilgrims: Popular Beliefs in Medieval England* (London: J. M. Dent, 1977).

Firth, K., *The Apocalyptic Tradition in Reformation Britain 1530–1645* (Oxford: Oxford University Press, 1979).

Flesseman van Leer, E., 'The Controversy about Scripture and Tradition Between Thomas More and William Tyndale', *Nederlands Archief voor Kerkesgeschiedenis* 43 (1959): 143–64.

——, 'The Controversy About Ecclesiology between Thomas More and William Tyndale', *Nederlands Archief voor Kerkesgeschiedenis* 44 (1960): 65–86.

Foucault, M., *The Order of Things: An Archaeology of the Human Sciences* (London: Routledge, 2002).

Foxe, J., *Acts and Monuments* (London, 1570).

Freeman, T. S., 'The importance of dying earnestly: the metamorphosis of the account of James Bainham in Foxe's *Book of Martyrs*', in R. N. Swanson (ed.), *The Church Retrospective*, Studies in Church History 33 (Woodbridge: Boydell & Brewer, 1997), pp. 267–88.

——, 'Early modern martyrs', *Journal of Ecclesiastical History* 52 (2001): 696–701.

——, 'Dissenters from a dissenting Church: the challenge of the Freewillers, 1550–1558', in P. Marshall and A. Ryrie (eds), *The Beginnings of English Protestantism* (Cambridge: Cambridge University Press, 2002), pp. 129–56.

——, 'The power of polemic: Catholic attacks on the calendar of martyrs in John Foxe's Acts and Monuments', *Journal of Ecclesiastical History* 61 (2010): 475–95.

Freeman, T. S. and Mayer, T. F., *Martyrs and Martyrdom in England, c. 1400–1700* (Woodbridge: Boydell & Brewer, 2007).

Freeman, T. S. and Wall, S. E., 'Racking the Body, Shaping the Text: The Account of Anne Askew in Foxe's "Book of Martyrs"', *Renaissance*

Quarterly 54, no. 4 (2001): 1165–96, doi:10.2307/1261970.

Frymire, J. M., *The Primacy of the Postils: Catholics, Protestants, and the Dissemination of Ideas in Early Modern Germany* (Leiden: Brill, 2010).

Fudge, T. A., 'Incest and Lust in Luther's Marriage: Theology and Morality in Reformation Polemics', *Sixteenth Century Journal* 34, no. 2 (2003): 319–45.

Fulton, E., 'Touching Theology with Unwashed Hands', in H. Parish, E. Fulton and P. Webster (eds), *The Search for Authority in Reformation Europe* (Farnham: Ashgate, 2015), pp. 89–95.

Gaskill, M., *Crime and Mentalities in Early Modern England* (Cambridge and New York: Cambridge University Press, 2000).

Gee, H. and Hardy, W. H., eds, *Documents Illustrative of English Church History* (New York: Macmillan, 1896).

Geertz, H., 'An Anthropology of Religion and Magic, I', *Journal of Interdisciplinary History* 6 (1975): 71–89.

Geisberg, M., *The German Single Leaf Woodcut 1500–1550* (New York: Hacker Art Book, 1974).

Gentilcore, D., *From Bishop to Witch: The System of the Sacred in Early Modern Terra d'Otranto* (Manchester: Manchester University Press, 1992).

Gerrish, B., *The Old Protestantism and the New: Essays on the Reformation Heritage* (Edinburgh: T&T Clark, 1982).

Gillis, J. R., ed., *Commemorations: The Politics of National Identity* (Princeton, NJ: Princeton University Press, 1996).

Gilmont, J.-F. *Jean Crespin: Un éditeur réformé du XVIe siècle*, Travaux d'Humanisme et de Renaissance 186 (Geneva: Droz, 1981).

Goertz, H.-J., *The Anabaptists* (London: Routledge, 1996).

——, 'Karlstadt, Müntzer and the Reformation of the Commoners', in J. Roth and J. Stayer, *A Companion to Anabaptism and Spiritualism* (Leiden: Brill, 2007).

Gogan, B., *The Common Corps of Christendom: Ecclesiological Themes in the Writings of Sir Thomas More* (Leiden: Brill, 1982).

Gordon, B., *The Swiss Reformation* (Manchester: Manchester University Press, 2004).

——, ed., *Protestant History and Identity in Sixteenth Century Europe*, 2 vols (Aldershot: Scolar Press, 1996).

Gordon, B. and Marshall, P., eds, *The Place of the Dead: Death and Remembrance in Late Medieval and Early Modern Europe* (Cambridge: Cambridge University Press, 2000).

Gowing, L., 'The Haunting of Susan Lay: Servants and Mistresses in Seventeenth-Century England', *Gender and History* 14 (2002): 183–201.

Grafton, A., *What was History? The Art of History in Early Modern Europe* (Cambridge and New York: Cambridge University Press, 2007).

Gray, G. J., 'Fisher's Sermons Against Luther', *The Library*, 3rd series, 4, no. 4 (1912): 55–63.

Greatrex, J., 'On Ministering to "certayne devoute and religiouse women": Bishop Fox and the Benedictine nuns of the Winchester diocese on the eve of the Dissolution', in W. J. Sheils and D. Wood (eds), *Women in the Church*, Studies in Church History, vol. 27 (Oxford: Blackwell, 1989), pp. 223–35.

Gregory, B., *Salvation at Stake: Christian Martyrdom in Early Modern Europe*, Harvard Historical Studies 134 (Cambridge, MA: Harvard University Press, 1999).

——, 'Persecutions and Martyrdom', in R. Po-Chia Hsia (ed.), *The Cambridge History of Christianity*, vol. 6: *Reform and Expansion 1500–1660* (Cambridge: Cambridge University Press, 2007), pp. 261–82.

——, *The Unintended Reformation* (Cambridge, MA: Harvard University Press, 2012).

Grell, O. P., ed., *Paracelsus: The Man and his Reputation, his Ideas and their Transformation* (Leiden: Brill, 1998).

Grell, O. P. and Scribner, R., eds, *Tolerance and Intolerance in the European Reformation* (Cambridge: Cambridge University Press, 1996).

Grieser, J. D., 'Anabaptism, Anticlericalism and the Creation of a Protestant Clergy', *Mennonite Quarterly Review* 71, no. 4 (1997): 515.

Hall, B., 'Puritanism: the Problem of Definition', in G .J. Cuming (ed.), *Studies in Church History*, vol. 2 (Oxford: Blackwell, 1965).

Hamm, B., 'Wie innovativ war die Reformation?', *Zeitschrift für Historische Forschung* 27 (2000): 481–97.

Hanstein, A. L., *Das Jubeljar der evangelischen Kirche: Vie vorbereitende Predigten* (Berlin: n.p., 1817).

Harrington, J. F., *Reordering Marriage and Society in Reformation Germany* (Cambridge: Cambridge University Press, 1995).

Harrington, J. F. and Smith, H., 'Confessionalization, Community, and State-Building in Germany, 1555–1870', *Journal of Modern History* 69 (1997): 77–101.

Haude, S., *In the Shadow of 'Savage Wolves': Anabaptist Munster and the German Reformation During the 1530s* (Leiden: Brill, 2000), p. 26.

Headley, J. M., 'The Reformation as a Crisis in the Understanding of Tradition', *Archiv für Reformationsgeschichte* 78 (1987): 5–22.

Heal, B., 'Images of the Virgin Mary and Marian devotion in Protestant Nuremberg', in B. Naphy and H. Parish (eds), *Religion and 'Superstition' in Reformation Europe* (Manchester: Manchester University Press, 2003).

——, 'Sacred image and sacred space in sixteenth-century Germany', in W. Coster and A. Spicer (eds), *Sacred Space: The Redefinition of Sanctity in Post-Reformation Europe* (Cambridge: Cambridge University Press, 2005).

——, *The Cult of the Virgin Mary in Early Modern Germany: Protestant and Catholic Piety, 1500–1648* (Cambridge: Cambridge University Press, 2007).

Heal, F., *The Reformation in Britain and Ireland* (Oxford: Oxford University Press, 2003).

——, 'What can King Lucius do for you? The reformation and the early British Church', *English Historical Review* 120 (2005): 593–614.

——, 'The bishops and the printers: Henry VII to Elizabeth', in F. M. Heal (ed.), *The Prelate in England and Europe 1300–1600* (York: York Mediaeval Press, 2014), pp. 142–72.

Heid, S., *Clerical Celibacy in the Early Church: The Beginnings of Obligatory Continence for Clerics in East and West*, trans. M. J. Muller (San Francisco: Ignatius Press, 2001).

Heinz, T., 'Die Deutsche Nation und Martin Luther', *Historisches Jahrbuch* 1052 (1985): 426–54.

Hendrix, S., '"We are all Hussites": Hus and Luther Revisited', *Archiv Fur Reformationsgeschichte* 65 (1974): 134–61.

——, 'In Quest of Vera Ecclesia: The Crises of Late Medieval Theology', *Viator* (1976): 347–78.

——, 'Luther on Marriage', *Lutheran Quarterly* 14, no. 3 (2000): 335–50.

Herl, J., *Worship Wars in Early Lutheranism: Choir, Congregation, and Three Centuries of Conflict* (Oxford and New York: Oxford University Press, 2004).

Hinrichs, C., 'Ranke's Lutherfragment von 1817 und der Ursprung seiner univeralhistorischen Anschauung', in R. Nürnberger (ed.), *Festschrift für Gerhard Ritter zu seinem 60. Geburtstag* (Tübingen: J. C. B. Mohr, 1950), pp. 299–321.

——, *Ranke und die Geschichtstheologie der Goethezeit* (Göttingen: Musterschmidt Wissenschaftlicher Verlag, 1954).

Hockenbery Dragseth, J., 'Martin Luther's Views on Bodies, Desire, and Sexuality', *Oxford Research Encyclopedias: Religion*, 2016: DOI:10.1093/acrefore/9780199340378.013.35.

Hohenberger, T., *Lutherische Rechtfertigungslehre in den reformatorischen Flugschriften der Jahre 1521–22* (Tübingen: J. C. B. Mohr, 1996).

Holborn, L., 'Printing and the Growth of a Protestant Movement in Germany from 1517 to 1524', *Church History* 11 (1942): 123–37.

Howard, T. A., 'Protestant Reformation Approaching 500', *First Things*, May 2013, https://www.firstthings.com/blogs/firstthoughts/2013/05/protestant-reformation-approaching (accessed 17 March 2017).

Howard, T. A. and Knoll, M. A., eds, *Protestantism after 500 Years* (Oxford: Oxford University Press, 2016).

Hoyer, S., 'Antiklerikalismus in den Forderungen und Aktionen der Aufstadnischen von 1524–5', in P. A. Dykema and H. A. Oberman (eds), *Anticlericalism in Late Medieval and Early Modern Europe* (Leiden: Brill, 1993), pp. 535–44.

Hruza, K., ed., *Propaganda, Kommunikation und Öffentlichkeit (11.–16. Jahrhundert)* (Vienna: Verlag der Österreichischen Akademie der Wissenschaften, 2002).

Hsia, R. Po-Chia, *Social Discipline in the Reformation: Central Europe, 1550–1750* (London: Routledge, 1989).

Hsu, F. L. K., *Exorcising the Trouble Makers: Magic, Science and Culture* (Westport, CT: Greenwood Press, 1983).

Huggarde, M., *The displaying of the Protestantes, and sondry of their practises, with a description of divers their abuses of late frequented within their malignaunte churche* (London: n.p., 1556), fos 54–5.

Hull, S., *Women According to Men* (Thousand-Oaks, CA, and London: AltaMira Press, 1996).

Hunt, A., *The Art of Hearing: English Preachers and their Audiences, 1590–1640* (Cambridge: Cambridge University Press, 2010).

Husken, U., *Negotiating Rites* (Oxford: Oxford University Press, 2012).

Hutton, R., 'The English Reformation and the Evidence of Folklore', *Past and Present* 148 (1995): 89–116.

Iserloh, E., *The Theses were not Posted: Luther Between Reform and Reformation* (Boston: Beacon Press, 1968).

Israel, J., *The Dutch Republic: Its Rise, Greatness and Fall 1477–1806* (Oxford: Clarendon, 1995).

Further Reading

Jewel, J., *Apology of the Church of England*, ed. J. E. Booty (Ithaca, NY: Cornell University Press, 1963).

Johnson, S., 'Luther's Reformation and (un)holy Matrimony', *Journal of Family History* 17, no. 3 (1992): 271–88.

Johnston, P. and Scribner, R., eds, *The Reformation in Germany and Switzerland* (Cambridge: Cambridge University Press, 1993).

Jordan, C., *Renaissance Feminism: Literary Texts and Politics Models* (Ithaca, NY: Cornell University Press, 1990).

Josephson-Storm, J. A., *The Myth of Disenchantment* (Chicago: University of Chicago Press, 2017).

Kaplan, B., *Divided by Faith: Religious Conflict and the Practice of Toleration in Early Modern Europe* (Cambridge, MA: Harvard University Press, 2007).

Kaplan, B., Moore, R., van Nierop, H. and Pollmann, J., eds, *Catholic Communities in Protestant States: Britain and the Netherlands, c.1570–1720* (Manchester: Manchester University Press, 2009).

Karant-Nunn, S., 'Continuity and Change: Some effects of the Reformation on the Women of Zwickau', *Sixteenth Century Journal* 13 (1982): 17–42.

——, 'The Reformation of Women', in R. Bridenthal, S. M. Stuard and M. E. Wiesner-Hanks, *Becoming Visible: Women in European History* (Boston: Houghton Mifflin, 1998), pp. 175–202.

——, 'Preaching the Word in Early Modern Germany', in L. Taylor (ed.), *Preachers and People in the Reformation and Early Modern Period* (Leiden: Brill, 2001).

Karant-Nunn, S. and Wiesner-Hanks, M. E., eds, *Luther on Women: A Sourcebook* (New York and Cambridge: Cambridge University Press, 2003).

Kastner, R., *Geistliche Rauffhandel: Form und Funktion der illustrierten Flugblatter zum Reformationsjubiläum 1617* (Frankfurt and Berne: Peter Lang, 1982).

——, 'The Reformer and Reformation Annivesaries', *History Today* 33 (1983): 22–3.

Kauffmann, K. H., *Michael Sattler – ein Märtyrer der Täuferbewegung* (Albstadt: Brosamen-Verlag, 2010).

Kess, A., *Johann Sleidan and the Protestant Vision of History* (Burlington: Ashgate, 2008).

Kewes, P., ed., *The Uses of History in Early Modern England* (San Marino, CA: Huntingdon Library, 2006).

Klassen, W., 'The Anabaptist Understanding of the Separation of the Church', *Church History* 46 (1977): 421–36.

——, ed., *Anabaptism in Outline: Selected Primary Sources* (Waterloo: Herald, 1981), p. 178.

Klein, J. L., ed, *Daughters, Wives and Widows: Writings by Men about Women and Marriage in England 1500–1640* (Urbana: University of Illinois Press, 1992).

Knott, J., *Discourses of Martyrdom in English Literature, 1563–1694* (Cambridge: Cambridge University Press, 1993).

Koerner, J. L., *The Reformation of the Image* (Chicago: University of Chicago Press, 2004).

Köhler, H. J., 'The *Flugschriften* and their Importance in Religious Debate: A Quantitative Approach', in P. Zambelli (ed.), *'Astrologi hallucinati': Stars and the End of the World in Luther's Time* (New York: W. de Gruyter, 1986), pp. 153–75.

Kolb, R., *For All the Saints: Changing Perceptions of Martyrdom and Sainthood in the Lutheran Reformation* (Macon, GA: Mercer University Press, 1987).

——, *Martin Luther as Prophet, Teacher and Hero* (Grand Rapids, MI: Baker Books, 1999).

Kolb, R. and Wengert, T., eds, *The Book of Concord: The Confessions of the Evangelical Lutheran Church* (Minneapolis, MN: Fortress Press, 2000).

Kreizer, B., *Reforming Mary: Changing Images of the Virgin Mary in Lutheran Sermons of the Sixteenth Century* (Oxford and New York: Oxford University Press, 2004).

Kuhn, T., *The Structure of Scientific Revolutions*, 2nd edn (Chicago: University of Chicago Press, 1975).

Kupisch, K., *Von Luther zu Bismarck: Zur Kritik einer historischen Idee: Heinrich von Treitschke* (Berlin: Verlag Haus & Schule, 1949).

Kurihara, K., *Celestial Wonders in Reformation Germany* (Abingdon: Routledge, 2014).

Kurtz, B. and Morris, J. G., *The Year-Book of the Reformation* (Baltimore, MD: Publication Rooms, 1844).

Lake, P., *Moderate Puritans and the Elizabethan Church* (Cambridge: Cambridge University Press, 1982).

——, 'Calvinism and the English Church 1570–1635', *Past and Present* 114 (1987): 32–76.

——, 'Defining Puritanism – again?', in F. J. Bremer (ed.), *Puritanism: Transatlantic Perspectives on a Seventeenth-Century Anglo-American*

Faith (Boston: Massachusetts Historical Society, distributed by Northeastern University Press, 1993).

——, 'Anti-Puritanism: The Structure of a Prejudice', in K. Fincham and P. Lake (eds), *Religious Politics in Post-Reformation England* (Woodbridge: Boydell, 2006).

Landry, S. M., 'That All May Be One? Church Unity and the German National Idea, 1866–1883', *Church History* 80, no. 2 (2011): 281–301.

Lavater, L., *De Spectris* (1683).

Lee, P., *Nunneries, Learning, and Spirituality in Late Medieval English Society: The Dominican Priory of Dartford* (Martlesham: Boydell & Brewer/York Medieval Press, 2000).

Lefebvre, H., *The Production of Space*, trans. D. Nicholson-Smith (Oxford: Wiley-Blackwell, 1991).

Lehrich, C., *The Language of Demons and Angels: Cornelius Agrippa's Occult Philosophy* (Leiden: Brill, 2003).

Leonard, A., *Nails in the Wall: Catholic Nuns in Reformation Germany* (Chicago and London: University of Chicago Press, 2005).

Letters and Papers, Foreign and Domestic, Henry VIII, Volume 3, 1519–1523, ed. J. S. Brewer (London, 1867), i.1193, *British History Online*, http://www.british-history.ac.uk/letters-papers-hen8/vol3 (accessed 4 May 2018).

Levi, A., *Renaissance and Reformation: The Intellectual Genesis* (New Haven, CT: Yale University Press, 2002).

Lewis, B., 'Protestantism, Pragmatism and Popular Religion: A Case Study of Early Modern Ghosts', in J. Bath and J. Newton (eds), *Early Modern Ghosts* (Durham: Centre for Seventeenth-Century Studies, 2002).

Lindberg, C., *Beyond Charity: Reformation Initiatives for the Poor* (Minneapolis, MN: Fortress Press, 1993).

——, *The European Reformations* (London: Wiley and Sons, 1996).

——, ed., *The European Reformations Sourcebook* (Malden, MA: Blackwell, 2000).

Lohse, B., *Martin Luther's Theology: Its Historical and Systematic Development*, ed. and trans. R. A. Harrisville (Minneapolis, MN: Fortress Press, 1999).

Lotz-Heumann, U., 'The Natural and Supernatural', in U. Rublack (ed.), *The Oxford Handbook of the Reformation* (Oxford: Oxford University Press, 2017), pp. 688–707.

Lotz-Heumann, U. and Pohlig, M., 'Confessionalization and Literature in the Empire, 1555–1700', *Central European History* 40 (2007): 35–61.

Lowenthal, D., *The Past is a Foreign Country* (Cambridge: Cambridge University Press, 1985).

Luther, M., D. *Martin Luthers Werke: Kritische Gesammtausgabe*, 121 vols (Weimar: Hermann Böhlau/H. Böhlaus Nachfolger, 1883–2009).

——, *Luther's Works*, ed. J. Pelikan and H. T. Lehmann, 55 vols (Philadelphia: Muhlenberg Press, 1957–86).

MacCulloch, D., *Tudor Church Militant: Edward VI and the Protestant Reformation* (London: Penguin, 1999).

——, 'Mary and Sixteenth-century Protestants', in R. N. Swanson (ed.), *The Church and Mary*, Studies in Church History 39 (Woodbridge: Boydell, 2004), pp. 191–207.

——, *Reformation: Europe's House Divided 1490–1700* (London: Penguin, 2004).

Machielsen, J., *Martin Delrio: Demonology and Scholarship in the Counter-Reformation* (Oxford: Oxford University Press, 2015).

Mackenzie, P. A., *Caritas Pirckheimer: A Journal of the Reformation Years, 1524–1528* (Cambridge: D. S. Brewer, 2006).

Maclean, I., *The Renaissance Notion of Woman* (Cambridge: Cambridge University Press, 1980).

Mangrum, B. D. and Scavizzi, G., *A Reformation Debate: Karlstadt, Emser and Eck on Sacred Images: Three Treatises in Translation*, 2nd edn (Toronto: University of Toronto Press, 1998).

Marius, R. C., 'Thomas More and the Early Church Fathers', *Traditio* 24 (1968): 379–407.

——, 'Thomas More's View of the Church', in L. A. Schuster, R. C. Marius and J. P. Lusardi (eds), *The Yale Edition of the Complete Works of St. Thomas More*, vol. 8: *The Confutation of Tyndale's Answer* (New Haven, CT: Yale University Press, 1969), pp. 1269–363.

——, *Martin Luther: The Christian between God and Death* (Cambridge, MA: Harvard University Press, 1999).

Marshall, P., 'The Debate over "Unwritten Verities" in Early Reformation England', in B. Gordon (ed.), *Protestant History and Identity in Sixteenth Century Europe* (Aldershot: Scolar Press, 1996), pp. 60–77.

——, *Beliefs and the Dead in Reformation England* (Oxford: Oxford University Press, 2002).

——, 'Deceptive Appearances: Ghosts and Reformers in Elizabethan and Jacobean England', in H. Parish and W. G. Naphy (eds), *Religion and Superstition in Reformation Europe* (Manchester: Manchester University Press, 2002), pp. 188–209.

——, 'Old Mother Leakey and the Golden Chain: Context and Meaning in an Early Stuart Haunting', in J. Bath and J. Newton (eds), *Early Modern Ghosts* (Durham: Centre for Seventeenth-Century Studies, 2002), pp. 93–109.

——, 'Anticlericalism Revested? Expressions of Discontent in Early Tudor England', in C. Burgess and E. Duffy (eds), *The Parish in Late Medieval England* (Donnington: Shaun Tyas, 2006).

——, *Mother Leakey and the Bishop: A Ghost Story* (Oxford: Oxford University Press, 2009).

——, 'Transformations of the Ghost Story in Post-Reformation England', in H. Conrad-O'Briain and J. A. Stevens (eds), *The Ghost Story from the Middle Ages to the Twentieth Century* (Dublin: Four Courts Press, 2010).

Martyrs Mirror, trans. I. D. Rupp (Lancaster, PA: David Miller, 1837).

Mayer, C. S., 'Henry VIII burns Luther's books, 12 May 1521', *Journal of Ecclesiastical History* 9 (1958): 173–87.

Mayer, T., 'Becket's Bones Burnt! Cardinal Pole and the Invention and Dissemination of an Atrocity', in T. S. Freeman and T. F. Mayer (eds), *Martyrs and Martyrdom in England, c.1400–1700* (Woodbridge: Boydell, 2007), pp. 126–43.

Mayes, D., *Communal Christianity: The Life and Loss of a Peasant Vision in Early Modern Germany* (Leiden: Brill, 2004).

McCullough, P. et al., *The Oxford Handbook of the Early Modern Sermon* (Oxford: Oxford University Press, 2011).

McGrath, A., *Luther's Theology of the Cross: Martin Luther's Theological Breakthrough* (Oxford: Blackwell, 1985).

——, *The Intellectual Origins of the European Reformation* (Oxford: Oxford University Press, 1987).

McKee, E., *Katherina Zell: Church Mother: The Writings of a Protestant Reformer in Sixteenth-Century Germany* (Chicago: University of Chicago Press, 2006).

McKim, D. K., *The Cambridge Companion to John Calvin* (Cambridge: Cambridge University Press, 2004).

McLaughlin, R. E., 'Radicals', in D. M. Whitford (ed.), *Reformation and Early Modern Europe* (Kirksville, MO: Truman State University Press, 2008).

McNamara, J., *Sisters in Arms: Catholic Nuns through Two Millennia* (Cambridge, MA: Harvard University Press, 1998).

McSheffrey, S., *Gender and Heresy: Women and Men in Lollard Communities, 1420–1530* (Philadelphia: University of Pennsylvania Press, 1995).

Melanchthon, P., *Apology of the Augsburg Confession*, 'The Marriage of Priests, article 23', in R. Kolb and T. Wengert (eds), *The Book of Concord: The Confessions of the Evangelical Lutheran Church* (Minneapolis, MN: Fortress Press, 2000).

Merrifield, R., *The Archaeology of Ritual and Magic* (London: Batsford, 1987).

Miles, M., *Visual Understanding in Western Christianity and Secular Culture* (Boston: Beacon Press, 1985).

Milner, M., *The Senses and the English Reformation* (Basingstoke: Routledge, 2011).

Moeller, B., 'Stadt und Buch: Bemerkungen zur Struktur der Reformatorischen Bewegung in Deutschland', in W. J. Mommsen (ed.), *Stadtbürgertum und Adel in der Reformation: Studien zur Socialgeschichte der Reformation in England und Deutschland* (Stuttgart: Klett-Cotta, 1979), pp. 5–39.

——, *Die Reformation und das Mittelalter. Kirchenhistorische Aufsätze* (The Reformation and the Middle Ages: Essays in Church History) (Göttingen: Vandenhoeck & Ruprecht, 1991).

More, T., *Responsio ad Lutherum*, in J. M. Headley, *The Yale Edition of the Complete Works of St. Thomas More* (CW) (New Haven and London: Yale University Press, 1969).

Morrissey, M., *Politics and the Paul's Cross Sermons 1558–1642* (Oxford: Oxford University Press, 2011).

Möseneder, K., *Paracelsus und die Bilder: über Glauben, Magie, und Astrologie im Reformationszeitalter* (Tübingen: Niemeyer, 2009).

Muller, J. A., ed., *The Letters of Stephen Gardiner* (Cambridge: Cambridge University Press, 1933).

Mullett, M., 'Martin Luther's Ninety-Five Theses', *History Today* 46 (September 2003).

Müntzer, T., *Protestation oder Entbietung*, in H. Brandt (ed.), *Thomas Müntzer, Sein Leben und seine Schriften* (Jena: E. Diederichs, 1933), p. 133–44.

Murray, A., 'Missionaries and Magic in Dark-Age Europe', *Past and Present* 136 (1992): 186–205.

Naphy, W. G., ed., *Documents on the Continental Reformation* (Basingstoke: Macmillan, 1996).

Nederman, C. J. and Laursen, J. C., eds, *Difference and Dissent: Theories of Tolerance in Medieval and Early Modern Europe* (Lanham, MD: Rowman & Littlefield, 1996).

Neuhaus, H., 'Martin Luther in Geschichte und Gegenwart: Neuerscheinungen Anläßlich des 500 Geburtstages des Reformators', *Archiv für Kulturgeschichte* 662 (1984): 425–79.

Neusner, J., Frerichs, E. and McCracken Flesher, P. V., eds, *Religion, Science, and Magic: In Concert and In Conflict* (Oxford: Oxford University Press, 1989).

Newman Brooks, P., 'A lily ungilded? Martin Luther, the Virgin Mary and the saints', *Journal of Religious History* 13 (1984): 136–49.

Nicholls, D., 'The Theatre of Martyrdom in the French Reformation', *Past and Present* 121 (1988): 49–73.

Nipperdey, T., 'Luther und die Bildung der Deutschen', in H. Löwe and C.-J. Roepke (eds), *Luther und die Folgen: Beiträge zur sozialgeschichtlichen Bedeutung der lutherischen Reformation* (Munich: Chr. Kaiser, 1983).

——, 'The Reformation and the modern world', in E. I. Kouri and T. Scott (eds), *Politics and Society in Reformation Europe: Essays for Sir Geoffrey Elton on his Sixty-fifth Birthday* (Basingstoke: Macmillan, 1987), pp. 535–45.

Oakley, F., *The Western Church in the Late Middle Ages* (Ithaca, NY: Cornell University Press, 1979).

Oberman, H., *The Harvest of Medieval Theology: Gabriel Biel and Late Medieval Nominalism* (Cambridge, MA: Harvard University Press, 1963).

——, *Dawn of the Reformation: Essays in Late Medieval and Early Reformation Thought* (Edinburgh: T&T Clark, 1986).

——, 'Via Antiqua and Via Moderna: Late Medieval Prolegomena to Early Reformation Thought', *Journal of the History of Ideas* 48, no. 1 (Jan–Mar 1987): 23–40.

——, *The Reformation: Roots and Ramifications*, trans. A. C. Gow (Edinburgh: T&T Clark, 1993).

——, 'The Virgin Mary in Evangelical Perspective', in H. Oberman, *The Impact of the Reformation* (Edinburgh: T&T Clark, 1994).

——, *Luther: Man between God and Devil*, trans. E. Walliser-Schwarzbart (New Haven, CT: Yale University Press, 2006).

——, ed., *Forerunners of the Reformation: The Shape of Late Medieval Thought Illustrated by Key Documents* (New York: Holt, Rinehart and Winston, 1966; Philadelphia: Fortress Press, 1981).

Oettinger, R. W., *Music as Propaganda in the German Reformation* (Aldershot: Ashgate, 2001).

Old, H. O., *The Shaping of the Reformed Baptismal Rite in the Sixteenth Century* (Grand Rapids, MI: Wm. B. Eerdmans, 1992).

Oliva, M., *The Convent and the Community in Late Medieval England* (London: Boydell, 1998).

Ozment, S., *The Age of Reform, 1250–1550: An Intellectual and Religious History of Late Medieval and Reformation Europe* (New Haven, CT: Yale University Press, 1980, 1981).

——, *When Fathers Ruled: Family Life in Reformation Europe* (Cambridge, MA: Harvard University Press, 1985).

——, 'Reinventing Family Life', *Christian History* 12, no. 3 (1993): 22.

——, *Flesh and Spirit: Private Life in Early Modern Germany* (New York: Viking, 1999).

——, ed., *The Reformation in Medieval Perspective* (Chicago: Quadrangle Books, 1971).

Paas, J. R., *The German Political Broadsheet 1600–1700*, 2 vols (Wiesbaden: Harrossowitz, 1986).

Parish, H. L., *Monks, Miracles and Magic: Reformation Representations of the Medieval Church* (London and New York: Routledge, 2005).

——, *Clerical Celibacy in the West 1100–1700* (Aldershot: Ashgate, 2011).

Parish, H. L. and Naphy, W. G., eds, *Religion and Superstition in Reformation Europe* (Manchester: Manchester University Press, 2002).

Parker, M., *Correspondence of Matthew Parker, Archbishop of Canterbury*, ed. J. Bruce (London: Wipf and Stock, 2005).

Patterson, J. A., 'The Church in History: Ecclesiological Ideals and Institutional Realities', in K. H. Easley and C. W. Morgan (eds), *The Community of Jesus: A Theology of the Church* (Nashville, TN: Broadman & Holman, 2013).

Peachey, P., 'The Radical Reformation, Political Pluralism, and the Corpus Christianum', in M. Lienhard (ed.), *The Origins and Characteristics of Anabaptism* (The Hague: Nijhoff, 1997), pp. 83–102.

Pelikan, J., *Mary Through the Centuries: Her Place in the History of Culture* (New Haven, CT, and London: Yale University Press, 1996).

Pettegree, A., 'Books, Pamphlets and Polemic', in A. Pettegree (ed.), *The Reformation World* (London: Routledge, 2000).

——, *Reformation and the Culture of Persuasion* (Cambridge: Cambridge University Press, 2005).

——, ed., *The Reformation: Critical Concepts in Historical Studies* (London: Routledge, 2004).

Pettegree, A. and Hall, M., 'The Reformation and the Book: A reconsideration', *Historical Journal* 47, no. 4 (2004): 785–808.

Phipps, W., *Clerical Celibacy, The Heritage* (London and New York: Continuum, 2004).

Plummer, M. E., 'Clerical Marriage and Territorial Reformation in Ernestine Saxony and the Diocese of Merseburg in 1522–1524', *Archiv für Reformationsgeschichte* 98 (2007): 45–70.

——, '"Partner in his Calamities": Pastors Wives, Married Nuns and the Experience of Clerical Marriage in the Early German Reformation', *Gender and History* 20, no. 2 (2008): 207–27.

——, *Priest's Whore to Pastor's Wife: Clerical Marriage and the Process of Reform in the Early German Reformation* (Farnham: Ashgate, 2012).

Porter, M., *Sex, Marriage and the Church: Patterns of Change* (Victoria, Australia: Dove, 1996).

Racault, L. and Ryrie, A., eds, *Moderate Voices in the European Reformation* (Aldershot: Ashgate, 2005).

Racaut, L., 'The Polemical use of the Albigensian Crusade during the French Wars of Religion', *French History* 13, no. 3 (1999): 261–79.

——, 'Religious polemic and Huguenot self-perception and identity, 1554–1619', in R. A. Mentzer and A. Spicer (eds), *Society and Culture in the Huguenot World 1559–1685* (Cambridge: Cambridge University Press, 2002), pp. 29–43.

Ramussen, T., 'Iconoclasm and Religious Images in the Early Lutheran Tradition', in K. Kolrud (ed.), *Iconoclasm from Antiquity to Modernity* (Farnham: Ashgate, 2014).

Ranke, L. von, *Deutsche Geschichte im Zeitalter der Reformation*, in L. von Ranke, *Sämmtliche Werke*, vols 1–6 (Berlin: Duncker & Humblot, 1867–90).

——, 'Fragment Uber Luther 1817', in L. von Ranke, *Aus Werk und Nachlass: Fruhe Schriften III*, ed. W. P. Fuchs (Munich: Oldenbourg Verlag, 1973).

Rastell, J., *A replie against an answer (false intitled) in Defence of the Truth* (Antwerp: n.p., 1565).

Razzall, L., '"A good Booke is the pretious life-blood of a master-spirit": Recollecting Relics in Post-Reformation English Writing', *Journal of the Northern Renaissance* 2, no. 1 (2010): 93–110.

Reeves, M., 'History and Eschatology: Mediaeval and Early Protestant Thought in Some English and Scottish Writings', *Medievalia et Humanistica*, New Series, 4 (1973): 99–123.

Reinhard, W., 'Reformation, Counter-Reformation, and The Early Modern State, a Reassessment', *Catholic Historical Review* 75, no. 3 (July 1989): 383–404.

Relations politiques des Pays-Bas et de L'Angleterre sous le règne de Philippe II, IV, ed. J. M. B. C. Kervyn de Lettenhove (1885).

Rider, C., *Magic and Religion in Medieval England* (London, Reaktion Books, distributed by University of Chicago Press, 2012).

Ringbom, S., 'Devotional Images and Imaginative Devotions', *Gazette des Beaux Arts*, Series 6, 73 (1969): 159–70.

Ritter, G., Bornkamm, H. and Scheel, O., 'Zur Neugestaltung unserer Zeitschrift', *Archiv für Reformationsgeschichte* 35 (1938): 1–7.

Roberts, P., 'Martyrologies and Martyrs in the French Reformation: Heretics to Subversives in Troyes', in D. Wood (ed.), *Studies in Church History, 30* (Oxford: Blackwell, 1993), pp. 221–9, doi:10.1017/S0424208400011712.

Robinson H., ed., *The Zurich Letters, Comprising the Correspondence of Several English Bishops and Others, with some of the Helvetian Reformers, During the Early Part of the Reign of Queen Elizabeth* (Cambridge: Parker Society, 1842).

Roper, L., 'Luther, Sex, Marriage and Motherhood', *History Today* 33 (1983): 33–8.

——, '"The Common Man", "The Common Good", "Common Women": Gender and Meaning in the German Reformation Commune', *Social History* 12 (1987): 1–21.

——, *The Holy Household: Women and Morals in Reformation Augsburg* (Oxford and New York: Oxford University Press, 1989).

——, 'Gender and the Reformation', *Archiv fur Reformationsgeschichte* 92 (2001): 290–302.

——, 'Martin Luther's Body: the "Stout Doctor" and his Biographers', *American Historical Review* 115, no. 2 (April 2010): 350–84.

——, *Oedipus and the Devil: Witchcraft, Religion and Sexuality in Early Modern Europe* (London: Routledge, 2013).

Roper, L., and Spinks, J., 'Karlstadt's Wagen: The First Visual Propaganda for the Reformation', *Art History: Journal of the Association of Art Historians* 40, no. 2 (April 2017): 256–85.

Roth, J. and Stayer, J., *A Companion to Anabaptism and Spiritualism* (Leiden: Brill, 2007).

Rubin, M., *Corpus Christi: The Eucharist in Late Medieval Culture* (Cambridge: Cambridge University Press, 1991).

Rublack, U., 'Grapho-Relics: Lutheranism and the Materialization of the Word', *Past and Present* 206 (supp. 5) (2010): 144–66.

Rummel, E., 'Biblical Scholarship: Humanist Innovators and Scholastic Defenders of Tradition', in E. Rummel (ed.), *The Humanist–Scholastic Debate in the Renaissance and Reformation* (Cambridge, MA: Harvard University Press, 1995).

——, *Erasmus on Women* (Toronto and London: University of Toronto Press, 1996).

——, *The Confessionalization of Humanism in Reformation Germany* (New York: Oxford University Press, 2000).

Russell, P. A., *Lay Theology in the Reformation: Popular Pamphleteers in Southwest Germany, 1521–1525* (Cambridge: Cambridge University Press, 2002).

Ryrie, A., 'The Problems of Legitimacy and Precedent in English Protestantism, 1539–47', in B. Gordon (ed.), *Protestant History and Identity in Sixteenth Century Europe* (Aldershot: Scolar, 1996).

——, *The Origins of the Scottish Reformation* (Manchester: Manchester University Press, 2006).

——, *Being Protestant in Reformation Britain* (Oxford: Oxford University Press, 2013).

Sattler, M., 'The Schleitheim Confession of Faith', 1527, *Mennonite Quarterly Review* 19, no. 4 (October 1945).

Schilling, H., *Konfessionskonflikt und Staatsbildung* (Gütersloh: Gütersloher Verlagshaus, 1981).

——, 'Confessionalization: Historical and Scholarly Perspectives of a Comparative and Interdisciplinary Paradigm', in J. M. Headley, H. J. Hillerbrand and A. J. Papalas (eds), *Confessionalization in Europe, 1555–1700: Essays in Honor and Memory of Bodo Nischan* (Burlington, VT: Ashgate, 2004).

Schilling, H., and Reinhard, W., 'Konfession und Konfessionalisierung in Europa', in W. Reinhard (ed.), *Bekenntnis und Geschichte: die Confessio Augustana im historischen Zusammenhang* (Munich: Verlag Ernst Vögel, 1981), pp. 165–89.

Schoepffer, J., *Lutherus non combustus sive enarratio de D. M. Luthero eiusque imagine singulari providentia dei T. O. M. duplici vice ab igne miraculosa* (Wittenberg: n.p., 1717).

Schuster, L., 'Reformation Polemic and Renaissance Values', *Moreana* 43–4 (1974): 47–54.

Schwab, W., *Entwicklung und Gestalt der Sakramententheologie bei*

Martin Luther (Frankfurt: P. Lang, 1977).

Schwitalla, J., *Deutsche Flugschriften, 1460–1525: Textortengeschichtliche Studien* (Tübingen: Niemeyer, 1983).

Scot, R., *Discoverie of Witchcraft*, London, pp. 152–3, https://www.bl.uk/collection-items/the-discovery-of-witchcraft-by-reginald-scot-1584 (accessed 4 May 2017).

Scribner, R., 'Incombustible Luther: The Image of the Reformer in Early Modern Germany', *Past and Present* 100 (1986): 36–68.

——, *Popular Culture and Popular Movements in Reformation Germany* (London: Hambledon, 1987).

——, 'Popular Piety and Modes of Visual Perception in Late Medieval and Reformation Germany', *Journal of Religious History* 15, no. 4 (1989): 448–69.

——, 'The impact of the Reformation on Daily Life', in *Mench and Objekt im Mittelalter und in der Fruhen Neuzeit. Leben-Alltag-Kultur* (Vienna: Verlag der Osterreichischen Akademie der Wissenschaften, 1990), pp. 316–443.

——, 'The Reformation, Popular Magic and the Disenchantment of the World', *Journal of Interdisciplinary History* 23 (1993): 475–94.

——, *For the Sake of Simple Folk: Popular Propaganda for the German Reformation* (Oxford: Clarendon, 1994).

——, 'Elements of Popular Belief', in T. Brady, H. Oberman and J. Tracey (eds), *Handbook of European History 1400–1600*, 2 vols (Leiden: Brill, 1994–5).

——, 'Reformation and Desacralisation: From Sacramental World View to Moralised Universe', in R. Scribner and R. Po-Chia Hsia (eds), *Problems in the Historical Anthropology of Early Modern Europe* (Wiesbaden: Harrassowitz, 1997).

Scribner, R. and Benecke, G., eds, *The German Peasant War of 1525 – New Viewpoints* (London: Unwin Hyman, 1979).

Seidemann, J. K., *Thomas Müntzer – Eine Biographie* (Dresden and Leipzig: In der Arnoldischen Buchhandlung, 1842).

Selderhuis, H., *Marriage and Divorce in the Thought of Martin Bucer*, trans. J. Vriend and L. Bierma (Kirksville, MO: Thomas Jefferson University Press at Truman State University Press, 1999).

Sessions, K. and Bebb, P. N., eds, *Pietas et Societas: New Trends in Reformation Social History – Essays in Memory of Harold J. Grimm* (Kirksville, MO: Sixteenth Century Journal Publishers, 1985).

Shagan, E., *Popular Politics and the English Reformation* (Cambridge:

Cambridge University Press, 2002).

Shakespeare, W., Sonnet 73, in *Shakespeare's Sonnets*, ed. K. Duncan-Jones (London: Arden Shakespeare, 2001).

Shaw, D., 'What is religious history?', *History Today* 38, no. 8 (1985).

Shorn-Schutte, L., 'Gefartin und Mitregentin: Zur Sozialgeschichte der evangelischen Pfarrfrau in der Fruhen Neuzeit', in H. Wunder and C. Wanj (eds), *Wandel der Geschlechterbeziehungen zu Beginn der Neuzeit* (Berlin: Suhrkamp Verlag, 1990).

Simpson, J., *Burning to Reading: English Fundamentalism and its Opponents* (Cambridge, MA: Harvard University Press, 2007).

Smith, P., *The Life and Letters of Martin Luther* (Boston and London: Hodder & Stoughton, 1911).

Snyder, C. A., *The Life and Thought of Michael Sattler* (Scottdale, PA: Herald Press, 1984).

Soergel, P. M., *Miracles and the Protestant Imagination: The Evangelical Wonder Book in Reformation Germany* (New York: Oxford University Press, 2012).

Sohm, R., *Kirchenrecht* (Leipzig: Duncher & Humblot, 1892).

Speier, H., *The Truth in Hell and Other Essays in Politics and Culture* (Oxford: Oxford University Press, 1999).

Spicer, A., 'Iconoclasm and adaptation: the reformation of the churches in Scotland and the Netherlands', in D. Gaimser and R. Gilchrist (eds), *The Archaeology of Reformation 1480–1580* (Barnsley: Society for Post-Medieval Archaeology, 2003), pp. 29–43.

——, 'Iconoclasm on the Frontier: le Cateau Cambresis, 1566', in K. Kolrud (ed.), *Iconoclasm from Antiquity to Modernity* (Aldershot: Ashgate, 2014).

Spicer, A. and Coster, W., eds, *Sacred Space in Early Modern Europe* (Cambridge: Cambridge University Press, 2005).

Spicer, A. and Hamilton, S. M., eds, *Defining the Holy: Sacred Space in Medieval and Early Modern Europe* (Aldershot: Ashgate, 2005).

Spierenburg, P., *The Broken Spell: A Cultural and Anthropological History of Preindustrial Europe* (Basingstoke: Macmillan, 1991).

Spohnholz, J., 'Multiconfessional Celebration of the Eucharist in Sixteenth-Century Wesel', *Sixteenth Century Journal* 39, no. 3 (2008): 705–29.

Stein, A., 'Martin Luthers Bedeutung dur die Anfange des Evangelischen Eherechts', *Osterreichisches Archiv fur Kirchenrecht* 34, nos 1–2 (1983–4): 29–95.

Steinmetz, D., 'Luther and Calvin on Church and Tradition', *Michigan Germanic Studies* 10 (Spring/Fall 1984): 98–111.

——, 'The Council of Trent', in D. Bagchi and D. Steinmetz (eds), *The Cambridge Companion to Reformation Theology* (Cambridge: Cambridge University Press, 2004).

Stephenson, B., *Performing the Reformation: Ritual in the City of Luther* (New York: Oxford University Press, 2010).

Stewart, A., 'Paper Festivals and Popular Entertainment: The Kermis Woodcuts of Hans Sebald Beham in Reformation Nuremberg', *Sixteenth Century Journal* 24, no. 2 (1993): 301–50.

Stjerna, K. I., *Women and the Reformation* (Malden, MA: Blackwell, 2009).

Strasser, U., 'Bones of Contention: Cloistered Nuns, Decorated Relics, and the Contest over Women's Place in the Public Sphere of Counter-Reformation Munich', *Archiv für Reformationsgeschichte* 90 (1999): 255–88.

——, *State of Virginity: Gender, Religion, and Politics in an Early Modern Catholic State* (Ann Arbor: University of Michigan Press, 2004).

Strauss, G., 'Local Anticlericalism in Reformation Germany', in P. A. Dykema and H. A. Oberman (eds), *Anticlericalism in Late Medieval and Early Modern Europe* (Leiden: Brill, 1993), pp. 625–38.

Tanner, N., *The Ages of Faith: Popular Religion in Late Medieval England and Western Europe* (London: I.B.Tauris, 2008).

——, ed., *Heresy Trials in the Diocese of Norwich 1428–31* (London: Camden Society, 1977).

Tavard, G. H., *Holy Writ or Holy Church: The Crisis of the Protestant Reformation* (London: Burns and Oates, 1959).

Taylor, L., ed. *Preachers and People in the Reformations and Early Modern Period* (Boston: Brill Academic, 2003).

Taylor, T., *The Prehistory of Sex: Four Million Years of Human Sexual Culture* (London: Fourth Estate, 1996).

Thieleman, J. van Braght, *The bloody theatre, or 'Martyrs' mirror', of the defenceless Christians, who suffered from the time of Christ until 1660*, trans. I. D. Rupp (Scottdale, PA: Herald Press, 1987).

Thomas, K., *Religion and the Decline of Magic: Studies in Popular Beliefs in Sixteenth- and Seventeenth-Century England* (London: Weidenfeld and Nicolson, 1971).

——, 'An Anthropology of Religion and Magic, II', *Journal of Interdisciplinary History* 6 (1975): 91–109.

Todd, M., *The Culture of Protestantism in Early Modern Scotland* (New Haven, CT: Yale University Press, 2002).

Troelstch, E., *Protestantism and Progress: The Significance of Protestantism for the Rise of the Modern World*, trans. W. Montgomery (London: Williams & Norgate, 1912).

——, 'Renaissance and Reformation', in L. Spitz (ed.), *The Reformation: Basic Interpretations* (Lexington, MA: Heath, 1972), pp. 261–96.

——, *The Social Teachings of the Christian Churches*, trans. O. Wyon (Louisville, KY: Westminster/John Knox Press, 1992).

Vandiver, E., Keen, R. and Frazel, T. D., eds, *The Deeds and Writings of Martin Luther from the Year of Our Lord 1517 to the Year 1546 Related Chronologically to all Posterity*, in *Luther's Lives: Two Contemporary Accounts of Martin Luther* (Manchester: Manchester University Press, New York: Palgrave, 2002).

Van Engen, J., 'The Christian Middle Ages as an Historiographical Problem', *American Historical Review* 91 (1986): 519–52.

van Liere, K., Ditchfield, S. and Louthan, H., *Sacred History: Uses of the Christian Past in the Renaissance World* (Oxford: Oxford University Press, 2012).

Vermigli, P. M., *The Oxford Treatise and Disputation on the Eucharist*, 1549, ed. and trans. J. C. McLelland, Sixteenth Century Essays and Studies, vol. 56 (Kirkland, MO: Truman State University Press, 2000).

Vinke, R., ed., *Lutherforschung im 20 Jahrhundert: Rückblick, Bilanz, Ausblick* (Mainz: P. von Zabern, 2004).

Vogler, G., 'Imperial City Nuremberg 1524–5: The Reformation in Transition', in R. Po-Chia Hsia (ed.), *The German People and the Reformation* (Ithaca, NY: Cornell University Press, 1988), pp. 33–51.

Voklmar, C., 'Turning Luther's Weapons against Him: the Birth of Catholic Propaganda in Saxony in the 1520s', in M. Walsby and G. Kemp (eds), *The Book Triumphant: Print in Transition in the Sixteenth and Seventeenth Centuries* (Leiden: Brill, 2011), pp. 115–31.

von Treitschke, H., 'Luther und die deutsche Nation', in H. von Treitschke, *Historische und politische Aufsätze*, vol. 4 (Berlin: S. Hirzel, 1897), pp. 378–94.

Waite, G., 'Between the Devil and the Inquisitor: Anabaptists, Diabolical Conspiracies and Magical Beliefs in the Sixteenth-Century Netherlands', in W. Packull and G. Dipple (eds), *Radical Reformation Studies: Essays Presented to James M. Stayer* (Aldershot: Ashgate, 1999), pp. 120–40.

——, *Eradicating the Devil's Minions: Anabaptists and Witches in Reformation Europe, 1525–1600* (Toronto: University of Toronto Press, 2007).

Walker, D. P., 'The Cessation of Miracles', in I. Merkel and A. Debus (eds), *Hermeticism and the Renaissance* (Washington, DC: Folger Shakespeare Library, 1988), pp. 111–24.

Walsham, A., 'Jewels for Gentlewomen: Religious Books as Artefacts in Late Medieval and Early Modern England', in R. N. Swanson (ed.), *The Church and the Book* (Woodbridge: Boydell & Brewer, 2005), pp. 123–42.

——, 'Miracles in post-reformation England', in K. Cooper and J. Gregory (eds), *Signs, Wonders, Miracles: Representations of Divine Power in the Life of the Church* (Woodbridge: Boydell, 2005), pp. 273–306.

——, *Charitable Hatred: Tolerance and Intolerance in England, 1500–1700* (Manchester: Manchester University Press, 2006).

——, 'Recording Superstition in Early Modern Britain: The Origins of Folklore', in S. A. Smith and A. Knight (eds), *The Religion of Fools? Superstition Past and Present*, Past and Present Supplement 3 (Oxford: Oxford University Press, 2008), pp. 178–206.

——, 'The Reformation and the Disenchantment of the World Reassessed', *Historical Journal* 51, no. 2 (2008): 497–528.

——, 'Like Fragments of a Shipwreck: Printed Images and Religious Antiquarianism in Early Modern England', in M. Hunter (ed.), *Printed Images in Early Modern Britain: Essays in Interpretation* (Aldershot: Ashgate, 2010), pp. 87–109.

——, 'Sermons in the Sky: Apparitions in Early Modern Europe', *History Today* (April 2010): 56–63.

——, 'Skeletons in the Cupboard: Relics after the English Reformation', *Past and Present* 206 (supp. 5) (2010): 121–43.

——, *The Reformation of the Landscape: Religion, Identity and Memory in Early Modern Britain and Ireland* (Oxford: Oxford University Press, 2011).

——, 'History, Memory and the English Reformation', *Historical Journal* 55 (2012): 899–938.

——, 'Migrations of the Holy: Religious Change in Medieval and Early Modern Europe', *Journal of Medieval and Early Modern Studies* 44 (2014): 241–80.

——, 'Domesticating the Reformation: Material Culture, Memory and Confessional Identity in Early Modern England', *Renaissance Quarterly* 69 (2016): 566–616.

Weber, M., *The Protestant Ethic and the Spirit of Capitalism*, trans. T. Parsons (London: George Allen & Unwin, 1930).

Further Reading

Wendel, L. P., *Always Among Us: Images of the Poor in Zwingli's Zurich* (Cambridge: Cambridge University Press, 1990).

——, *Voracious Idols and Violent Hands: Iconoclasm in Reformation Zurich, Strasbourg and Basel* (Cambridge and New York: Cambridge University Press, 1995).

White, H., *Tudor Books of Saints and Martyrs* (Madison: University of Wisconsin Press, 1963).

Wiesner, M. E., 'Nuns, Wives and Mothers: Women and the Reformation in Germany', in S. Marshall (ed.), *Women in Reformation and Counter-Reformation Europe: Public and Private Worlds* (Bloomington: Indiana University Press, 1989).

Wiesner-Hanks, M., 'Luther and Women: The death of two Marys', in J. Obelkevich, L. Roper and R. Samuel (eds), *Disciplines of Faith: Studies in Religion, Politics and Patriarchy* (London and New York: Routledge, 1987).

——, 'Women's response to the Reformation', in R. Po-Chia Hsia, *The German People and the Reformation* (Ithaca, NY: Cornell University Press, 1988).

——, *Christianity and Sexuality in the Early Modern World: Regulating Desire, Reforming Practice* (New York: Routledge, 2000).

——, *Women and Gender in Early Modern Europe*, 2nd edn (Cambridge: Cambridge University Press, 2000).

Witte, J., *From Sacrament to Contract: Marriage, Religion and Law in the Western Tradition* (Louisville, KY: Westminster John Knox Press, 1997).

Wood, D., ed. *Martyrs and Martyrologies: Papers Read at the 1992 Summer Meeting and the 1993 Winter Meeting of the Ecclesiastical History Society*, Studies in Church History 30 (Oxford: Blackwell, 1993).

Woolf, D., *The Social Circulation of the Past: English Historical Culture 1500–1730* (Oxford: Oxford University Press, 2003).

Wright, T., ed., *Three Chapters of Letters Relating to the Suppression of the Monasteries*, 1st series, 26 (London: Camden Society, 1843).

Wunder, H., *He is the Sun, She is the Moon: Women in Early Modern Germany* (Cambridge: Cambridge University Press, 1988).

Yost, J. K., 'The Reformation Defence of Clerical Marriage in the Reigns of Henry VIII and Edward VI', *Church History* 50 (1981): 152–65.

Zapalac, K., *'In His Likeness': Political Iconography and Religious Change in Regensburg, 1500–1600* (Ithaca, NY: Cornell University Press, 1990).

Zika, C., 'Writing the Visual into History: Changing Cultural Perceptions of Late Medieval and Reformation Germany', *Parergon* 11, no. 2 (Dec. 1993): 107–34.

——, 'Reformation Jubilee of 1617: Appropriating the Past through Centenary Celebration', in D. E. Kennedy (ed.), *Authorized Pasts: Essays in Official History* (Melbourne: Melbourne University, 1995), pp. 75–112.

Notes

INTRODUCTION

1 G. Benrath, *Reformierte Kirchengeschichtsschreibung an der Universitat Heidelbert im 16. Und 17. Jahrhundert* (Speyer: Zechnersche Buchdruckerei, 1963), pp. 37–9.

2 J. Schoepffer, *Lutherus non combustus sive enarratio de D. M. Luthero eiusque imagine singulari providentia dei T. O. M. duplici vice ab igne miraculosa* (Wittenberg, 1717).

3 *Das Jubeljar der evangelischen Kirche: Vie vorbereitende Predigten* (Berlin, 1817), p. 31.

4 Papal bull, *Exsurge Domine*, 1520; J. Cochlaeus, *Commentaria de actis et scriptis Martini Lutheri ex ordine ab Anno Domini MDXVII usque ad Annum MDXLVI inclusive, fideliter conscripta* (Mainz: Franz Behem, 1549); *The Deeds and Writings of Martin Luther from the Year of Our Lord 1517 to the Year 1546 Related Chronologically to all Posterity*, in *Luther's Lives: Two Contemporary Accounts of Martin Luther*, trans. and annotated by E. Vandiver, R. Keen and T. D. Frazel (Manchester: Manchester University Press; New York: Palgrave, 2002), pp. 53–5; C. Voklmar, 'Turning Luther's Weapons against Him: the Birth of Catholic Propaganda in Saxony in the 1520s', in *The Book Triumphant: Print in Transition in the Sixteenth and Seventeenth Centuries*, ed. M. Walsby and G. Kemp (Leiden: Brill, 2011), pp. 115–31; D. Bagchi, *Luther's Earliest Opponents: Catholic Controversialists, 1518–1525* (Minneapolis: Fortress, 1991).

5 See, for example, A. G. Dickens and J. Tonkin, *The Reformation in Historical Thought* (Cambridge, MA: Harvard University Press, 1985); B. Gordon (ed.), *Protestant History and Identity in Sixteenth Century*

Europe, 2 vols (Aldershot: Scolar Press, 1996); A. Grafton, *What was History? The Art of History in Early Modern Europe* (Cambridge and New York: Cambridge University Press, 2007); P. Kewes (ed.), *The Uses of History in Early Modern England* (San Marino, CA: Huntingdon Library Press, 2006); K. van Liere, S. Ditchfield and H. Louthan, *Sacred History: Uses of the Christian Past in the Renaissance World* (Oxford: Oxford University Press, 2012); I. Backus, *Historical Method and Confessional Identity in the Era of the Reformation (1378–1615)* (Leiden: Brill, 2003); B. Gregory, 'Persecutions and Martyrdom', in *Cambridge History of Christianity: Reform and Expansion 1500–1660*, Vol. 6, ed. R. Po-Chia Hsia (Cambridge: Cambridge University Press, 2007), pp. 261–82; P. Burschel, *Sterben und Unsterblichkeit: Zur Kultur des Martyriums in der frühen Neuzeit*, Ancien Régime, Aufklärung und Revolution 35 (Munich: Oldenbourg, 2004); B. Gregory, *Salvation at Stake: Christian Martyrdom in Early Modern Europe*, Harvard Historical Studies 134 (Cambridge, MA: Harvard University Press, 1999); R. Kolb, *For All the Saints: Changing Perceptions of Martyrdom and Sainthood in the Lutheran Reformation* (Macon, GA: Mercer University Press, 1987); D. Nicholls, 'The Theatre of Martyrdom in the French Reformation', *Past and Present* 121 (1988): 49–73; J.-F. Gilmont, *Jean Crespin: Un éditeur réformé du XVIe siècle*. Travaux d'Humanisme et de Renaissance 186 (Geneva: Droz, 1981); D. Wood (ed.), *Martyrs and Martyrologies: Papers Read at the 1992 Summer Meeting and the 1993 Winter Meeting of the Ecclesiastical History Society*, Studies in Church History 30 (Oxford: Blackwell, 1993); J. Knott, *Discourses of Martyrdom in English Literature, 1563–1694* (Cambridge: Cambridge University Press, 1993); H. C. White, *Tudor Books of Saints and Martyrs* (Madison: University of Wisconsin Press, 1963).

6   Van Liere, Ditchfield and Louthan, *Sacred History*, p. 186; E. Cameron, 'Primitivism, Patristics and Polemic in Protestant Visions of Early Christianity', in Van Liere, Ditchfield and Louthan, *Sacred History*, pp. 27–51; F. M. Heal, 'What can King Lucius do for you? The reformation and the early British Church', *English Historical Review* 120 (2005): 593–614.

7   C. Zika, 'Reformation Jubilee of 1617: Appropriating the Past through Centenary Celebration', in *Authorized Pasts: Essays in Official History*, ed. D. E. Kennedy (Melbourne: Melbourne University Press, 1995); R. Kastner, *Geistliche Rauffhandel: Form und Funktion der illustrierten*

Flugblatter zum Reformationsjubilaum 1617 (Frankfurt and Berne: Peter Lang, 1982); R. Kastner, 'The Reformer and Reformation Annivesaries', *History Today* 33 (1983): 22–3; J. R. Paas, *The German Political Broadsheet 1600–1700*, 2 vols (Wiesbaden: Harrossowitz, 1986).

8 *Göttlicher Schrifftmessiger, woldenckwürdiger Traum, welchen der Hochlöbliche ... Churfürst zu Sachsen ... dreymal nach einander gehabt hat ...* (London: British Museum, 1880, 0710.299).

9 B. Kurtz and J. G. Morris, *The Year-Book of the Reformation* (Baltimore, MD: Publication Rooms, 1844), pp. 48ff.

10 R. Scribner, 'Incombustible Luther: the Image of the Reformer in Early Modern Germany', *Past and Present* 110 (1986): 38–68.

11 J. L. Kerner, *The Reformation of the Image* (London: Reaktion, 2004).

12 C. Linberg, *The European Reformations* (London: Wiley and Sons, 1996); R. Kolb, *Martin Luther as Prophet, Teacher and Hero* (Grand Rapids, MI: Baker Books, 1999).

13 *Vorlesungen uber die Philosophie der Geschichte.*

14 L. von Ranke, 'Fragment Uber Luther 1817', in L. von Ranke, *Aus Werk und Nachlass: Fruhe Schriften III*, ed. W. P. Fuchs (Munich: Oldenbourg Verlag, 1973); L. von Ranke, *German History in the Age of the Reformation*, 6 vols (Berlin: Duncker & Humblot, 1839–47); A. G. Dickens, *Ranke as a Reformation Historian* (Reading: University of Reading, 1980); C. Hinrichs, 'Ranke's Lutherfragment von 1817 und der Ursprung seiner univeralhistorischen Anschauung', in *Festschrift für Gerhard Ritter zu seinem 60. Geburtstag*, ed. Richard Nürnberger (Tübingen: J. C. B. Mohr, 1950), pp. 299–321; G. Berg, *Leopold von Ranke als akademischer Lehrer: Studien zu seinen Vorlesungen und seinem Geschichtsdenken* (Göttingen: Vandenhoeck & Ruprecht, 1968), pp. 109–13; C. Hinrichs, *Ranke und die Geschichtstheologie der Goethezeit* (Göttingen: Musterschmidt Wissenschaftlicher Verlag, 1954); L. von Ranke, *Deutsche Geschichte im Zeitalter der Reformation*, in L. von Ranke, *Sämmtliche Werke*, vols 1–6 (Berlin: Duncker & Humblot, 1867–90).

15 K. Kupisch, *Von Luther zu Bismarck: Zur Kritik einer historischen Idee: Heinrich von Treitschke* (Berlin: Verlag Haus & Schule, 1949); S. M. Landry, 'That All May Be One? Church Unity and the German National Idea, 1866–1883', *Church History* 80, no. 2 (2011): 281–301; H. von Treitschke, 'Luther und die deutsche Nation', in H. von Treitschke, *Historische und politische Aufsätze*, vol. 4 (Berlin: S. Hirzel, 1897),

pp. 378–94; T. Nipperdey, 'Luther und die Bildung der Deutschen', in *Luther und die Folgen: Beiträge zur sozialgeschichtlichen Bedeutung der lutherischen Reformation*, ed. H. Löwe and C.-J. Roepke (Munich: Chr. Kaiser, 1983), p. 27.

16 G. Ritter, H. Bornkamm and O. Scheel, 'Zur Neugestaltung unserer Zeitschrift', *Archiv für Reformationsgeschichte* 35 (1938): 1–7.

17 The origins of this approach are seen most clearly in, for example, H. Oberman, *The Harvest of Medieval Theology: Gabriel Biel and Late Medieval Nominalism* (Cambridge, MA: Harvard University Press, 1963; Grand Rapids, MI: Baker Academic, 2001); H. Oberman, *Dawn of the Reformation: Essays in Late Medieval and Early Reformation Thought* (Edinburgh: T&T Clark, 1986); H. Oberman, *The Reformation: Roots and Ramifications*, trans. A. C. Gow (Edinburgh: T&T Clark, 1993); H. Oberman (ed.), *Forerunners of the Reformation: The Shape of Late Medieval Thought* (New York: Holt, Rinehart and Winston, 1966; Philadelphia: Fortress Press, 1981); R. J. Bast and A. C. Gow (eds), *Continuity and Change: The Harvest of Late Medieval and Reformation History: Essays Presented to Heiko A. Oberman on His 70th Birthday* (Leiden: Brill, 2000); S. Ozment (ed.), *The Reformation in Medieval Perspective* (Chicago: Quadrangle Books, 1971); S. Ozment, *The Age of Reform, 1250–1550: An Intellectual and Religious History of Late Medieval and Reformation Europe* (New Haven, CT: Yale University Press, 1980, 1981). See also P. Blickle, *Die Gemeindereformation: Die Menschen des 16. Jahrhunderts auf dem Weg zum Heil* (Munich: Oldenbourg, 1987); B. Moeller, *Die Reformation und das Mittelalter. Kirchenhistorische Aufsätze* [The Reformation and the Middle Ages: Essays in Church History] (Göttingen: Vandenhoeck & Ruprecht, 1991); B. Hamm, 'Wie innovativ war die Reformation?', *Zeitschrift für Historische Forschung* 27 (2000): 481–97; A. Levi, *Renaissance and Reformation: The Intellectual Genesis* (New Haven, CT: Yale University Press, 2002).

18 H. Schilling, *Konfessionskonflikt und Staatsbildung* (Gütersloh, Germany: Gütersloher Verlagshaus, 1981); W. Reinhard, 'Konfession und Konfessionalisierung in Europa', in *Bekenntnis und Geschichte: die Confessio Augustana im historischen Zusammenhang*, ed. W. Reinhard (Munich: Verlag Ernst Vögel, 1981), pp. 165–89; H. Schilling, 'Confessionalization: Historical and Scholarly Perspectives of a Comparative and Interdisciplinary Paradigm', in *Confessionalization in Europe, 1555–1700: Essays in Honor and Memory of Bodo Nischan*,

ed. J. M. Headley, H. J. Hillerbrand and A. J. Papalas (Burlington, VT: Ashgate, 2004); W. Reinhard, 'Reformation, Counter-Reformation, and The Early Modern State a Reassessment', *Catholic Historical Review* 75, no. 3 (July 1989): 383; Cf. T. A. Brady, Jr, 'Confessionalization: The Career of a Concept', in *Confessionalization in Europe, 1555–1700: Essays in Honor and Memory of Bodo Nischan*, ed. J. M. Headley, H. J. Hillerbrand and A. J. Papalas (Burlington, VT: Ashgate, 2004), pp. 1–20. See also the synthesis in J. F. Harrington and H. W. Smith, 'Confessionalization, Community, and State-Building in Germany, 1555–1870', *Journal of Modern History* 69 (1997): 77–101.

19 R. Po-Chia Hsia, *Social Discipline in the Reformation: Central Europe, 1550–1750* (London: Routledge, 1989); E. Rummel, *The Confessionalization of Humanism in Reformation Germany* (New York: Oxford University Press, 2000); C. S. Dixon, *The Reformation and Rural Society: The Parishes of Brandenburg-Ansbach-Kulmbach, 1528–1603* (Cambridge: Cambridge University Press, 2002); B. Kaplan, *Divided by Faith: Religious Conflict and the Practice of Toleration in Early Modern Europe* (Cambridge, MA: Harvard University Press, 2007); J. Spohnholz, 'Multiconfessional Celebration of the Eucharist in Sixteenth-Century Wesel', *Sixteenth Century Journal* 39, no. 3 (2008); U. Lotz-Heumann and M. Pohlig, 'Confessionalization and Literature in the Empire, 1555–1700', *Central European History* 40 (2007); C. S. Dixon, C. Scott, D. Freist and M. Greengrass (eds), *Living with Religious Diversity in Early Modern Europe* (Farnham: Ashgate, 2009); O. P. Grell and R. Scribner (eds), *Tolerance and Intolerance in the European Reformation* (Cambridge: Cambridge University Press, 1996); B. Kaplan, R. Moore, H. van Nierop and J. Pollmann (eds), *Catholic Communities in Protestant States: Britain and the Netherlands, c.1570–1720* (Manchester: Manchester University Press, 2009; C. J. Nederman and J. C. Laursen (eds), *Difference and Dissent: Theories of Tolerance in Medieval and Early Modern Europe* (Lanham, MD: Rowman & Littlefield, 1996); L. Racault and A. Ryrie (eds), *Moderate Voices in the European Reformation* (Aldershot: Ashgate, 2005); A. Walsham, *Charitable Hatred: Tolerance and Intolerance in England, 1500–1700* (Manchester: Manchester University Press, 2006).

20 M. Wiesner-Hanks, *Christianity and Sexuality in the Early Modern World: Regulating Desire, Reforming Practice* (New York: Routledge, 2000); S. C. Karant-Nunn and M. E. Wiesner-Hanks (eds), *Luther on Women: A Sourcebook* (Cambridge: Cambridge University Press, 2003);

L. Roper, *The Holy Household: Women and Morals in Reformation Augsburg* (New York: Oxford University Press, 1989; L. Roper, *Oedipus and the Devil: Witchcraft, Religion and Sexuality in Early Modern Europe* (London: Routledge, 2013); K. I. Stjerna, *Women and the Reformation* (Malden, MA: Blackwell, 2009); M. Plummer, *Priest's Whore to Pastor's Wife: Clerical Marriage and the Process of Reform in the Early German Reformation*, St. Andrews Studies in Reformation History (Farnham: Ashgate, 2012); S. Ozment, *When Fathers Ruled: Family Life in Reformation Europe* (Cambridge, MA: Harvard University Press, 1985).

21 The 1545 edition of the Luther Bible shows the Whore of Babylon (from the *Book of Revelation*) wearing the papal tiara; see also Luther's 1520 pamphlet *Babylonian Captivity of the Church*, and Lucas Cranach the Elder's illustrations for Luther's German translation of the *New Testament* (1522). K. Firth, *The Apocalyptic Tradition in Reformation Britain 1530–1645* (Oxford: Oxford University Press, 1979), and R. Bauckham, *Tudor Apocalypse: Sixteenth Century Apocalypticism, Millenarianism, and the English Reformation from John Bale to John Foxe and Thomas Brightman*, Courtenay Library of Reformation Classics, vol. 8 (Oxford: Sutton Courtenay Press, 1978). For the nature of medieval prophecies of Antichrist and the influence of such prophecies, especially that of Joachim of Fiore, on Protestant polemic, see Bauckham, *Tudor Apocalypse*, pp. 10–33; Firth, *The Apocalyptic Tradition*, pp. 1–15; M. Reeves, 'History and Eschatology: Mediaeval and Early Protestant Thought in Some English and Scottish Writings', *Medievalia et Humanistica*, New Series, 4 (1973): 99–123.

22 R. W. Scribner, *For the Sake of Simple Folk: Popular Propaganda for the German Reformation* (Cambridge: Cambridge University Press, 1981); M. Edwards, *Printing, Propaganda, and Martin Luther* (Berkeley: University of California Press, 1994); L. Febvre and H.-J. Martin, *L'apparition du livre* (Paris: A. Michel, 1958); L. Febvre and H.-J. Martin, *The Coming of the Book: The Impact of Printing, 1450–1800*, 3rd edn (London: Verso, 2000); K. Hruza (ed.), *Propaganda, Kommunikation und Öffentlichkeit (11.–16. Jahrhundert)* (Vienna: Verlag der Österreichischen Akademie der Wissenschaften, 2002); P. A. Russell, *Lay Theology in the Reformation: Popular Pamphleteers in Southwest Germany, 1521–1525* (Cambridge: Cambridge University Press, 2002); A. Pettegree, *Reformation and the Culture of Persuasion* (Cambridge: Cambridge University Press, 2005); E. L. Eisenstein, *The*

Printing Press as an Agent of Change (Cambridge: Cambridge University Press, 1979); E. L. Eisenstein, 'An Unacknowledged Revolution Revisited', *American Historical Review* 107, no. 1 (2002): 87–105; E. L. Eisenstein, *The Printing Revolution in Early Modern Europe*, 2nd edn (Cambridge: Cambridge University Press, 2005); J. Schwitalla, *Deutsche Flugschriften, 1460–1525: Textortengeschichtliche Studien* (Tübingen: Niemeyer, 1983); L. Roper and J. Spinks, 'Karlstadt's Wagen: The First Visual Propaganda for the Reformation', *Art History: Journal of the Association of Art Historians* 40, no. 2 (April 2017): 256–85.

23 M. Milner, *The Senses and the English Reformation* (London: Routledge, 2011); W. de Boer and C. Göttler (eds), *Religion and the Senses in Early Modern Europe* (Leiden: Brill, 2012); J. M. Frymire, *The Primacy of the Postils: Catholics, Protestants, and the Dissemination of Ideas in Early Modern Germany* (Leiden: Brill, 2010); C. Brown, *Singing the Gospel: Lutheran Hymns and the Success of the Reformation* (Cambridge, MA: Harvard University Press, 2005); L. Taylor (ed.), *Preachers and People in the Reformations and Early Modern Period* (Boston: Brill Academic, 2003); R. W. Oettinger, *Music as Propaganda in the German Reformation* (Aldershot: Ashgate, 2001); A. Walsham, *The Reformation of the Landcape: Religion, Identity and Memory in Early Modern Britain and Ireland* (Oxford: Oxford University Press, 2011); A. Walsham, 'Recording Superstition in Early Modern Britain: The Origins of Folklore', in *The Religion of Fools? Superstition Past and Present*, Past and Present Supplement 3, ed. S. A. Smith and A. Knight (Oxford: Oxford University Press, 2008), pp. 178–206; A. Walsham, 'Like Fragments of a Shipwreck: Printed Images and Religious Antiquarianism in Early Modern England', in *Printed Images in Early Modern Britain: Essays in Interpretation*, ed. M. Hunter (Aldershot: Ashgate, 2010), pp. 87–109; A. Walsham, 'History, Memory and the English Reformation', *Historical Journal* 55 (2012): 899–938.

24 A. Walsham, 'Domesticating the Reformation: Material Culture, Memory and Confessional Identity in Early Modern England', *Renaissance Quarterly* 69 (2016): 566–616; C. C. Christensen, *Art and the Reformation in Germany* (Athens: Ohio University Press, 1979; J. Dillenberger, *Images and Relics: Theological Perceptions and Visual Images in Sixteenth-Century Europe* (New York: Oxford University Press, 1999); A. Walsham, 'Migrations of the Holy: Religious Change in Medieval and Early Modern Europe', *Journal of Medieval and Early Modern Studies* 44 (2014): 241–80; J. L. Koerner, *The Reformation of*

the Image (Chicago: University of Chicago Press, 2004); B. Heal, *The Cult of the Virgin Mary in Early Modern Germany: Protestant and Catholic Piety, 1500–1648* (Cambridge: Cambridge University Press, 2007).

25 R. W. Scribner, *Popular Culture and Popular Movements in Reformation Germany* (London: Hambledon, 1987); K. Thomas, *Religion and the Decline of Magic: Studies in Popular Beliefs in Sixteenth- and Seventeenth-Century England* (London: Weidenfeld and Nicolson, 1971); C. S. Dixon, D. Freist and M. Greengrass (eds), *Living with Religious Diversity in Early Modern Europe* (Farnham: Ashgate, 2009); D. Mayes, *Communal Christianity: The Life and Loss of a Peasant Vision in Early Modern Germany* (Leiden: Brill, 2004); W. Coster and A. Spicer (eds), *Sacred Space in Early Modern Europe* (Cambridge: Cambridge University Press, 2005); M. Todd, *The Culture of Protestantism in Early Modern Scotland* (New Haven, CT: Yale University Press, 2002).

CHAPTER 1: IN THE POWER OF GOD ALONE?

1 For an accessible introduction to the shift from ecclesiastical history to religious history in recent scholarship, see D. Shaw, 'What is religious history?', *History Today* 38, no. 8 (1985).

2 R. J. Bast, *The Reformation of Faith in the Context of Late Medieval Theology and Piety* (Leiden: Brill, 2004); A. E. McGrath, *The Intellectual Origins of the European Reformation* (Oxford: Oxford University Press, 1987); S. Ozment, *The Age of Reform, 1250–1550: An Intellectual and Religious History of Late Medieval and Reformation Europe* (New Haven, CT: Yale University Press, 1981).

3 D. Bagchi and D. Steinmetz (eds), *The Cambridge Companion to Reformation Theology* (Cambridge: Cambridge University Press, 2006), pp. 4–5.

4 F. Capon, *Newsweek*, 12 February 2015, http://www.newsweek.com/martin-luther-playmobil-toy-sells-out-germany-following-record-breaking-demand-306329.

5 E. Iserloh, *The Theses were not Posted: Luther Between Reform and Reformation* (Boston: Beacon Press, 1968).

6 Ibid., pp. 66–73.

7 The same vocabulary is evident in Brad Gregory's assessment of the

impact of Protestantism, *The Unintended Reformation* (Boston, MA: Harvard University Press, 2012).

8   M. Mullett, 'Martin Luther's Ninety-Five Theses', *History Today* 46 (September 2003).

9   B. Stephenson, *Performing the Reformation: Ritual in the City of Luther* (New York: Oxford University Press, 2010), p. 91; U. Husken, *Negotiating Rites* (Oxford: Oxford University Press, 2012), p. 91.

10 See, for example, M. Arnold, 'De l'hérétique Allemand au témoin œcumenique de Jesus-Christ: La biographie de Martin Luther au XXe siècle, a la croisée des ecoles historiographiques Françaises et Allemandes', *Revue d'Allemagne* 334 (2001): 395–412; H. Neuhaus, 'Martin Luther in Geschichte und Gegenwart: Neuerscheinungen Anläßlich des 500 Geburtstages des Reformators', *Archiv für Kulturgeschichte* 662 (1984): 425–79; R. Vinke (ed.), *Lutherforschung im 20 Jahrhundert: Rückblick, Bilanz, Ausblick* (Mainz: P von Zabern, 2004); R. H. Bainton, *Here I Stand: A Life of Martin Luther* (Peabody, MA: Hendrickson, 2009); M. Brecht, *Martin Luther*, trans. James L Schaaf, 3 vols (Philadelphia: Fortress, 1985); R. Marius, *Martin Luther: The Christian between God and Death* (Cambridge, MA: Harvard University Press, 1999); H. Oberman, *Luther: Man between God and Devil*, trans. E. Walliser-Schwarzbart (New Haven, CT: Yale University Press, 2006); T. Heinz, 'Die Deutsche Nation und Martin Luther', *Historisches Jahrbuch* 1052 (1985): 426–54; C. Bultmann, V. Leppin and A. Lindner (eds), *Luther und das monastische Erbe* (Tübingen: Mohr Siebeck, 2007); W. Schwab, *Entwicklung und Gestalt der Sakramententheologie bei Martin Luther* (Frankfurt: P. Lang, 1977); P. Althaus, *The Theology of Martin Luther*, trans. R. C. Schultz (Philadelphia: Fortress, 1966); B. Lohse, *Martin Luther's Theology: Its Historical and Systematic Development*, ed. and trans. R. A. Harrisville (Minneapolis: Fortress, 1999); T. Hohenberger, *Lutherische Rechtfertigungslehre in den reformatorischen Flugschriften der Jahre 1521–22* (Tübingen: J. C. B. Mohr, 1996); A. McGrath, *Luther's Theology of the Cross: Martin Luther's Theological Breakthrough* (Oxford: Blackwell, 1985).

11 M. Luther, *Luther's Works* [hereafter, *LW*], ed. J. Pelikan and H. T. Lehmann, 55 vols (Philadelphia: Muhlenberg Press, 1957–86), XLVIII, 24.

12 For a discussion of these themes in a variety of contexts, see N. Tanner, *The Ages of Faith: Popular Religion in Late Medieval England and Western Europe* (London: I.B.Tauris, 2008), and, in the English

context, G. Bernard, *The Late Medieval English Church: Vitality and Vulnerability Before the Break with Rome* (New Haven, CT: Yale University Press, 2012).

13 A. McGrath, *The Intellectual Origins of the European Reformation* (Oxford: Wiley, 2004), p. 27.

14 The term 'harvest of medieval theology' is taken from Heiko Oberman's book of the same name, *The Harvest of Medieval Theology: Gabriel Biel and Late Medieval Nominalism* (Cambridge, MA: Harvard University Press, 1963). See also Bast, *The Reformation of Faith*; A. E. McGrath, *The Intellectual Origins of the European Reformation* (Oxford: Oxford University Press, 1987); S. Ozment, *The Age of Reform, 1250–1550: An Intellectual and Religious History of Late Medieval and Reformation Europe* (New Haven, CT: Yale University Press, 1981).

15 W. G. Naphy (ed.), *Documents on the Continental Reformation* (Basingstoke: Macmillan, 1996), no. 11.

16 Ibid., no. 12.

17 P. Johnston and R. Scribner (eds), *The Reformation in Germany and Switzerland* (Cambridge: Cambridge University Press, 1993), p. 13.

18 M. Bachmann (ed.), *Lutherische und neue Paulusperspektive: Beiträge zu einem Schlüsselproblem der gegenwärtigen exegetischen Diskussion* (Tübingen: Mohr Siebeck, 2005); T. Hohenberger, *Lutherische Rechtfertigungslehre in den reformatorischen Flugschriften der Jahre 1521–22* (Tübingen: J. C. B. Mohr, 1996); A. McGrath, *Luther's Theology of the Cross: Martin Luther's Theological Breakthrough* (Oxford: Blackwell, 1985).

19 *LW* 26: 26, 116.

20 *LW* 26: 136, 198, 285, 395.

21 *LW* 26: 30, 224, 247.

22 *LW* 26: 26–7.

23 C. Lindberg, *The European Reformations* (London: John Wiley and Sons, 1999), p. 161; A. Pettegree (ed.), *The Reformation: Critical Concepts in Historical Studies* (London: Routledge, 2004), p. 257; A. Ryrie, *The Origins of the Scottish Reformation* (Manchester: Manchester University Press, 2006), p. 36; B. Gordon, *The Swiss Reformation* (Manchester: Manchester University Press, 2004), p. 54; Oberman, *Man Between God and the Devil*.

24 These questions are addressed in more detail in Chapter 2, below.

25 M. Luther, *D. Martin Luthers Werke: Kritische Gesammtausgabe* [hereafter, *WA*], 121 vols (Weimar: Hermann Böhlau; H. Böhlaus

Nachfolger, 1883–2009), 2.42.22; S. Hendrix, '"We are all Hussites": Hus and Luther Revisited', *Archiv Fur Reformationsgeschichte* 65 (1974): 134–61; S. Hendrix, 'In Quest of Vera Ecclesia: The Crises of Late Medieval Theology', *Viator* (1976): 347–78.

26 Gregory, *The Unintended Reformation*, p. 86.

27 F. Oakley, *The Western Church in the Late Middle Ages* (Ithaca, NY: Cornell University Press, 1979), p. 157; H. Oberman, *Forerunners of the Reformation: The Shape of Late Medieval Thought* (New York: Hold, Rinehart and Winston, 1966); H. A. Oberman, 'Via Antiqua and Via Moderna: Late Medieval Prolegomena to Early Reformation Thought', *Journal of the History of Ideas* 48, no. 1 (January–March 1987): 23–40; J. Brevicoxa, '*A Treatise on Faith, the Church, the Roman Pontiff, and the General Council*', trans. in *Forerunners of the Reformation*, ed. Heiko A. Oberman (Philadelphia: Fortress, 1981); G. Biel, *Exposition of the Canon of the Mass* (1495).

28 Oberman, *Man Between God and the Devil*, p. 118.

29 *WA*: 6.322. 1ff.

30 *WA*: 6.322. 1ff.

31 The statements were added by the first editor of Luther's collected works, George Rorer.

CHAPTER 2: THE REFORMATION AND DISSEMINATION OF IDEAS

1 *Calendar of State Papers Relating To English Affairs in the Archives of Venice, Volume 3, 1520–1526*, ed. R. Brown (London, 1869), 121 n.208, *British History Online*, http://www.british-history.ac.uk/cal-state-papers/venice/vol3 (accessed 4 May 2018); C. S. Mayer, 'Henry VIII burns Luther's books, 12 May 1521', *Journal of Ecclesiastical History* 9 (1958): 173–87.

2 G. J. Gray, 'Fisher's Sermons Against Luther', *The Library*, 3rd series, 4, no. 4 (1912): 55–63; F. Heal, 'The bishops and the printers: Henry VII to Elizabeth', in M. Heal (ed.), *The Prelate in England and Europe 1300–1600* (York: York Mediaeval Press, 2014), pp. 142–72.

3 Mayer, 'Henry VIII burns Luther's books', 174, 176.

4 *Letters and Papers, Foreign and Domestic, Henry VIII, Volume 3, 1519–1523*, ed. J. S. Brewer (London, 1867), i.1193, *British History Online*, http://www.british-history.ac.uk/letters-papers-hen8/vol3 (accessed 4 May 2018).

5   God's gift was granted notwithstanding the possibility that the greed and self-interest of the printers might at times obstruct the enactment of this ambition. John Foxe, *Acts and Monuments* (London, 1570), p. 837; E. Eisenstein, *The Printing Press as an Agent of Change: Communications and Cultural Transformations in Early Modern Europe*, 2 vols (Cambridge: Cambridge University Press, 1979), I, p. 373.

6   A. G. Dickens, *Reformation and Society in Sixteenth Century Europe* (New York: Harcourt, 1966), p. 51.

7   Ibid. See also L. Holborn, 'Printing and the Growth of a Protestant Movement in Germany from 1517 to 1524', *Church History* 11 (1942): 123–37; Eisenstein, *The Printing Press as an Agent of Change*, 1, pp. 303–450; B. Moeller, 'Stadt und Buch: Bemerkungen zur Struktur der Reformatorischen Bewegung in Deutschland', in Wolfgang J. Mommsen (ed.), *Stadtbürgertum und Adel in der Reformation: Studien zur Socialgeschichte der Reformation in England und Deutschland* (Stuttgart: Klett-Cotta, 1979), pp. 25–39.

8   Dickens, *Reformation and Society*, p. 51.

9   Eisenstein, *The Printing Press as an Agent of Change*, p. 450.

10 M. U. Edwards, *Printing, Propaganda, and Martin Luther* (Berkeley: University of California Press, 1994), p. 1.

11 See H.-J. Köhler, 'The *Flugschriften* and their Importance in Religious Debate: A Quantitative Approach', in Paola Zambelli (ed.), *'Astrologi hallucinati': Stars and the End of the World in Luther's Time* (New York: W. de Gruyter, 1986), pp. 153–75.

12 T. Hohenberger, *Lutherische Rechtfertigungslehre in den reformatorischen Flugschriften der Jahre 1521–1522* (Tübingen: J. C. B. Mohr, 1996), p. 396.

13 Edwards, *Printing*, p. 28.

14 A. Pettegree and M. Hall, 'The Reformation and the Book: A reconsideration', *Historical Journal* 47, no. 4 (2004): 785.

15 A. Pettegree, 'Books, Pamphlets and Polemic' in A. Pettegree (ed.), *The Reformation World* (London: Routledge, 2000), p. 109.

16 Edwards, *Printing*, p. 8.

17 A. Pettegree, *Reformation and the Cultures of Persuasion* (Cambridge: Cambridge University Press, 2005), pp. 156–8.

18 Edwards, *Printing*, introduction.

19 P. Smith, *The Life and Letters of Martin Luther* (Boston and London: Hodder & Stoughton, 1911), pp. 43–4.

20 M. U. Chrisman, *Lay Culture, Learned Culture: Books and Social Change in Strasbourg, 1480–1599* (New Haven, CT: Yale University Press, 1982).

21 M. Morrissey, *Politics and the Paul's Cross Sermons 1558–1642* (Oxford: Oxford University Press, 2011); A. Hunt, *The Art of Hearing: English Preachers and their Audiences, 1590–1640* (Cambridge: Cambridge University Press, 2010); P. McCullough et al., *The Oxford Handbook of the Early Modern Sermon* (Oxford: Oxford University Press, 2011). Morrissey concludes that the text recorded in manuscript or print may safely be treated as a 'different version' of the words delivered in the pulpit, and 'not a separate composition'. S. C. Karant-Nunn, 'Preaching the Word in Early Modern Germany', in L. Taylor (ed.), *Preachers and People in the Reformation and Early Modern Period* (Leiden: Brill: 2001), pp. 203–4; A. Ryrie, *Being Protestant in Reformation Britain* (Oxford: Oxford University Press, 2013), pp. 351–62.

22 J. Crick and A. Walsham, *The Uses of Script and Print 1300–1700* (Cambridge: Cambridge University Press, 2003), p. 152.

23 See, for example, C. B. Brown, *Singing the Gospel: Lutheran Hymns and the Success of the Reformation* (Cambridge, MA: Harvard University Press, 2005); J. Herl, *Worship Wars in Early Lutheranism: Choir, Congregation, and Three Centuries of Conflict* (Oxford and New York: Oxford University Press, 2004); and R. W. Oettinger, *Music as Propaganda in the German Reformation* (Burlington: Ashgate, 2001); Edwards *Printing*, p. 39.

24 Brown, *Singing the Gospel*, pp. 8–9, 86–7.

25 R. W. Scribner, *Popular Culture and Popular Movements in Reformation Germany* (London: Hambledon, 1987), pp. 61–2, 104.

26 The best introduction to the visual propaganda for the German Reformation is R. Scribner, *For the Sake of Simple Folk: Popular Propaganda for the German Reformation* (Oxford: Clarendon, 1994). See also Chrisman, *Lay Culture*; Edwards, *Printing*; R. G. Cole, 'The Use of Reformation Woodcuts by Sixteenth-Century Printers as a Mediator Between the Elite and Popular Cultures', *Journal of Popular Culture* 21, no. 3 (1987): 111–30; A. Stewart, 'Paper Festivals and Popular Entertainment: The Kermis Woodcuts of Hans Sebald Beham in Reformation Nuremberg', *Sixteenth Century Journal* 24, no. 2 (1993): 301–50; M. Geisberg, *The German Single Leaf Woodcut 1500–1550* (New York: Hacker Art Book, 1974); R. Cole, 'Pamphlet Woodcuts in the Communication Process of Reformation Germany', in K. Sessions

and P. N. Bebb (eds), *Pietas et Societas: New Trends in Reformation Social History – Essays in Memory of Harold J. Grimm* (Kirksville, MO: Sixteenth Century Journal, 1985).

27 For a fuller discussion, see Scribner, *For the Sake of Simple Folk*, p. 203.

28 For more on the evolution of Luther's image, see L. Roper, 'Martin Luther's Body: the "Stout Doctor" and his Biographers', *American Historical Review* 115, no. 2 (April 2010): 350–84.

29 R. Scribner, 'Images of Luther, 1519–25', in Scribner, *For the Sake of Simple Folk*, pp. 14–36; R. Scribner, 'Incombustible Luther: The Image of the Reformer in Early Modern Germany', *Past and Present* 100 (1986): 36–68.

30 H. Speier, *The Truth in Hell and Other Essays in Politics and Culture* (Oxford: Oxford University Press, 1999), p. 202.

CHAPTER 3: THE REFORMATION AND THE IMAGE

1 *Relations politiques des Pays-Bas et de L'Angleterre sous le règne de Philippe II*, IV, ed. J. M. B. C. Kervyn de Lettenhove (1885), pp. 337–9, 341–4.

2 For a fuller discussion of these themes, see A. Spicer, 'Iconoclasm and adaptation: the reformation of the churches in Scotland and the Netherlands', in D. Gaimser and R. Gilchrist (eds), *The Archaeology of Reformation 1480–1580* (Barnsley: Society for Post-Medieval Archaeology, 2003), pp. 29–43; J. Israel, *The Dutch Republic: Its Rise, Greatness and Fall 1477–1806* (Oxford: Clarendon, 1995), pp. 146ff.; A. Duke, *Reformation and Revolt in the Low Countries* (London: Hambledon, 1996).

3 Henry Gee and W. H. Hardy (eds), *Documents Illustrative of English Church History* (New York: Macmillan, 1896), pp. 417–42.

4 For a fuller discussion, see J. Simpson, *Burning to Reading: English Fundamentalism and its Opponents* (Cambridge, MA: Harvard University Press, 2007), p. 15; D. MacCulloch, *Tudor Church Militant: Edward VI and the Protestant Reformation* (London: Penguin, 1999), ch. 2; F. Heal, *The Reformation in Britain and Ireland* (Oxford: Oxford University Press, 2003), pp. 157–66; M. Aston, *The King's Bedpost: Reformation and Iconography in a Tudor Group Portrait* (Cambridge: Cambridge University Press, 1993).

5 M. Miles, *Visual Understanding in Western Christianity and Secular*

Culture (Boston: Beacon Press, 1985); R. W. Scribner, 'Ritual and Popular Religion in Catholic Germany at the time of the Reformation', in R. W. Scribner, *Popular Culture and Popular Movements in Reformation Germany* (London: Hambledon, 1987), pp. 23–31.

6 *Rationale Divinorum Officiorum*, trans. T. M. Thibodeau (New York and Chichester: Columbia University Press, 2007), 2.13, 3.7.

7 S. Ringbom, 'Devotional Images and Imaginative Devotions', *Gazette des Beaux Arts*, Series 6, 73 (1969); R. W. Scribner, 'Popular Piety and Modes of Visual Perception in Late Medieval and Reformation Germany', *Journal of Religious History* 15, no. 4 (1989): 448–69.

8 J. Wycliffe, *Tractatus de Mandatis Divinis*, ed. J. Loserth and F. D. Matthew (London: Wyclif Society, 1922), p. 156.

9 Ibid., pp. 152–5. For a fuller discussion, see M. Aston, *Lollards and Reformers: Images and Literacy in Late Medieval Religion* (London: Hambledon, 1984), ch. 5.

10 J. A. Muller (ed.), *The Letters of Stephen Gardiner* (Cambridge: Cambridge University Press, 1933), p. 273.

11 Several cases are well documented in N. P. Tanner (ed.), *Heresy Trials in the Diocese of Norwich 1428–31* (London: Camden Society, 1977).

12 D. Erasmus, *Opera Omnia Desiderii Erasmi Roterodami* (Amsterdam: North-Holland, 1969–), vol. 5: 1187–8; *In Praise of Folly*; *De amabili Ecclesiae Concordia*, in *Opera Omnia*, vol. 5: 501.

13 C. M. N. Eire, *War Against the Idols: The Reformation of Worship from Erasmus to Calvin* (Cambridge: Cambridge University Press, 1986); C. Christensen, *Art and the Reformation in Germany* (Athens: Ohio University Press, 1979); L. P. Wendel, *Always Among Us: Images of the Poor in Zwingli's Zurich* (Cambridge: Cambridge University Press, 1990); L. P. Wendel, *Voracious Idols and Violent Hands: Iconoclasm in Reformation Zurich, Strasbourg and Basel* (Cambridge and New York: Cambridge University Press, 1995); K. Zapalac, *'In His Likeness': Political Iconography and Religious Change in Regensburg, 1500–1600* (Ithaca, NY: Cornell University Press, 1990); B. Heal, *The Cult of the Virgin Mary in Early Modern Germany: Protestant and Catholic Piety 1500–1648* (Cambridge: Cambridge University Press, 2007).

14 M. Luther, *Wider die himmlischen Propheten von Bildern und Sakramenten* (Against the Heavenly Prophets).

15 See, for example, Luther's *Sermon on Indulgences* (1518) or the *Commentary on Deuteronomy* (1529).

16 Christensen, *Art and the Reformation* p. 27.

17 i Das wir bilder in Kirchen vñ gots hewßern habē / ist vnrecht / vnd wider das erste gebot. Du solst nicht frombde gotter haben. ii Das geschnitzte vnd gemalthe Olgotzen vff den altarien stehnd ist noch schadelicher vnd Tewffellischer. iii Drumb ists gut / notlich / loblich / vñ gottlich / das wir sie abthun / vñ ire recht vñ vrteyl der schrifft gebē.

18 B. D. Mangrum and G. Scavizzi, *A Reformation Debate: Karlstadt, Emser and Eck on Sacred Images: Three Treatises in Translation*, 2nd edn (Toronto: University of Toronto Press, 1998), pp. 21–42.

19 For a fuller discussion, see L. P. Wendel, *Voracious Idols and Violent Hands: Iconoclasm in Reformation Zurich, Strasbourg, and Basel* (Cambridge and New York: Cambridge University Press, 1995).

20 A. Spicer, 'Iconoclasm on the Frontier: le Cateau Cambresis, 1566', in K. Kolrud (ed.), *Iconoclasm from Antiquity to Modernity* (Aldershot: Ashgate, 2014), p. 126.

21 J. Calvin, *Institutes of the Christian Religion* (Louisville, KY: Westminster John Knox Press, 2001), book 1, ch. 11; see also Calvin's Sermon on Galatians 1.8–9, in *Ioannis Calvini opera quae supersunt omnia*, ed. G. Baum, E. Cunitz and E. Reuss, 59 vols, Corpus Reformatorum 29–87 (Brunswick: Schwetschke, 1863–1900), vol. 1, 326; J. Calvin, *John Calvin: Selections From His Writings*, ed. John Dillenberger (Garden City, NY: Doubleday Anchor, 1971), p. 151.

22 D. K. McKim, *The Cambridge Companion to John Calvin* (Cambridge: Cambridge University Press, 2004), pp. 214–15.

23 J. Balserak, *John Calvin as Sixteenth Century Prophet* (Oxford: Oxford University Press, 2014), p. 123.

24 For a fuller discussion, see D. Crouzet, *Les guerriers de Dieu. La violence au temps des troubles de religion, vers 1525–vers 1610* (Champ Vallon: Seyssel, 1990), chs 7–8.

25 B. Heal, *The Cult of the Virgin Mary in Early Modern Germany: Protestant and Catholic Piety, 1500–1648* (Cambridge: Cambridge University Press, 2007); B. Heal, 'Sacred image and sacred space in sixteenth-century Germany', in W. Coster and A. Spicer (eds), *Sacred Space: The Redefinition of Sanctity in Post-Reformation Europe* (Cambridge: Cambridge University Press, 2005); B. Heal, 'Images of the Virgin Mary and Marian devotion in Protestant Nuremberg', in W. Naphy and H. Parish (eds), *Religion and Superstition in Reformation Europe* (Manchester: Manchester University Press, 2003).

26 See, for example, J. L. Koerner, *The Reformation of the Image* (Chicago: University of Chicago Press, 2004); P. Collinson, *From Iconoclasm to*

Iconophobia: The Cultural Impact of the Second English Reformation (Reading: University of Reading Press, 1986), esp. p. 8: '[the Reformation] is hostile to false art but not anti-art, since its hostility implies a true and acceptable art, applied to a laudable purpose'.

27 *WA* 31.1.415; *WA* 36.35.

28 For a fuller discussion of Luther on justification, see pp. 31–4 above.

29 T. Ramussen, 'Iconoclasm and Religious Images in the early Lutheran tradition', in Kolrud, *Iconoclasm from Antiquity to Modernity*. The Lutheran *Passionale Christi und Antichristi* provides a clear example of the potency of the image in conversion, while R. W. Scribner's work on the 'incombustible Luther' explores the appropriation of traditional iconography, and sometimes cultic tendencies, in evangelical visual propaganda.

30 J. Budd, 'Rethinking Iconoclasm in early modern England: The case of the Cheapside cross', *Journal of Early Modern History* 4, nos 3–4 (2000): 371–404; M. Driver, *the Image in Print: Book Illustration in Late Medieval England and its Sources* (London: British Library, 2004); M. Aston, 'Gods, Saints and Reformers: Portraiture and Protestant England', in L. Ghent (ed.), *Albion's Classicism* (London: Yale University Press, 1995), pp. 181–220; P. Corby, *Seeing Beyond the Word: Visual Arts and the Calvinist Tradition* (Grand Rapids, MI, and Cambridge: W. B. Eerdmans, 1999); M. Todd, *The Culture of Protestantism in Early Modern Scotland* (New Haven, CT: Yale University Press, 2002).

31 R. W. Scribner, 'Reformation, carnival, and the world turned upside down', in Scribner, *Popular Culture and Popular Movements*, ch. 4.

32 John Foxe, *Acts and Monuments* (London, 1563), fol. 590.

33 J. Edwards and R. Truman, *Reforming Catholicism in the England of Mary Tudor: The Achievement of Friar Bartolomé Carranza* (Aldershot and Burlington, VT: Ashgate, 2005), p. 129.

34 W. Shakespeare, Sonnet 73, in *Shakespeare's Sonnets*, ed. K. Duncan-Jones (London: Arden Shakespeare, 2001).

35 E. Shagan, *Popular Politics and the English Reformation* (Cambridge: Cambridge University Press, 2002), ch. 5.

36 The best recent discussion of these themes is A. Walsham, *The Reformation of the Landscape: Religion, Identity and Memory in Early Modern Britain and Ireland* (Oxford: Oxford University Press, 2011). For discussions of the changing understanding of sacred space in this period, see A. Spicer and S. M. Hamilton (eds), *Defining the Holy: Sacred Space in Medieval and Early Modern Europe* (Aldershot:

Ashgate, 2005); A. Spicer and W. Coster (eds), *Sacred Space in Early Modern Europe* (Cambridge: Cambridge University Press, 2005).

37 Spicer, 'Iconoclasm and adaptation', pp. 38–9.

38 H. Lefebvre, *The Production of Space*, trans. D. Nicholson-Smith (Oxford: Wiley-Blackwell, 1991), p. 254.

39 R. W. Scribner, 'The Reformation, popular magic and the disenchantment of the World', *Journal of Interdisciplinary History* 23 (1993): 475–94; R. W. Scribner, 'The Impact of the Reformation on Daily Life', in *Mensch und Mittelalter und in der fruhen Neuzeit. Leiben, Altag, Kultur* (Vienna: Verlag der Osterreichischen Akademie der Wissenschaften, 1990), pp. 316–443.

40 Scribner, 'Popular Piety and Modes of Visual Perception'; C. Zika, 'Writing the Visual into History: changing cultural perceptions of late medieval and Reformation Germany', *Parergon* 11, no. 2 (December 1993): 107–34.

CHAPTER 4: THE REFORMATION, AUTHORITY AND RADICALISM

1 M. Luther, *Defence and Explanation of all the Articles*, in *LW*, vol. 32, pp. 9–10.

2 A. Ryrie, 'The Problems of Legitimacy and Precedent in English Protestantism, 1539–47', in Bruce Gordon (ed.), *Protestant History and Identity in Sixteenth-Century Europe* (Aldershot: Scolar, 1996), p. 78.

3 M. Luther, *Address to the Christian Nobility* (1520); D. Steinmetz, 'Luther and Calvin on Church and Tradition', *Michigan Germanic Studies* 10 (Spring/Fall, 1984): 98–111.

4 D. Steinmetz, 'The Council of Trent', in D. Bagchi and D. Steinmetz (eds), *The Cambridge Companion to Reformation Theology* (Cambridge: Cambridge University Press, 2004), p. 236ff.; G. R. Evans, *Problems of Authority in the Reformation Debates* (Cambridge: Cambridge University Press, 1992).

5 P. M. Vermigli, *The Oxford Treatise and Disputation on the Eucharist*, 1549, ed. and trans. J. C. McLelland, Sixteenth Century Essays and Studies, vol. 56 (Kirkland, MO: Truman State University Press, 2000), p. 209.

6 J. Jewel, *Apology of the Church of England*, ed. J. E. Booty (Ithaca, NY: Cornell University Press, 1963), p. 85.

7 Evans, *Problems of Authority in the Reformation Debates*, p. 56.

8   E. Rummel, 'Biblical Scholarship: Humanist Innovators and Scholastic Defenders of Tradition', in E. Rummel (ed.), *The Humanist–Scholastic Debate in the Renaissance and Reformation* (Cambridge, MA: Harvard University Press, 1995).

9   J. Rastell, *A replie against an answer (false intitled) in Defence of the Truth* (Antwerp, 1565).

10 T. More, *Responsio ad Lutherum*, in J. M. Headley, *The Yale Edition of the Complete Works of St. Thomas More* (CW) (New Haven and London: Yale University Press, 1969), vol. 5, pp. 236–7; *Confutation of Tyndale's Answer* (CW, 8), p. 728.

11 Y.-M. Congar, *Tradition and Traditions: An Historical and a Theological Essay* (London: Burns and Oates, 1966), p. 91; L. Schuster, 'Reformation Polemic and Renaissance Values', *Moreana* 43–4 (1974): 50; Evans, *Problems of Authority in the Reformation Debates*, ch. 2.

12 P. Marshall, 'The debate over unwritten verities in early reformation England', in B. Gordon (ed.), *Protestant History and Identity in Sixteenth-Century Europe* (Aldershot: Scolar, 1996), pp. 60–77; Steinmetz, 'The Council of Trent', pp. 233–47; Evans, *Problems of Authority in the Reformation Debates*, p. 72; E. Fulton, 'Touching Theology with Unwashed Hands', in H. Parish, E. Fulton and P. Webster (eds), *The Search for Authority in Reformation Europe* (Farnham: Ashgate, 2015), pp. 89–95; H. Oberman, *The Harvest of Medieval Theology: Gabriel Biel and Late Medieval Nominalism* (Cambridge, MA: Harvard University Press, 1963); H. Oberman, *Forerunners of the Reformation: The Shape of Late Medieval Thought Illustrated by Key Documents* (New York: Holt, Rinehart and Winston, 1966; Philadelphia: Fortress Press, 1981).

13 *Corpus Reformatorum* 4.367–8, quoted in Evans, *Problems of Authority in the Reformation Debates*, p. 73.

14 P. Marshall, 'The Debate over "Unwritten Verities" in Early Reformation England', in B. Gordon (ed.), *Protestant History and Identity in Sixteenth Century Europe* (Aldershot: Scolar Press, 1996); Evans, *Problems of Authority in Reformation Debates*; B. Gerrish, *The Old Protestantism and the New: Essays on the Reformation Heritage* (Edinburgh: T&T Clark, 1982); G. H. Tavard, *Holy Writ or Holy Church: The Crisis of the Protestant Reformation* (London: Burns and Oates, 1959); E. Flesseman van Leer, 'The Controversy About Ecclesiology between Thomas More and William Tyndale', *Nederlands Archief voor Kerkesgeschiedenis* 44 (1960): 65–86; E. Flesseman van Leer, 'The Controversy about

Scripture and Tradition Between Thomas More and William Tyndale',
Nederlands Archief voor Kerkesgeschiedenis 43 (1959): 143–64; B.
Gogan, *The Common Corps of Christendom: Ecclesiological Themes
in the Writings of Sir Thomas More* (Leiden: Brill, 1982); J. M. Headley,
'The Reformation as a Crisis in the Understanding of Tradition', *Archiv
für Reformationsgeschichte* 78 (1987): 5–22; R. C. Marius, 'Thomas
More and the Early Church Fathers', *Traditio* 24 (1968): 379–407; R. C.
Marius, 'Thomas More's View of the Church', in L. A. Schuster, R. C.
Marius and J. P. Lusardi (eds), *The Yale Edition of the Complete Works
of St. Thomas More Volume 8: The Confutation of Tyndale`s Answer*
(New Haven, CT: Yale University Press, 1969), pp. 1269–363.

15 D. Erasmus, 'Two Forewords to the Latin Translation of the New
Testament', in *The Praise of Folly and Other Writings*, trans. R. M.
Adams (New York: Norton, 1989), p. 121.

16 Marshall, 'The Debate over "Unwritten Verities"', p. 62.

17 *Martyrs Mirror*, trans. I. D. Rupp (Lancaster, PA: David Miller, 1837),
pp. 379–82.

18 Anna's husband may well have fallen victim to the persecution of
Anabaptists in England in 1538; he certainly leaves no trace in the
record after this date.

19 C. A. Snyder, *The Life and Thought of Michael Sattler* (Scottdale, PA:
Herald Press, 1984); K.-H. Kauffmann, *Michael Sattler – ein Märtyrer
der Täuferbewegung* (Albstadt: Brosamen-Verlag, 2010); J. van Braght,
Thieleman, *The bloody theatre, or 'Martyrs' mirror', of the defenceless
Christians, who suffered from the time of Christ until 1660* (Scottdale,
PA: Herald Press, 1987), pp. 416–18.

20 For a fuller discussion of this theme, see P. Roberts, 'Martyrologies and
Martyrs in the French Reformation: Heretics to Subversives in Troyes', in
D. Wood (ed.), *Studies in Church History, 30* (Oxford: Blackwell, 1993),
pp. 221–9, doi:10.1017/S0424208400011712; L. Racaut, 'Religious
polemic and Huguenot self-perception and identity, 1554–1619', in R.
A. Mentzer and A. Spicer (eds), *Society and Culture in the Huguenot
World 1559–1685* (Cambridge: Cambridge University Press, 2002), pp.
29–43; L. Racaut, 'The Polemical use of the Albigensian Crusade during
the French Wars of Religion', *French History* 13, no. 3 (1999): 261–79;
T. S. Freeman and S. E. Wall, 'Racking the Body, Shaping the Text:
The Account of Anne Askew in Foxe's "Book of Martyrs"', *Renaissance
Quarterly* 54, no. 4 (2001): 1165–96, doi:10.2307/1261970; E. Beilin
(ed.), *The Examinations of Anne Askew* (Oxford: Oxford University

Press, 1996); L. P. Fairfield, *John Bale: Mythmaker for the English Reformation* (West Lafayette, IN: Purdue University Press, 1976); T. S. Freeman and T. F. Mayer, *Martyrs and Martyrdom in England, c. 1400–1700* (Woodbridge: Boydell & Brewer, 2007); T. S. Freeman, 'The power of polemic: Catholic attacks on the calendar of martyrs in John Foxe's Acts and Monuments', *Journal of Ecclesiastical History* 61 (2010): 475–95; T. S. Freeman, 'Dissenters from a dissenting Church: the challenge of the Freewillers, 1550–1558', in P. Marshall and A. Ryrie (eds), *The Beginnings of English Protestantism* (Cambridge: Cambridge University Press, 2002), pp. 129–56; T. S. Freeman, 'Early modern martyrs', *Journal of Ecclesiastical History* 52 (2001): 696–701; T. S. Freeman, 'The importance of dying earnestly: the metamorphosis of the account of James Bainham in Foxe's *Book of Martyrs*', in R. N. Swanson (ed.), *The Church Retrospective*, Studies in Church History 33 (Woodbridge: Boydell & Brewer, 1997), pp. 267–88.

21 A. G. Dickens, 'The Radical Reformation', *Past and Present* 27 (1964): 124.

22 C. Lindberg, *The European Reformations* (London: Wiley and Sons, 2011), p. 215.

23 See, for example, C. S. Dixon, *Contesting the Reformation* (Oxford: Wiley Blackwell, 2012), pp. 88–95; M. Driedger, 'Anabaptism and Religious Radicalism', in A. Ryrie (ed.), *The European Reformations* (Basingstoke: Macmillan, 2006), pp. 212–32.

24 E. Troelstch, *The Social Teachings of the Christian Churches*, trans. O. Wyon (Louisville, KY: Westminster/John Knox Press, 1992), vol. 2, pp. 479–82.

25 K. Depperman, 'The Anabaptists and the State Churches', in K. von Greyerz (ed.), *Religion and Society in Early Modern Europe, 1500–1800* (London: German Historical Institute, 1984), p. 95.

26 See, for example, the use of the word 'Puritan' in Elizabethan and Stuart England. For fuller discussion, see B. Hall, 'Puritanism: the Problem of Definition', in G. J. Cuming (ed.), *Studies in Church History*, vol. 2 (Oxford: Blackwell, 1965); P. Collinson, *English Puritanism* (London: Historical Association, 1983); P. Collinson, 'A Comment: Concerning the Name Puritan', *Journal of Ecclesiastical History* 10 (1980): 483–8; P. Collinson, *The Elizabethan Puritan Movement* (London: Jonathan Cape, 1967); P. Collinson, 'Ecclesiastical Vitriol: Religious Satire in the 1590s and the Invention of Puritanism', in J. Guy (ed.), *The Reign of Elizabeth I* (Cambridge: Cambridge University Press, 1995); P. Lake,

Moderate Puritans and the Elizabethan Church (Cambridge: Cambridge University Press, 1982); P. Lake, 'Calvinism and the English Church 1570– 1635', *Past and Present* 114 (1987): 32–76; P. Lake, 'Defining Puritanism – again?', in F. J. Bremer (ed.), *Puritanism: Transatlantic Perspectives on a Seventeenth-Century Anglo-American Faith* (Boston: Massachusetts Historical Society, distributed by Northeastern University Press, 1993); P. Lake, 'Anti-Puritanism: The Structure of a Prejudice', in K. Fincham and P. Lake (eds), *Religious Politics in Post-Reformation England* (Woodbridge: Boydell, 2006).

27 C.-P. Clasen, *Anabaptism, a Social History* (Ithaca, NY: Cornell University Press, 1972); H. Goertz, *The Anabaptists* (London: Routledge, 1996); R. E. McLaughlin, 'Radicals', in D. M. Whitford (ed.), *Reformation and Early Modern Europe* (Kirksville, MO: Truman State University Press, 2008); J. Roth and J. Stayer, *A Companion to Anabaptism and Spiritualism* (Leiden: Brill, 2007).

28 G. Waite, 'Between the Devil and the Inquisitor: Anabaptists, Diabolical Conspiracies and Magical Beliefs in the Sixteenth-Century Netherlands', in W. Packull and G. Dipple (eds), *Radical Reformation Studies: Essays Presented to James M. Stayer*, (Aldershot: Ashgate, 1999), p. 121.

29 M. Sattler, 'The Schleitheim Confession of Faith', 1527, *Mennonite Quarterly Review* 19, no. 4 (October 1945).

30 E. Cameron, *The European Reformation* (Oxford: Oxford University Press, 1991), p. 159.

31 T. Müntzer, *Protestation oder Entbietung*, in H. Brandt (ed.), *Thomas Müntzer, Sein Leben und seine Schriften* (Jena: E. Diederichs, 1933), pp. 133–44; H. O. Old, *The Shaping of the Reformed Baptismal Rite in the Sixteenth Century* (Grand Rapids, MI: Wm. B. Eerdmans, 1992), p. 79ff.

32 C. Lindberg (ed.), *The European Reformations Sourcebook* (Malden, MA: Blackwell, 2000), p. 134.

33 M. Luther, 'Concerning Rebaptism', 1528. See, for example, the condemnation at the Diet of Speyer (1526) of those who denied the value of infant baptism, repeated in the Confession of Augsburg (1530), and the use of the Justinian code to justify the death penalty for rebaptism. B. Scribner and G. Benecke (eds), *The German Peasant War of 1525 – New Viewpoints* (London: Unwin Hyman, 1979), p. 278; Waite, 'Between the Devil and the Inquisitor', p. 128

34 Roth and Stayer, *A Companion to Anabaptism and Spiritualism*, p. 484; W. Klassen, 'The Anabaptist Understanding of the Separation of

the Church', *Church History* 46 (1977): 422.

35 W. Klaasen, ed., *Anabaptism in Outline: Selected Primary Sources* (Waterloo: Herald, 1981), p. 178.

36 P. A. Dykema and H. A. Oberman (eds), *Anticlericalism in Late Medieval and Early Modern Europe* (Leiden: Brill, 1993); T. Brady, *Communities, Politics, and Reformation in Early Modern Europe* (Leiden: Brill, 1998).

37 G. Vogler, 'Imperial City Nuremberg 1524–5: The Reformation in Transition', in R. Po-Chia Hsia, *The German People and the Reformation* (Ithaca, NY: Cornell University Press, 1988), pp. 33–51.

38 P. Blickle, *Gemeindereformation: Die Menschen des 16..Jahrhunderts auf Dem Weg zum Heil* (Munich: Oldenbourg, 1985).

39 S. Hoyer, 'Antiklerikalismus in den Forderungen und Aktionen der Aufstadnischen von 1524–5', in P. A. Dykema and H. A. Oberman (eds), *Anticlericalism in Late Medieval and Early Modern Europe* (Leiden: Brill, 1993), pp. 535–44.

40 G. Strauss, 'Local Anticlericalism in Reformation Germany', in P. A. Dykema and H. A. Oberman (eds), *Anticlericalism in Late Medieval and Early Modern Europe* (Leiden: Brill, 1993), pp. 625–38; J. D. Grieser, 'Anabaptism, Anticlericalism and the Creation of a Protestant Clergy', *Mennonite Quarterly Review* 71, no. 4 (1997); C. S. Dixon and L. Schorn-Schutte, *The Protestant Clergy of Early Modern Europe* (Basingstoke: Macmillan, 2003); P. Marshall, 'Anticlericalism Revested? Expressions of Discontent in Early Tudor England', in C. Burgess and E. Duffy (eds), *The Parish in Late Medieval England* (Donnington: Shaun Tyas, 2006).

41 G. Waite, *Eradicating the Devil's Minions: Anabaptists and Witches in Reformation Europe, 1525–1600* (Toronto: University of Toronto Press, 2007), p. 141.

42 H. J. Goertz, 'Karlstadt, Müntzer and the Reformation of the Commoners', in J. Roth and J. Stayer, *A Companion to Anabaptism and Spiritualism* (Leiden: Brill, 2007), p. 39

43 Ibid., p. 13.

44 Ibid., p. 14.

45 Ibid., pp. 24–5.

46 J. K. Seidemann, *Thomas Müntzer – Eine Biographie* (Dresden and Leipzig: In der Arnoldischen Buchhandlung, 1842), appendix 5, p. 110.

47 H.-J. Goertz, *The Anabaptists* (London: Routledge, 1996), p. 41.

48 Waite, *Eradicating the Devil's Minions*, p. 141.

49 Depperman, 'The Anabaptists and the State Churches', pp. 97, 95.

50 Goertz, *The Anabaptists*, p. 129.

51 P. Peachey, 'The Radical Reformation, Political Pluralism, and the Corpus Christianum', in M. Leihard (ed.), *The Origins and Characteristics of Anabaptism* (The Hague: Nijhoff, 1997); J. A. Patterson, 'The Church in History: Ecclesiological Ideals and Institutional Realities', in K. H. Easley and C. W. Morgan (eds), *The Community of Jesus: A Theology of the Church* (Nashville, TN: Broadman & Holman, 2013), p. 173ff.

52 Gary K. Waite, 'Between the Devil and the Inquisitor', pp. 121–2.

53 Peachey, 'The Radical Reformation', pp. 83–102, at p. 10.

54 R. Sohm, *Kirchenrecht* (Leipzig: Duncher & Humblot, 1892), p. 138.

55 The best recent study of Sleidan and his work is A. Kess, *Johann Sleidan and the Protestant Vision of History* (Burlington: Ashgate, 2008).

56 S. Haude, *In the Shadow of 'Savage Wolves': Anabaptist Munster and the German Reformation During the 1530s* (Leiden: Brill, 2000), p. 26.

57 Waite, 'Between the Devil and the Inquisitor'.

CHAPTER 5: THE REFORMATION, WOMEN AND MARRIAGE

1 P. Smith, *The Life and Letters of Martin Luther* (New York: Barnes and Noble, 1968), p. 175.

2 LW 45.36.

3 Smith, *The Life and Letters of Martin Luther*, p. 178.

4 S. Ozment, *When Fathers Ruled: Family Life in Reformation Europe* (Cambridge, MA: Harvard University Press, 1983), p. 17.

5 Smith, *The Life and Letters of Martin Luther*, p. 176

6 H. L. Parish, *Clerical Celibacy in the West 1100–1700* (Aldershot: Ashgate, 2011), pp. 144–6.

7 A. Stein, 'Martin Luthers Bedeutung dur die Anfange des Evangelischen Eherechts', *Osterreichisches Archiv fur Kirchenrecht* 34, nos 1 –2 (1983–4): 29–95; S. Johnson, 'Luther's Reformation and (un)holy Matrimony', *Journal of Family History*, 17, no. 3 (1992): 271–88; L. Roper 'Luther, Sex, Marriage and Motherhood', *History Today* 33 (1983): 33–8; T. A. Fudge, 'Incest and Lust in Luther's Marriage: Theology and Morality in Reformation Polemics', *Sixteenth Century Journal* 34, no. 2 (2003): 319–45; J. K. Yost, 'The Reformation Defence of Clerical Marriage in the Reigns of Henry VIII and Edward VI', *Church History* 50 (1981): 152–65; E. Carlson, 'Clerical Marriage and the English Reformation',

Journal of British Studies 31 (1992): 1–31; M. Porter, *Sex, Marriage and the Church: Patterns of Change* (Victoria, Australia: Dove, 1996); M. E. Plummer, 'Clerical Marriage and Territorial Reformation in Ernestine Saxony and the Diocese of Merseburg in 1522–1524', *Archiv für Reformationsgeschichte* 98 (2007): 45–70; M. E. Plummer, '"Partner in his Calamities": Pastors Wives, Married Nuns and the Experience of Clerical Marriage in the Early German Reformation', *Gender and History* 20, no. 2 (2008): 207–27; W. A. Coupe, *German Political Satires from the Reformation to the Second World War*, 3 vols (White Plains, NY: Kraus International Publications, 1993), vol. 1, p. 109.

8   For a fuller discussion, see Parish, *Clerical Celibacy in the West*.

9   M. E. Plummer, *From Priest's Whore to Pastor's Wife: Clerical Marriage and the Process of Reform in the Early German Reformation* (Farnham: Ashgate, 2012).

10 For a fuller discussion of the case, see J. Witte, *From Sacrament to Contract: Marriage, Religion and Law in the Western Tradition* (Louisville, KY: Westminster John Knox Press, 1997), pp. 44–6; T. A. Fudge, 'Incest and Lust in Luther's Marriage: Theology and Morality in Reformation Polemic', *Sixteenth Century Journal* 34, no. 2 (2003): 319–45 at 328ff.

11 For a fuller discussion of the Hedio case, see T. Brady, *Communities, Politics, and Reformation in Early Modern Europe* (Leiden: Brill, 1998), p. 194ff.

12 Plummer, 'Clerical Marriage and Territorial Reformation', pp. 45–70.

13 *LW* 1: 135.

14 S. Ozment, 'Reinventing Family Life', *Christian History* 12, no. 3 (1993): 22; J. Brundage, *Law, Sex and Christian Society in Medieval Europe* (Chicago: University of Chicago Press, 1990).

15 *LW* 54: 441.

16 E. Clark (ed.), *St Augustine on Marriage and Sexuality* (Washington, DC: Catholic University of America Press, 1996).

17 Luther, *A Sermon on the Estate of Marriage* (1519); *LW* 44: 8.

18 Luther, *A Sermon on the Estate of Marriage* (1519); *LW* 44: 10–12.

19 *LW* 44: 10.

20 *LW* 45: 39; Table Talk (*WA* TR 1: 974).

21 *LW* 44: 8.

22 W. Phipps, *Clerical Celibacy, The Heritage* (London and New York: Continuum, 2004), p. 61, suggests that Paul made this recommendation not with any real enthusiasm, but as a concession to the ascetically-minded Corinthians.

23 P. Brown, *The Body and Society: Men, Women and Sexual Renunciation* (New York: Columbia University Press, 1988), p. 55.

24 For the suggestions that it was celibacy rather than asceticism that was at stake here, see S. Heid, *Clerical Celibacy in the Early Church: The Beginnings of Obligatory Continence for Clerics in East and* West, trans. M. J. Muller (San Francisco: Ignatius Press, 2001), pp. 38–9.

25 *LW* 28.11; *LW* 28.12, 16, 17.

26 *LW* 28.22, 24, 25.

27 J. Calvin, *Institutes of the Christian Religion*, trans. F. Battles (Philadelphia: Library of Christian Classics, 1960).

28 M. Luther, *To the Christian Nobility of the German Nation* (1520); *LW* 44: 176.

29 M. Luther, *The Babylonian Captivity of the Church* (1520); *LW* 36: 92.

30 *LW* 36: 92.

31 *LW* 45: 11–49.

32 S. Hendrix, 'Luther on Marriage', *Lutheran Quarterly* 14, no. 3 (2000): 335–50; S. M. Johnson, 'Luther's Reformation and (un)holy matrimony', *Journal of Family History* 17 (1992): 271–88; E. J. Carlson, *Marriage and the English Reformation* (Oxford: Clarendon Press, 1994); J. F. Harrington, *Reordering Marriage and Society in Reformation Germany* (Cambridge: Cambridge University Press, 1995); S. Ozment, *Flesh and Spirit: Private Life in Early Modern Germany* (New York: Viking, 1999).

33 M. Luther, *The Estate of Marriage* (1522); *LW* 45: 18; P. Melanchthon, *Apology of the Augsburg Confession*, 'The Marriage of Priests, article 23', in R. Kolb and T. Wengert (eds), *The Book of Concord: The Confessions of the Evangelical Lutheran Church* (Minneapolis, MN: Fortress Press, 2000), pp. 247–60.

34 *LW* 39.290–1.

35 D. MacCulloch, *Reformation: Europe's House Divided 1490–1700* (London: Penguin, 2004), p. 647. Some of the most useful analysis of perceptions of women in Renaissance and Reformation Europe is to be found in C. Jordan, *Renaissance Feminism: Literary Texts and Politics Models* (Ithaca, NY: Cornell University Press, 1990); P. J. Benson, *The Invention of the Renaissance Woman* (Pittsburgh: Penn State University Press, 1992); I. Maclean, *The Renaissance Notion of Woman* (Cambridge: Cambridge University Press, 1980); E. Rummel, *Erasmus on Women* (Toronto and London: University of Toronto Press, 1996); J. L. Klein (ed.), *Daughters, Wives and Widows: Writings by Men about*

Women and Marriage in England 1500–1640 (Urbana: University of Illinois Press, 1992); S. W. Hull, *Women According to Men* (Thousand-Oaks, CA, and London: AltaMira Press, 1996).

36 S. Ozment, *Age of Reform 1250–1550: An intellectual and Religious History* (New Haven, CT: Yale University Press, 1981), p. 381; Witte, *From Sacrament to Contract*, p. 42ff.

37 R. H. Bainton, *Here I Stand: A Life of Martin Luther* (Peabody, MA: Hendrickson, 2009), p. 233.

38 This point has been developed at greater length by Carter Lindberg. Evangelical theology, he suggests, demanded the development of new social and legislative structures for addressing welfare needs. Social ethics was regarded as the continuation of community worship, but this sense of social obligation was also evident in the changing status of marriage and family in Reformation Germany. C. Lindberg, *Beyond Charity: Reformation Initiatives for the Poor* (Minneapolis, MN: Fortress Press, 1993).

39 *LW* 45: 46.

40 S. Ozment, *When Fathers Ruled: Family Life in Reformation Europe* (Cambridge, MA: Harvard University Press, 1985); M. Wiesner-Hanks, 'Luther and Women: The death of two Marys', in J. Obelkevich, L. Roper and R. Samuel (eds), *Disciplines of Faith: Studies in Religion, Politics and Patriarchy* (London and New York: Routledge, 1987); M. Weisner-Hanks, *Women and Gender in Early Modern Europe*, 2nd edn (Cambridge: Cambridge University Press, 2000); L. Roper, *The Holy Household: Women and Morals in Reformation Augsburg* (Oxford: Oxford University Press, 1989); L. Roper '"The Common Man", "The Common Good", "Common Women": Gender and meaning in the German Reformation Commune', *Social History* 12 (1987): 1–21; L. Shorn-Schutte, 'Gefartin und Mitregentin: Zur Sozialgeschichte der evangelischen Pfarrfrau in der Fruhen Neuzeit', in H. Wunder and C. Wanja (eds), *Wandel der Geschlechterbeziehungen zu Beginn der Neuzeit* (Berlin: Suhrkamp Verlag, 1990).

41 For a fuller discussion of these questions, see Roper, '"The Common Man"', S. Karant-Nunn, 'Continuity and Change: Some effects of the Reformation on the Women of Zwickau', *Sixteenth Century Journal* 13 (1982): 17–42; S. Karant-Nunn, 'The Reformation of Women', in R. Bridenthal, S. M. Stuard, M. E. Wiesner-Hanks, *Becoming Visible: Women in European History* (Boston: Houghton Mifflin, 1998), pp. 175–202; H. Wunder, *He is the Sun, She is the Moon: Women in Early*

Modern Germany (Cambridge: Cambridge University Press, 1988).

42 Ozment, *When Fathers Ruled*, pp. 10–23; J. D. Douglass, 'Women and the Continental Reformation', in R. R. Ruether, *Religion and Sexism: Images of Woman in the Jewish and Christian Traditions* (New York: Simon and Schuster, 1974), passim.

43 M. E. Wiesner, 'Nuns, Wives and Mothers: Women and the Reformation in Germany', in S. Marshall (ed.), *Women in Reformation and Counter-Reformation Europe: Public and Private Worlds* (Bloomington: Indiana University Press, 1989), p. 26.

44 Roper, *The Holy Household*.

45 U. Strasser, *State of Virginity: Gender, Religion, and Politics in an Early Modern Catholic State* (Ann Arbor: University of Michigan Press, 2004), p. 120; U. Strasser, 'Bones of Contention: Cloistered Nuns, Decorated Relics, and the Contest over Women's Place in the Public Sphere of Counter-Reformation Munich', *Archiv für Reformationsgeschichte* 90 (1999): 255–88.

46 A. Leonard, *Nails in the Wall: Catholic Nuns in Reformation Germany* (Chicago and London: University of Chicago Press, 2005).

47 Ibid.

48 J. McNarama, *Sisters in Arms: Catholic Nuns through Two Millennia* (Cambridge, MA: Harvard University Press, 1998), pp. 419–50.

49 The best modern edition of her 'Journal of the Reformation' is P. A. Mackenzie, *Caritas Pirckheimer: A Journal of the Reformation Years, 1524–1528* (Cambridge: D. S. Brewer, 2006). Its 69 chapters set out the conflict between Pirckheimer and the city council, via letters and commentaries.

50 P. Lee, *Nunneries, Learning, and Spirituality in Late Medieval English Society: The Dominican Priory of Dartford* (Martlesham: Boydell & Brewer, 2000); C. Cross, 'Community Solidarity among Yorkshire Religious after the Dissolution', in J. Loades (ed.), *Monastic Studies: The Continuity of Tradition* (Bangor: Headstart History, 1990), p. 245; J. Greatrex, 'On Ministering to "certayne devoute and religiouse women": Bishop Fox and the Benedictine nuns of the Winchester diocese on the eve of the Dissolution', in W. J. Sheils and D. Wood (eds), *Women in the Church*, Studies in Church History, vol. 27 (Oxford: Blackwell, 1989), pp. 223–35; M. Oliva, *The Convent and the Community in Late Medieval England* (London: Boydell, 1998).

51 M. E. Plummer, '"Partner in his Calamities": Pastors Wives, Married Nuns and the Experience of Clerical Marriage in the Early German

Reformation', *Gender and History* 20, no. 2 (2008): 217–9; *From Priest's Whore to Pastor's Wife.*

52 Mackenzie, *Caritas Pirckheimer.*

53 S. C. Karant-Nunn and M. E. Wiesner-Hanks (eds), *Luther on Women: A Sourcebook* (New York and Cambridge: Cambridge University Press, 2003).

54 B. Heal, *The Cult of the Virgin Mary in Early Modern Germany: Protestant and Catholic Piety, 1500–1648* (Cambridge: Cambridge University Press, 2007), p. 1.

55 J. Pelikan, *Mary Through the Centuries: Her Place in the History of Culture* (New Haven, CT, and London: Yale University Press, 1996), p. 153; Heal, *The Cult of the Virgin Mary*, p. 3; D. MacCulloch, 'Mary and Sixteenth-century Protestants', in R. N. Swanson (ed.), *The Church and Mary*, Studies in Church History 39 (Woodbridge: Boydell, 2004); P. Newman Brooks , 'A lily ungilded? Martin Luther, the Virgin Mary and the saints', Journal of Religious History 13 (1984): 136–49; B. Kreizer, *Reforming Mary: Changing Images of the Virgin Mary in Lutheran Sermons of the Sixteenth Century* (Oxford and New York: Oxford University Press, 2004).

56 *WA* X.3: 312ff.; reproduced and translated in Karant-Nunn and Wiesner-Hanks, *Luther on Women.*

57 *WA* XII.608–17 (Sermon on the Feast of the Visitation, July 1523).

58 Pelikan, *Mary Through the Centuries*, p. 157; Heal, *The Cult of the Virgin Mary*, p. 4; H. Düfel, *Luthers Stellung zur Marienverehrung* (Göttingen: Vandenhoeck u. Ruprecht, 1968); H. O. Oberman, 'The Virgin Mary in Evangelical Perspective', in H. O. Oberman, *The Impact of the Reformation* (Edinburgh: T&T Clark, 1994).

59 Plummer, 'Partner in his calamities', p. 211.

60 Ibid., pp. 207–9; R. Bainton, *Women of the Reformation in Germany and Italy* (Minneapolis, MN: Fortress, 1971); N. Z. Davis, 'City women and religious change', in *Society and Culture in Early Modern France* (Stanford, CA: Stanford University Press, 1975); M. U. Chrisman, 'Women and the Reformation in Strasbourg 1490–1530', *Archiv fur Reformationsgeschichte* 63 (1972): 143–68; L. Roper, 'Gender and the Reformation', *Archiv fur Reformationsgeschichte* 92 (2001): 290–302.

61 E. McKee, *Katherina Zell: Church Mother: The Writings of a Protestant Reformer in Sixteenth-Century Germany* (Chicago: University of Chicago Press, 2006), p. 1.

62 The relationship between clerical concubinage and clerical marriage is

worth further reflection. Plummer notes that in 1521–1, marriage to concubines accounted for two-thirds of all clerical marriage, around one-third in the period 1523–7, and around half in the period 1528–30. Such marriages certainly did little to improve the standing of clergy wives, thus perpetuating the belief that marriage to a priest was only an attractive option for those seeking to make an existing relationship legitimate.

63 McKee, *Katherina Zell,* p. 59ff.

64 H. Selderhuis, *Marriage and Divorce in the Thought of Martin Bucer,* trans. J. Vriend and L. Bierma (Kirksville, MO: Thomas Jefferson University Press at Truman State University, 1999); McKee, *Katherina Zell,* pp. 48–9.

65 M. Wiesner, 'Women's response to the Reformation', in R. Po-Chia Hsia, *The German People and the Reformation* (Ithaca, NY: Cornell University Press, 1988), p. 160.

66 Cross-reference here to the authority chapter.

67 S. McSheffrey, *Gender and Heresy: Women and Men in Lollard Communities, 1420–1530* (Philadelphia: University of Pennsylvania Press, 1995).

68 M. Aston, 'Lollard Women Priests?', *Journal of Ecclesiastical History* 31, no. 4 (1980): 441–61.

69 T. Taylor, *The Prehistory of Sex: Four Million Years of Human Sexual Culture* (London: Fourth Estate, 1996), p. 7, discussed in MacCulloch, *Reformation,* p. 608.

70 J. Hockenbery Dragseth, 'Martin Luther's Views on Bodies, Desire, and Sexuality', *Oxford Research Encyclopedias: Religion,* 2016: DOI:10.1093/acrefore/9780199340378.013.35.

71 Ozment, 'Reinventing Family Life', p. 22.

72 S. Burghartz, 'Ordering Discourse and Society: Moral Politics, Marriage, and Fornication during the Reformation and Confessionalisation Process in Germany and Switzerland', in H. Roodenburg and O. Spierenburg (eds), *Social Control in Europe Volume 1: 1500–1800* (Columbus: Ohio State University Press, 2004), pp. 78–98.

73 Witte, *From Sacrament to Contract,* p. 92.

74 K. Crowther, 'From Seven Sins to Lutheran Devils: Sin and Social Order in an Age of Confessionalization', in P. Gilli (ed.), *Les pathologies du pouvoir* (Leiden: E. J. Brill, 2016), pp. 481–520.

CHAPTER 6: THE REFORMATION AND THE SUPERNATURAL

1 K. Kurihara, *Celestial Wonders in Reformation Germany* (Abingdon: Routledge, 2014), pp. 23, 45; A. Walsham, 'Sermons in the Sky: Apparitions in Early Modern Europe', *History Today* (April 2010): 56–63; U. Lotz-Heumann, 'The Natural and Supernatural', in U. Rublack (ed.), *The Oxford Handbook of the Reformation* (Oxford: Oxford University Press, 2017), pp. 688–707.

2 K. Thomas, *Religion and the Decline of Magic* (London: Weidenfeld and Nicholson, 1971); H. Geertz, 'An Anthropology of Religion and Magic, I', *Journal of Interdisciplinary History* 6 (1975): 71–89; K. Thomas, 'An Anthropology of Religion and Magic, II', *Journal of Interdisciplinary History* 6 (1975): 91–109.

3 M. Weber, *The Protestant Ethic and the Spirit of Capitalism*, trans. T. Parsons (London: George Allen & Unwin, 1930); E. Troeltsch, *Protestantism and Progress: The Significance of Protestantism for the Rise of the Modern World*, trans. W. Montgomery (London: Williams & Norgate, 1912).

4 A. J. Carroll, 'Disenchantment, Rationality, and the Modernity of Max Weber', *Forum Philosophicum* 16, no. 1 (2001): 119.

5 J. A. Josephson-Storm, *The Myth of Disenchantment* (Chicago: University of Chicago Press, 2017), pp. 294–5.

6 E. Troeltsch, 'Renaissance and Reformation', in L. Spitz (ed. and trans.), *The Reformation: Basic Interpretations* (Lexington, MA: Heath, 1972), pp. 261–96; Thomas, *Religion and the Decline of Magic*; E. Cameron, *Enchanted Europe: Superstition, Reason and Religion 1350–1750* (Oxford: Oxford University Press, 2010); A. Walsham, 'The Reformation and the Disenchantment of the World Reassessed', *Historical Journal* 51, no. 2 (2008): 497–528.

7 T. Kuhn, *The Structure of Scientific Revolutions*, 2nd edn (Chicago: University of Chicago Press, 1975); M. Foucault, *The Order of Things: An Archaeology of the Human Sciences* (London: Routledge, 2002).

8 Thomas, *Religion and the Decline of Magic*, pp. 646–8.

9 Ibid., p. 37.

10 Ibid., ch. 1, 'The magic of the medieval church'; D. Gentilcore *From Bishop to Witch: The System of the Sacred in Early Modern Terra d'Otranto* (Manchester: Manchester University Press, 1992); M. Rubin, *Corpus Christi: The Eucharist in Late Medieval Culture* (Cambridge: Cambridge University Press, 1991).

11 C. Rider, *Magic and Religion in Medieval England* (London, Reaktion Books, distributed by University of Chicago Press, 2012), p. 39.

12 E. Cameron, *Enchanted Europe: Superstition, Reason and Religion 1350–1750* (Oxford: Oxford University Press, 2010), p. 42.

13 Rider, *Magic and Religion*, p. 70.

14 Cameron, *Enchanted Europe*, p. 62.

15 Rider, *Magic and Religion*, p. 8.

16 Cameron, *Enchanted Europe*, p. 42.

17 Thomas, *Religion and the Decline of Magic*, p. 643.

18 A. Walsham, *The Reformation of the Landscape: Religion, Identity and Memory in Early Modern Britain and Ireland* (Oxford: Oxford University Press, 2011).

19 Cameron, *Enchanted Europe*, p. 143.

20 F. L. K. Hsu, *Exorcising the Trouble Makers: Magic, Science and Culture* (Westport, CT: Greenwood Press, 1983); R. Merrifield, *The Archaeology of Ritual and Magic* (London: Batsford, 1987); A. Murray, 'Missionaries and Magic in Dark-Age Europe', *Past and Present* 136 (1992): 186–205; J. Neusner, E. Frerichs, and P. V. McCracken Flesher (eds), *Religion, Science, and Magic: In Concert and In Conflict* (Oxford: Oxford University Press, 1989); J. Van Engen, 'The Christian Middle Ages as an Historiographical Problem', *American Historical Review* 91 (1986): 519–52.

21 R. van Dülmen, 'The Reformation and the modern age', in C. S. Dixon (ed.), *The German Reformation: The Essential Readings* (Oxford: Oxford University Press, 1999), pp. 196–221; T. Nipperdey, 'The Reformation and the modern world', in E. I. Kouri and T. Scott (eds), *Politics and Society in Reformation Europe: Essays for Sir Geoffrey Elton on his Sixty-fifth Birthday* (Basingstoke: Macmillan, 1987), pp. 535–45; P. Spierenburg, *The Broken Spell: A Cultural and Anthropological History of Preindustrial Europe* (Basingstoke: Macmillan, 1991).

22 Cameron, *Enchanted Europe*.

23 Ibid.; H. Parish and W. G. Naphy, *Religion and Superstition in Reformation Europe* (Manchester: Manchester University Press, 2002).

24 R. Scribner, 'Reformation and Desacralisation: From Sacramental World to Moralised Universe', in R. Po-Chia Hsia and R. Scribner (eds), *Problems in the Historical Anthropology on Early Modern Europe* (Wiesbaden: Harrassowitz, 1997), p. 78; R. Scribner, 'The impact of the Reformation on Daily Life', in *Mench and Objekt im Mittelalter und in der Fruhen Neuzeit. Leben-Alltag-Kultur* (Vienna: Verlag der

Osterreichischen Akademie der Wissenschaften, 1990), pp. 316–443; Walsham, 'The Reformation and the Disenchantment of the World Reassessed', pp. 497–528.

25 Cameron, *Enchanted Europe*, p. 219.

26 Ibid., pp. 228–31.

27 L. Daston, 'Marvelous Facts and Miraculous Evidence in Early Modern Europe', *Critical Inquiry* 18 (1991): 93–124; A. Walsham, 'Miracles in post-reformation England', in K. Cooper and J. Gregory (eds), *Signs, Wonders, Miracles: Representations of Divine Power in the Life of the Church* (Woodbridge: Boydell, 2005), pp. 273–306; S. Clark, 'The rational witchfinder: conscience, demonological naturalism and popular superstition', in S. Pumfrey and P. Rossi (eds), *Science, Culture and Popular Belief in Renaissance Europe* (Manchester: Manchester University Press, 1992), pp. 222–48; S. Clark, *Vanities of the Eye: Vision in Early Modern European Culture* (Oxford: Oxford University Press, 2007); D. P. Walker, 'The Cessation of Miracles', in I. Merkel and A. Debus, *Hermeticism and the Renaissance* (Washington, DC: Folger Shakespeare Library, 1988), pp. 111–24.

28 O. P. Grell (ed.), *Paracelsus: The Man and his Reputation, his Ideas and their Transformation* (Leiden: Brill, 1998), p. 45.

29 C. S. Dixon, *Contesting the Reformation* (Oxford: Blackwell, 2012), p. 194 (confessional cultures, notes 131, 132, 133).

30 C. M. N. Eire, *Reformations: The Early Modern World* (New Haven, CT: Yale University Press, 2016), p. 747ff.

31 J. Delumeau, *Catholicism between Luther and Voltaire: A New View of the Counter-Reformation* (London: Burns and Oates, 1977).

32 Eire, *Reformations*, pp. 707–16.

33 The 'incombustible Weber' provides the starting point for an essay by Carlos Eire, in a play on Scribner's own discussion of the 'incombustible Luther', images of the reformer that were immune to the flames. See C. M. N. Eire, 'Incombustible Weber: How the Protestant Reformation Really Disenchanted the World', in A. Sterk and N. Caputo (eds), *Historians, Religion, and the Challenge of Objectivity* (New York: Cornell University Press, 2014), ch. 8.

34 R. Scribner, 'Reformation, Popular Magic and the Disenchantment of the World', *Journal of Interdisciplinary History* 23 (1993): 475–94; R. Scribner, *Popular Culture and Popular Movements in Reformation Germany* (London: Hambledon, 1987), pp. xii–xiv; Scribner, 'Reformation and Desacralisation', p. 76; Scribner, 'Reformation,

Popular Magic, and the Disenchantment of the World', p. 483; Scribner, 'Reformation and Desacralisation', pp. 77–8.

35 R. Scribner, 'Incombustible Luther: The Image of the Reformer in Early Modern Germany', *Past and Present* 100 (1986): 36–68.

36 C. S. Dixon, *The Reformation and Rural Society: The Parishes of Brandenburg-Ansbach-Kulmbach, 1528–1603* (Cambridge: Cambridge University Press, 2002), pp. 173–4.

37 E. Duffy, *Stripping of the Altars: Traditional Religion in England c.1400–c.1580* (New Haven, CT, and London: Yale University Press, 1993), pp. 136–8, 578; Thomas, *Religion and the Decline of Magic*, pp. 71–4.

38 R. C. Finucane, *Miracles and Pilgrims: Popular Beliefs in Medieval England* (London: J. M. Dent, 1977), ch. 12; H. L. Parish, *Monks, Miracles and Magic: Reformation Representations of the Medieval Church* (London and New York: Routledge, 2005), pp. 79–81; T. F. Mayer, 'Becket's Bones Burnt! Cardinal Pole and the Invention and Dissemination of an Atrocity', in T. S. Freeman and T. F. Mayer (eds), *Martyrs and Martyrdom in England, c.1400–1700* (Woodbridge: Boydell & Brewer, 2007), pp. 126–43; T. Wright (ed.), *Three Chapters of Letters Relating to the Suppression of the Monasteries*, 1st series, 26 (London: Camden Society, 1843), pp. 219–21.

39 H. Robinson (ed.), *The Zurich Letters, Comprising the Correspondence of Several English Bishops and Others, with some of the Helvetian Reformers, During the Early Part of the Reign of Queen Elizabeth* (Cambridge: Parker Society, 1842), p. 44; A. Walsham, 'Skeletons in the Cupboard: Relics after the English Reformation', *Past Present* 206 (suppl. 5) (2010): 121–43; M. Aston, 'English Ruins and English History: The Dissolution and the Sense of the Past', *Journal of the Warburg and Courtauld Institutes* 36 (1973): 231–55; E. Shagan, *Popular Politics and the English Reformation* (Cambridge: Cambridge University Press, 2002); A. Spicer and W. Coster (eds), *Sacred Space in Early Modern Europe* (Cambridge: Cambridge University Press, 2005).

40 M. Huggarde, *The displaying of the Protestantes, and sondry of their practises, with a description of divers their abuses of late frequented within their malignaunte churche* (London, 1556), fos 54–5; J. Foxe, *Acts and Monuments* (London, 1570), pp. 2196–7.

41 L. Razzall, '"A good Booke is the pretious life-blood of a master-spirit": Recollecting Relics in Post-Reformation English Writing', *Journal of the Northern Renaissance* 2, no. 1 (2010): 93–110.

42 A. Walsham, 'Jewels for Gentlewomen: Religious Books as Artefacts in Late Medieval and Early Modern England', in R. N. Swanson (ed.), *The Church and the Book* (Woodbridge: Boydell & Brewer), pp. 123–42.

43 D. Lowenthal, *The Past is a Foreign Country* (Cambridge: Cambridge University Press, 1985), pp. 238–59; J. Fentress and C. Wickham, *Social Memory* (Oxford: Oxford University Press, 1992).

44 Scribner, 'The Reformation, Popular Magic, and the Disenchantment of the World', pp. 475–94; Scribner, 'Reformation and Desacralisation', pp. 75–92; A. Walsham, 'Introduction: Relics and Remains', *Past Present* 206 (suppl. 5) (2010): 9–36; U. Rublack, 'Grapho-Relics: Lutheranism and the Materialization of the Word', *Past Present* 206 (suppl. 5) (2010): 144–66; Walsham, 'Skeletons in the Cupboard', pp. 121–43.

45 D. Woolf, *The Social Circulation of the Past: English Historical Culture 1500–1730* (Oxford: Oxford University Press, 2003).

46 Thomas, *Religion and the Decline of Magic*, p. 703.

47 P. Marshall, *Beliefs and the Dead in Reformation England* (Oxford: Oxford University Press, 2002), p. 245.

48 R. Scot, *Discoverie of Witchcraft*, London, pp. 152–3, https://www.bl.uk/collection-items/the-discovery-of-witchcraft-by-reginald-scot-1584 (accessed 4 May 2017).

49 R. W. Scribner, 'Elements of Popular Belief', in T. Brady, H. Oberman and J. Tracey (eds), *Handbook of European History 1400–1600*, 2 vols (Leiden: Brill, 1994–5), vol. 1, p. 237.

50 For a fuller discussion, see B. Lewis, 'Protestantism, Pragmatism and Popular Religion: A Case Study of Early Modern Ghosts' in Newton (ed.), *Early Modern Ghosts*, p. 85; J. Bath, '"In the Divells likeness", interpretation and confusion in popular ghosts belief' in J. Bath and J. Newton (eds), *Early Modern Ghosts* (Durham: Centre for Seventeenth-Century Studies, 2002), pp. 70–8; M. Gaskill, *Crime and Mentalities in Early Modern England* (Cambridge and New York: Cambridge University Press, 2000).

51 T. Brown, *The Fate of the Dead: A Study in Folk-Eschatology in the West Country after the Reformation* (Ipswich: D. S. Brewer, 1979), pp. 8, 83.

52 See, for example, Marshall, *Beliefs and the Dead*; B. Gordon and P. Marshall (eds), *The Place of the Dead: Death and Remembrance in Late Medieval and Early Modern Europe* (Cambridge: Cambridge University Press, 2000); P. Marshall, 'Old Mother Leakey and the Golden Chain: Context and Meaning in an Early Stuart Haunting', in

J. Bath and J. Newton (eds), *Early Modern Ghosts* (Durham: Centre for Seventeenth-Century Studies, 2002), pp. 93–109; P. Marshall, 'Deceptive Appearances: Ghosts and Reformers in Elizabethan and Jacobean England', in H. Parish and W. G. Naphy (eds), *Religion and Superstition in Reformation Europe* (Manchester: Manchester University Press, 2002), pp. 188–209; P. Marshall, *Mother Leakey and the Bishop: A Ghost Story* (Oxford: Oxford University Press, 2009); P. Marshall, 'Transformations of the Ghost Story in Post-Reformation England', in H. Conrad-O'Briain and J. A. Stevens (eds), *The Ghost Story from the Middle Ages to the Twentieth Century* (Dublin: Four Courts, 2010); K. Edwards, *Leonarde's Ghost: Popular Piety and 'The Appearance of a Spirit' in 1628*, ed. and trans. in collaboration with S. Speakman Sutch (Kirksville, MO: Truman State University Press, 2008). For discussions of the relationship between ghosts and witchcraft, see G. Bennett, 'Ghost and Witch in the Sixteenth and Seventeenth Centuries', *Folklore* 96, (1986): 3–14; R. Hutton, 'The English Reformation and the Evidence of Folklore', *Past and Present* 148, (1995): 89–116; L. Gowing, 'The Haunting of Susan Lay: Servants and Mistresses in Seventeenth-Century England', *Gender and History* 14 (2002): 183–201; J. Bossy, *Christianity in the West 1400–1700* (Oxford: Oxford University Press, 1985), p. 29.

53 M. Parker, *Correspondence of Matthew Parker, Archbishop of Canterbury*, ed. J. Bruce (London: Wipf and Stock, 2005), p. 222; Marshall, 'Deceptive Appearances', p. 188.

54 Thomas, *Religion and the Decline of Magic*, p. 703; D. Cressy, *Birth, Marriage and Death* (Oxford: Oxford University Press, 1997), p. 403.

55 L. Lavater, *De Spectris* (1683); Marshall, *Beliefs and the Dead*, p. 262.

56 Marshall, *Beliefs and the Dead*, p. 260.

57 Marshall, 'Deceptive Appearances', p. 189; Marshall, *Mother Leakey and the Bishop*; S. Clark, *Thinking with Demons: The Idea of Witchcraft in Early Modern Europe* (Oxford: Oxford University Press, 1997); Clark, *Vanities of the Eye*; C. Lehrich, *The Language of Demons and Angels: Cornelius Agrippa's Occult Philosophy* (Leiden: Brill, 2003); M. Bailey, *Fearful Spirits: The Boundaries of Superstition in Late Medieval Europe* (Ithaca, NY: Cornell University Press, 2013); J. Machielsen, *Martin Delrio: Demonology and Scholarship in the Counter-Reformation* (Oxford: Oxford University Press, 2015); K. Möseneder, *Paracelsus und die Bilder: über Glauben, Magie, und Astrologie im Reformationszeitalter* (Tübingen: Niemeyer, 2009).

58 Walsham, 'The Reformation and the Disenchantment of the World Reassessed', p. 527.

59 A. Walsham, *Providence in Early Modern England* (Oxford: Oxford University Press, 1999), p. 2; Dixon, *The Reformation and Rural Society*, pp. 201–2; P. M. Soergel, *Miracles and the Protestant Imagination: The Evangelical Wonder Book in Reformation Germany* (New York: Oxford University Press, 2012).

EPILOGUE

1 http://www.vatican.va/roman_curia/pontifical_councils/chrstuni/lutheran-fed-docs/rc_pc_chrstuni_doc_2013_dal-conflitto-alla-comunione_en.html#New_challenges_for_the_2017_commemoration_ (accessed 17 March 2018).

2 On ideas about memory and commemoration, see D. W. Cohen, *The Combing of History* (Chicago: University of Chicago Press, 1994); J. R. Gillis (ed.), *Commemorations: The Politics of National Identity* (Princeton, NJ: Princeton University Press, 1996); T. A. Howard, 'Protestant Reformation Approaching 500', *First Things*, May 2013; http://www.vatican.va/roman_curia/pontifical_councils/chrstuni/lutheran-fed-docs/rc_pc_chrstuni_doc_2013_dal-conflitto-alla-comunione_en.html (accessed 17 March 2018).

3 The phrase is borrowed from G. Bernard, *The Late Medieval English Church: Vitality and Vulnerability Before the Break with Rome* (New Haven, CT: Yale University Press, 2012).

4 B. S. Gregory, *The Unintended Reformation: How a Religious Revolution Secularised Society* (Cambridge, MA: Harvard University Press, 2012).

5 See, for example, the Luther memorial in Worms, around which sit Peter Waldes, John Wycliffe, Jan Hus and Girolamo Savonarola, as well as Frederick, Elector of Saxony, Philip Melanchthon, Philip of Hesse and Johannes Reuchlin, and the Calvin Wall in Geneva.

6 D. Daniell, *The Bible in English: History and Influence* (New Haven, CT: Yale University Press, 2003); D. Daniell, *William Tyndale: A Biography* (New Haven, CT, and London: Yale University Press, 1994).

7 T. A. Howard and M. A. Knoll (eds), *Protestantism after 500 Years* (Oxford: Oxford University Press, 2016), p. 1.

Index

Index